Women and Sex Therapy

Women and Sex Therapy

Ellen Cole, PhD
Esther D. Rothblum, PhD
Editors

The Haworth Press
New York • London

Women and Sex Therapy has also been published as *Women & Therapy*, Volume 7, Numbers 2/3, 1988.

The Haworth Press, Inc., 12 West 32 Street, New York, NY 10001
EUROSPAN/Haworth, 3 Henrietta Street, London WC2E 8LU England

Library of Congress Cataloging-in-Publication Data

Women and sex therapy.

"Has also been published as Women & therapy, volume 7, numbers 2/3, 1988"—T.p. verso.

Includes bibliographical references.

1. Sex therapy. 2. Feminist therapy. 3. Women—Sexual behavior. I. Cole, Ellen. II. Rothblum, Esther D.

RC557.W65 1988 616.85′83′0088042 88-11068

ISBN 0-86656-808-5

Women and Sex Therapy

CONTENTS

ABOUT THE EDITORS

Ellen Cole, PhD, has devoted 25 years to the practice of psychology. She currently conducts a private practice in sex therapy, is a professor of psychology at Goddard College, and chairs the Committee on Women and Minorities of the Vermont Psychological Association. In addition, she co-edited, with Esther Rothblum, the book *Another Silenced Trauma*, which received a 1987 Distinguished Publication Award from the Association for Women in Psychology.

Esther D. Rothblum, PhD, currently chairs the Women's Studies Program at the University of Vermont. She is planning a trip to the Antarctic to study gender differences in stress and coping. Currently a Kellogg Fellow, Dr. Rothblum will be traveling to Africa to study women's mental health. In addition, she co-edited the books *The Stereotyping of Women: Its Effects on Mental Health* and *Another Silenced Trauma*.

Preface

For centuries, the idea of "sex" as anything but a biological given has hardly if ever been mentioned; it was considered automatic that "sex" meant a set of activities including "foreplay" followed by "vaginal penetration" and "intercourse," usually ending with male ejaculation.

In recent years, women have begun a new dialogue about the nature of sexuality, and in particular, what we as women feel – and what other definitions of "sex" might be. One of the aspects of this ongoing questioning and redefinition of "sex" has been the discussion by women about the stimulation by which most women have orgasm. In the 1970s, women asserted that it is just as "normal" for a woman to want and need clitoral stimulation to orgasm as to have orgasm during intercourse – in fact, the majority of women orgasm more easily with exterior stimulation. Further important issues women are addressing about sexuality now include: How linked are "sex" and orgasm? Must "sex" lead to intercourse? Should much of our terminology be changed, e.g., why shouldn't "vaginal penetration" be also called "penile covering"? Why is sensuality so downplayed? Is sensuality between two women "lesbian"? Is heterosexuality a culturally imposed "norm"? A biological given for some? What could a new, more individually defined sexual/body expression be? Could it have new cultural meanings? Was sexuality defined differently in early pre-history?

This renaming of sexuality goes along with the overall renaming of reality and our lives that women everywhere are currently involved in; change in thinking is happening so quickly that what yesterday seemed radical, today seems unremarkable. This shows how far we have come, and yet, there are opposing forces: some would have us turn back to a society in which individuals have no right to decide their own destiny or define their own lives, but rather, the state or biology would again rule our position in the world. If God is male and he is the father, then similarly, the father is head of the household in a family, in legal charge of "his" wife and children. Thus would the chance for a truly democraticized household be lost, in a return to a hierarchical family system not freely chosen.

Individual women all over the world, of all political persuasions and religions, all ages and backgrounds, are now in the midst of a profound questioning of their priorities. Scholars in this volume are making a great contribution to this reshaping of "reality."

This volume and the valuable and diverse ideas presented by these outstanding scholars will surely enrich enormously the possibilities for all therapists and counselors to discuss with their clients and patients the many layers of feeling we all experience, so that, in dialogue, we can all gradually reinvent our world.

Shere Hite

Introduction

. . . Freud came to see his hypotheses as if they were facts.

Hannah Lerman

I first envisioned this volume at an international menopause conference in Miami, Florida in 1984. Many, indeed most, of the world's "leading authorities" on menopause were there, and the vast majority were men. All of the conference planners were men, and most of the presenters were men. The few presentations by women seemed to be more poorly attended than the others, and tended to address the "less serious" aspects of menopause: self-help groups; phenomenological rather than quantitative research; social science rather than medical science. Recognizing that the perspective of women was not being adequately represented at this conference, 17 of us–from Australia, Canada, England, Italy, Sweden, and the United States–met to form a women's caucus. Since that time, 14 other women have added their names to the list. And so began, perhaps for many of us who attended that meeting, a searching look at the wider field of sexology, through a feminist lens.

The original plan for this volume was to solicit manuscripts that presented a feminist critique of current practices in sex therapy and sex research, and several of the articles in this anthology do exactly that. One author, for example, challenges the sexual dysfunction nomenclature; another takes on sex research; two authors present a case for more woman-sensitive training programs for clinicians.

However, the eventual scope of the collection has turned out to be far broader than a feminist critique. Several articles examine issues central to women's sexual development that have not been adequately addressed in existing sex therapy literature, such as the relationship between sex and food. The sexual difficulties experienced by women with interstitial cystitis is but one of several topics addressing the relationship between female sexuality and physical conditions usually discussed only in the physician's office. In addition, several of the articles present a women's view of sexuality not as a critique of existing paradigms, but as a celebration of new visions, new possibilities. One author, for instance, writes about women and sexual ecstacy; another imagines alternatives to current thought.

This collection then is for the sex therapist interested in the woman's perspective, and the mental health practitioner interested in current issues in sex therapy that pertain to women. It is the beginning of a dialogue – long, long overdue – between the feminist therapist who may have no special training in sex therapy, and the sex therapist who has not considered the importance of the feminist perspective.

We have made a careful effort to include groups often overlooked in the mainstream literature: disabled women, for example; women from ethnic and racial minorities; and bisexual women. We have tried scrupulously to avoid the heterosexism of much of the sex therapy literature, by explicitly reminding authors to be aware of this issue and by including two articles that specifically address lesbianism. And, finally, we have included articles of great contemporary significance: about women and AIDS, for instance, and the new reproductive options.

I would like to appreciate here those who first opened my eyes to a concept of female sexuality that was true to my own experience: Lonnie Barbach, Shere Hite, Virginia Johnson and William Masters come immediately to mind. I find it inspiring that these modern pioneers have continued to innovate. Lonnie Barbach has begun to publish erotica by and for women; Shere Hite's most recent book is about women in relationships; Masters and Johnson have developed programs for incest survivors and have intensified their efforts to make sex therapy available to working class couples. Where there were once just a few, now there are many more who are extending our knowledge of women and sexuality. This collection begins with the concept that sexuality cannot be understood unless the woman's perspective is taken fully into account. It takes us one step further toward closing the circle of sexual knowledge.

Many people contributed behind-the-scenes efforts to the development of this volume. Thank you to Debbie Alicen, Hannah Lerman, Doug North, Margie Ripper, Sarah Rodriguez, Camille Ross, and Cassady Winner for your cheerful, thoughtful assistance. And a special thank you to Gale Golden, Jean Lathrop, and Dian Mueller for being so extraordinarily generous with your time and your wisdom.

Ellen Cole

REFERENCE

Lerman, H. (1986). *A mote in Freud's eye: From psychoanalysis to the psychology of women*. New York: Springer Publ. Co.

SECTION I: HISTORICAL AND POLITICAL PERSPECTIVES

A Feminist Critique of the Sexual Dysfunction Nomenclature

Leonore Tiefer

Although we think of formal "sex therapy" as a recent development within psychotherapy (Kaplan, 1974), the treatment of women for sexual problems obviously has a long and, to a feminist, tarnished history (Morgan, 1970). This paper will focus on the degree to which the current nomenclature describing women's sexual problems serves women's interests. Our text, since its classification system and terminology are widely used by therapists, researchers,

Leonore Tiefer, PhD, began specializing in sexuality with a dissertation on hamster mating behavior in 1969, and now finds herself doing research and clinical evaluations on men with erectile problems who come to the Urology Department at Beth Israel Medical Center in New York looking for a "quick fix." It's a great area for research and theory!

This paper was presented in an earlier form at the annual meeting of the Society for the Scientific Study of Sexuality in St. Louis, MO, November 1986.

academics and the media, is the *Diagnostic and Statistical Manual* of the American Psychiatric Association known as the DSM-III (APA, 1980).* Is it an improvement over what it replaced?

PAST VIEWS OF WOMEN'S SEXUAL PROBLEMS

A vast historical literature (e.g., of personal accounts, medical and religious treatises, legal and social writings) bears on the classification, etiology and treatment of women's sexual problems over the past centuries, although no thorough historical analyses yet exist. Indeed, interest in such "social" history is itself only a recent project. Shorter (1982) has argued that because of injury and suffering associated with reproduction, women's sexual lives prior to 1900 were essentially filled with pain, revulsion, and fear of pregnancy and disease. Although women were said in treatises and folklore to have insatiable sexual desires, and even to need orgasm in order to conceive, Shorter holds that:

> traditional women were sexually cowed and emotionally brutalized by men. They found it impossible to escape intercourse, and sought solace for its unpleasant consequences only in the company of other women. Not until women solved the problem of abortion, contraception, and safe childbirth would they be able to relax about marital sexuality. (Shorter, 1982, p. 16)

Whether this interpretation is valid remains for future historians to decide, but it does seem likely, for a wide variety of social and cultural reasons, that prior to the late 19th century women did not see sexual difficulties as "health" problems appropriate for professional consultation or treatment. During the 19th century, medical authorities adopted the Catholic (formerly Jewish) system of classification (by then incorporated into secular law) which considered non-procreative sexual acts, including use of birth control, as

---

Editor's Note: Although the DSM-IIIR has been published since this article was written, the article's major points are still valid.

"crimes against nature" indicative of physical or psychological pathology and needing correction (Kinsey, Pomeroy, Gebhard, & Martin, 1953; Weeks, 1981). Women who showed too much, too little or the wrong kind of sexual interests became increasingly likely to be labeled abnormal or perverse, and, in the 20th century, deviant or frigid.

It is important to note, however, how our understanding of the sexual experiences of people of earlier eras is fraught with mystery. Words such as "passion," "love," and "desire" are frequently present in the letters and diaries of pre-20th century women, but because of the contexts and consequences of these writings we know these words cannot have meant all the same things then that they do now (Smith-Rosenberg, 1985). It will be some time before we have any clear sense of what women in earlier times felt, wanted and did. Nor will it be easy to figure out how they construed authorities' opinions about female sexuality.

In the 20th century, as part of the medical profession's consolidation of authority, various approved national and international classification systems of medical disorders appeared. The listing of sexual problems went through many changes, primarily following the lead of the psychiatric profession. The American Psychiatric Association's first and second diagnostic classification manuals (APA, 1952; APA, 1968) both included a category for "Sexual Deviations." No subdivisions were specified in 1952, but "homosexuality" was specified as a subcategory in 1968. In both editions, the category "Psychophysiologic Disorders" was defined as a "group of disorders characterized by physical symptoms that are caused by emotional factors. . . ." It included a subdivision, "Psychophysiological Genito-Urinary Disorders," that mentioned women's sexual problems. The definition of this subcategory read:

> This diagnosis applies to genito-urinary disorders such as disturbances in menstruation and micturition, dyspareunia [pain during intercourse], and impotence in which emotional factors play a causative role. (APA, 1968, p. 47)

CURRENT OFFICIAL NOMENCLATURE FOR WOMEN'S SEXUAL PROBLEMS

In 1980, the APA's manual exploded from 119 pages to 494 twice-as-large pages, and the space given to sexuality expanded accordingly, from 3 to 22 pages. The first major sexual category, *Psychosexual Disorders*, includes several specific items which are alleged not to pertain much to women. Transsexualism is claimed to have a male-female frequency ratio of eight to one. Regarding Paraphilias (fetishism, transvestism, zoophilia, pedophilia, exhibitionism, and voyeurism), the manual states:

> virtually all reported cases have been in males, with the exception of sexual sadism and sexual masochism, which, however, occur far more commonly in males. (APA, 1980, p. 268)

The second major category, *Psychosexual Dysfunctions*, derives directly from Masters' and Johnson's influential physiological research which defined and described a "human sexual response cycle," apparently identical for all men and women, consisting of four phases: excitement, plateau, orgasm, and resolution (Masters & Johnson, 1966). The diagnostic manual relies on the authority of this cycle model, indeed assumes its veridicality, without discussing it as a model at all. "The essential feature [of psychosexual dysfunctions] is inhibition in the appetitive or psychophysiological changes that characterize the [sic] complete sexual response cycle" (APA, 1980, p. 275). The specific disorders in this category are:

– inhibited sexual desire (gender not mentioned)
– inhibited sexual excitement (in males, erectile problems; in females, "partial or complete failure to attain or maintain the lubrication-swelling response of sexual excitement until completion of the sexual act." [p. 279])
– inhibited female orgasm ("recurrent and persistent inhibition of the female orgasm as manifested by a delay in or absence of orgasm following a normal sexual excitement phase during sexual activity that is judged by the clinician to be adequate in focus, intensity, and duration." [p. 279])

– inhibited male orgasm
– premature ejaculation
– functional dyspareunia (genital pain during intercourse for no known medical reason)
– functional vaginismus (involuntary tightening of the outer vaginal muscles preventing intercourse)

We will discuss, below, the legitimacy of using this model normatively. While the standards are before us, however, it is important to notice how oriented they are to mechanical and heterosexual intercourse. Sexual disorders *are* physical failures in the performance of heterosexual intercourse.

The third and final category of sexual disorders in DSM-III is the catchall *Other Psychosexual Disorders* which includes, first, "Ego-dystonic homosexuality." This disorder has been deleted in the 1987 DSM-IIIR (revision), partly because of prolonged political activity by psychologists and psychiatrists who were opposed to any and all pathologizing of homosexuality. The elimination of homosexuality per se as a disorder (recall that it was listed as such in the 1968 edition) occurred in 1973 after a bitter fight within the American Psychiatric Association (Bayer, 1981). Women's role in the politics of that change remains to be documented since there seems to be no gender analysis in any of the gay liberation or social science literature cited. "Ego-dystonic" homosexuality, the substitute developed by the nomenclature committee after bitter debate between 1973 and 1978, "is reserved for those homosexuals for whom changing sexual orientations is a persistent concern" (APA, 1980, p. 281), but it is not clear whether men and women were thought to suffer from this problem equally often.

The remaining item in this last category, "Psychosexual Disorder Not Elsewhere Classified" includes ". . . psychological disturbances related to sexuality not covered by any of the other specific categories" (APA, 1980, p. 283) and explicitly mentions gender issues in at least one of its examples. Unfortunately, the text is extremely terse:

> Examples include the following: (1) marked feelings of inadequacy related to self-imposed standards of masculinity or femininity, such as body habitus, size and shape of sex organs, or sexual performance; (2) impaired pleasure during the normal physiologic pelvic responses of orgasm; (3) Don Juanism; (4) confusion about preferred sexual orientation. (APA, 1980, p. 283)

Because formal sex therapy deals with the so-called Psychosexual Dysfunctions, I will deal only with that category in the remainder of the paper. The Psychosexual Disorders (e.g., paraphilias, and ego-dystonic homosexuality) are more obviously cultural and historical constructions, and as recent experience has shown, can be directly addressed from a political point of view. The appropriateness of political analyses of what seems to be a straightforward biophysical category is less obvious.

CAN A NORMATIVE MODEL BE FEMINIST?

The DSM-III model of sexual response is obviously a normative one, deriving its prescriptive authority from the Masters and Johnson physiological research. Like other normative models, it specifies a standard of behavior and defines deviations as ab-normal instances. Were the norm statistical, deviations would be numerically unusual according to some frequency determination. Were the norm cultural, then deviations would be socially unexpected or improper. In the case of a clinical norm such as that embodied in the medical model of the DSM-III, the deviations are called pathology, disorder, illness.

Feminist discourse is explicitly committed to individual and social diversity, yet occasionally we can find a document which presents feminist norms. The following is taken from the Prologue of *An International Feminist Mental Health Agenda for the Year 2000*, a working paper put together by a committee convened by the Association for Women in Psychology (AWP).[1] The paper was presented at Forum '85, the Nongovernmental World Meeting for Women in Nairobi, Kenya, in July, 1985. Interestingly, it begins with a discussion of the dangers for women of normative discourse:

> Almost everywhere, standards of mental health, for women as well as for men, have been established by men and often reflect cultural and social norms in which inequality, discrimination, and the undervaluation of women are an accepted pattern of life. Such norms, perpetuated in schools, religious institutions, the home, and the workplace, directly undermine and interfere with a woman's ability to maintain the psychological and emotional quality of her life. . . . Women are raised to believe in and accept such norms, leading women to undervalue themselves. (p. 3)

In other words, feminists are typically suspicious of norms because of their historic function in social control. Socialization, the internalization of social norms, is a chief means of social control in the feminist analysis. Yet, the AWP document goes on to identify some feminist standards:

> When feminists speak of women's mental health, we refer to psychological and emotional *quality of life*, which includes:
>
> a. a sense of dignity, beauty and worth
> b. the capacity to love oneself and others
> c. the continuing acquisition of survival skills
> d. the valuing of daughters as much as sons
> e. the ability to offer and ask for assistance
> f. the enjoyment of life, of work, of nature
> g. the right to experience and express the full range of emotions including indignation and anger at injustice
> h. the right to take appropriate action toward equality, including resistance, organizing, and collective protest against injustice. (p. 3)

In answer to our first question, then, a normative model can be feminist, but the origin of its norms will have to be in women's experience and women-generated goals, established by women of diverse experiences and backgrounds. While the particular norms listed in the AWP document may not provide enough specificity or direction regarding the domain of sexuality, the method by which they were determined may be useful.

WHAT DO WOMEN SAY ARE THEIR SEXUAL PROBLEMS?

If we look to women's experience for guidelines as to women-defined sexual problems, we immediately come up against a lack of studies. Most research assumes the validity of the sexual response cycle model, and asks women to indicate any difficulties with arousal, orgasm, etc.

By contrast, Shere Hite (1976) began her survey of women's sexual practices and preferences by rejecting "experts'" standards and norms (p. xi). Rather, she asked women to describe, in open-ended answers, their practices, experiences, preferences, dissatisfactions, etc. Anyone interested in woman-defined standards of satisfaction and dissatisfaction could do worse than start here, and someone really should try to develop a system of classification based on Hite's data. Let me give some examples of the types of dissatisfaction very different from the classical dysfunctions that Hite's respondents mentioned:

> "I would like more love and gentleness instead of bare sexual stimulation, more emotion and communication." (p. 367)
>
> "I'd like to kiss mouth to mouth more." (p. 367)
>
> "More kisses, more time, more tenderness. Why don't men like to be touched in other parts of their bodies?" (p. 367)
>
> "More passion. Often he is in too much of a hurry and he pays too much attention to my vagina . . . I would like petting-type genital stimulation, with clothes on, pushing up my dress . . . I would like to be free enough to do anything and everything without embarrassment." (p. 368)
>
> "Many men think sex is just fucking, or something to do with hands, mouth, and cock, but not the rest of the body. Men don't feel that their whole bodies are beautiful or that the touch of thigh and thigh is a caress." (p. 368)
>
> "No matter what I do or say, most men simply won't believe that having my ears and the back of my neck kissed is really important." (p. 368)
>
> "I would like to have leisurely sex with a man more often,

> talking and fooling around and entertaining each other. Feeling relaxed." (p. 368)
>
> "I have viewed married love as a growing together in the ability to express love and pleasure. . . . My husband doesn't seem to enjoy anything besides intercourse . . . I don't feel my husband is emotionally involved during sex. . . . He forgets half the things I tell him that turn me on or off." (p. 370-71)
>
> "My best sexual experiences were all the heavy petting I did before I had intercourse at about nineteen. I used to do that for hours and fantasize afterwards." (p. 375)
>
> "Most of the excitement is about holding and being held." (p. 377)
>
> "Touching is the most important part of sex." (p. 386)

These quotations communicate women's dissatisfactions. But if these women are getting aroused and having orgasms, the official nosology would have nowhere to put their complaints. Their complaints would be invisible, without legitimacy.

A study on sexual problems reported by Ellen Frank and colleagues in 1978 got a great deal of publicity because of its choice of a "normal" sample, rather than one derived from a sex therapy clinic or practice (Frank, Anderson, & Rubinstein, 1978). One hundred white middle class couples, predominantly Christian and well-educated, with about half married for more than nine years, were recruited for a study of marriages that were working, were "happy." Each participant was asked to indicate on a checklist any sexual problems currently occurring in his or her marriage. Two types of sexual problems were defined: problems that could be labeled "dysfunctions" based on the DSM-III nosology; and "dissatisfactions," complaints that did not fit into the nosology. The authors justify the distinction as

> . . . to some extent an arbitrary one that we have chosen because we believe that it preserves the distinction between problems of performance on the one hand, which seem to be of such pressing concern to present-day people, and problems, on the other hand, that are more related to the emotional tone of sexual relations. (Frank et al., 1978, p. 111-112)

What is the evidence that the "emotional and relational" problems are *not* of "pressing concern"? In fact where are the data anywhere that ask people to rank order or rate the importance of all sorts of sexual problems? In contrast to what Frank et al. say, it seems to me that their distinction separates problems that fit the official psychiatry nosology ("dysfunctions") from everything else ("dissatisfactions").

As shown in Table 1, Frank and her colleagues found that in these happily married couples, 63% of women and 40% of men reported experiencing some sort of problem that fit the familiar dysfunction categories, while 77% of the women and 50% of the men indicated the other sort of difficulty.

The first noteworthy item is the higher level with which the wives reported both types of problems as compared with the husbands. The wording is not precisely comparable, however, since the commonest dysfunction for women was "difficulty getting excited," whereas men were asked if they had difficulty getting an erection. Men significantly underestimated the occurrence of sexual dysfunction in their wives, whereas women's estimates of men's problems closely approximated their husbands' reports.

Looking at the relationship between the two categories of sexual problem (i.e., dysfunction and difficulty) and overall ratings of satisfaction, we find that whereas women's ratings of sexual satisfaction are significantly correlated both with their own and their spouse's dysfunctions as well as their own and their spouse's difficulties, the highest correlation is with their own difficulties. That is, factors such as women's inability to relax or disinterest in sex most strongly predict women's sexual satisfaction. Interestingly, men's reports of their own sexual satisfaction is significantly correlated only with their reports of their wives' sexual difficulties (but not dysfunctions). Thus, for both these husbands and wives, sexual satisfaction is most clearly related to women's experience of the more emotional and relational aspects of sexuality including factors like negotiation, compromise and power issues; experience of anxiety or tension; non-genital physical and emotional communication; quantity of foreplay and of tenderness; being "turned off" or disinterested. These findings strongly echo Hite's (1976).

Finding that sexual satisfaction is more related to emotional fac-

Table 1

Sexual problem frequencies[a]

I. Frequency of dysfuntion-type sexual problems:

Women (%)		Men (%)	
difficulty getting excited	48	difficulty getting erection	7
difficulty maintaining excitement	33	difficulty maintaining erection	9
reach orgasm too quickly	11	ejaculating too quickly	36
difficulty reaching orgasm	46	difficulty ejaculating	0
inability to have an orgasm	15	inability to ejaculate	0
one or more listed	63%	one or more listed	40%

II. Frequency of sexual difficulties (emotional-type problems):

	Women (%)	Men (%)
partner chooses inconvenient time	31	16
inability to relax	47	12
attraction to person other than mate	14	21
disinterest	35	16
different sexual practices or habits	10	12
"turned off"	28	10
too little foreplay before intercourse	38	21
too little tenderness after intercourse	25	17

[a]from Frank Anderson and Rubinstein (1978).

tors than to smooth performance of the sexual response cycle actually does not come as new data. Many previous studies had shown poor correlations between "normal function," usually considered as frequency of sexual orgasm and women's ratings of both marital and sexual satisfaction. (Chester & Walker, 1980; Clark & Wallin, 1965; Fisher, 1973; Heiman, Gladue, Roberts, & LoPiccolo, 1986; Jayne, 1981; Tavris & Sadd, 1977; Waterman & Chiauzzi, 1982). Most of these studies had also shown that the emotional climate of the relationship was the best predictor of sexual satisfaction.

The inescapable conclusion, therefore, is that what is really important to women in sexual life has been neglected by those who are "officially" in charge of defining and describing norms for sexuality in favor of a nosology which focuses exclusively on physical performance elements. In fact, many of women's concerns about intimacy, negotiation, spontaneity, communication, remembering preferences, etc. *are* addressed in formal sex therapy and may even take up the bulk of the therapy time and work. But these complaints are usually addressed only because it seems that they need to be in order for the couple to regain their ability to perform the normal intercourse-oriented sexual response cycle. Certainly it is the rare couple that would come for sex therapy saying, "We have no trouble with sexual frequency, intercourse and orgasm, but we feel there's a lack of tenderness and communication." I've never heard of such a case. What would the therapist put down for a diagnosis on the insurance form, and would it be accepted?

ANTIFEMINIST IMPLICATIONS OF A MEDICALIZED SEXUALITY

There are serious implications to the fact that the DSM-III does not reflect the real type of problems women are having with sex. Through its influence, the DSM-III's sexuality nomenclature serves to repress women's sexuality through silence, neglect and misplaced emphases. By endorsing and legitimizing certain types of problems, others are de-legitimized. The DSM-III's classification system, as has been discussed, derives from the physiological research of Masters and Johnson (1966) which gave greater specificity to the amorphous category of "Psychophysiological Genito-Urinary Disorders." The locus of problems remained squarely in the medicalized domain, without concern for real people's real complaints. Reissman (1983) recently offered some insights into the negative consequences of medicalization for women, insights we can adapt to our discussion of sexuality (Tiefer, 1987).

Reissman emphasizes three consequences of medicalization which ill-serve women. First, through *mystification* people come to rely increasingly on professionals and experts to explain and advise them as to the nature of reality and, therefore, as to appropriate goals. Once sexuality is professionally defined as a matter of correct response cycle performance rather than self-defined enjoyment, couples and individuals are dependent on experts to guide them towards "normal and healthy" sexuality. Given the likelihood that few officially-sanctioned experts will have an economically disinterested, woman-centered view, this dependence will result in advice that serves the experts' interests more than women's.

Second, placing norms for sexuality within the scientific and medical domain introduces an illusory and damaging element of *moral neutrality*. If norms for sex are matters of scientific discovery, then it makes no sense to start with women's experience to develop diverse concepts. It is assumed that there is an objective "natural" reality that has already defined the conduct and purposes of sexuality and that deviation from that natural norm is inappropriate. Sex is no longer a human arena for negotiation, but an arena where there is an objective standard against which performance can be measured. In the past, women have been intimidated and oppressed by these allegedly "objective" readings of nature.

Third, and perhaps worst of all from a feminist point of view, medicalization of a phenomenon inevitably *individualizes* it in people's minds and in terms of social policy. Medicalization denies, obscures and ignores the social construction of sexuality, and the social contributions to people's sexual complaints. From the medicalized point of view, an individual person has a sexual problem, or, in the really modern view, a couple has a sexual problem. The social origins of sexuality problems—rigid sex roles, unrelenting standards of performance, relationships of unequal power, absence of positive sexuality training or education, sexuality having to fulfill displaced needs for self-esteem and worth in a bureaucratic world, increasing awareness of sex brought about by the commercial exploitation of sexual images, histories of sexual violence – are never treated (Schmidt, 1983; Tiefer, 1986). Insofar as an individual or couple has a history of sexual victimization or has too high performance standards, etc., this will be discussed as a problem for them to overcome, but to overcome as individuals, not on a societal level.

Thus, by maintaining a medicalized vision of what sexuality is, what it should be, and what types of things constitute problems, the official nosology controls public and personal sexuality discourse. In our view, however, it misdirects public attention and requires repeated feminist analyses.

TOWARDS A FEMINIST NOSOLOGY OF SEXUAL PROBLEMS

Suppose we discard the DSM-III dysfunction-based nosology as too tied to a procreative definition of sex, too tied to an intercourse focus with orgasm as the goal, too based on a normative model that gives priority to a medical perspective. Suppose instead we specify that feminist norms for sexuality *should never* valorize a *particular* set of behaviors or responses, but that feminist norms for sexuality would endorse those ways of enjoying and communicating with the body practiced by people with feminist political views.

To go back to the Association for Women in Psychology's list, people with feminist political views value women, their rights, their feelings, their dignity, their beauty, their capacity to love. Sexual problems would then be due to interference with these values in the practice of intimate physical communication and expression. An analysis of sexual problems would focus on the sources of depreciation of women. Sex therapy, insofar as an individualized treatment focus was needed, would have as its goal to remedy the inappropriate aspects of a relationship – sort of relationship treatment for politically incorrect relationships. Although she doesn't challenge the individualistic focus of therapy itself, Cammaert (1984) has something like this perspective in mind when she recommends that

> the focus [of sex therapy] could change from the genital functioning related to orgasmic dysfunction, vaginismus, painful intercourse, and impotence to much more emphasis on sex role definition, examination of beliefs about sexuality, negotiations in relationships, and responsibility for one's own sexuality. (p. 258)

With respect for the political aspects of a relationship as they bear on sexuality, Seidler-Feller (1985) has argued that women's sexual dysfunctions such as lack of interest or lack of arousal are often forms of resistance to inequality and exploitation in a relationship, and are positive expressions of self-ownership and the right to privacy. She rejects sex therapy treatments which utilize merely a mechanical and technical approach, and disregard these "functional" aspects of "dysfunctions." Any therapy approach which respected feminist norms would have these issues in the foreground, and would not address the "dysfunctions" a couple presented as "the" problems.

CONCLUSION

Soble (1987) has recently discussed how the medicalized construction of sexual problems exclusively as performance difficulties, i.e., "machines in disrepair (p. 120)," fits nicely into familiar contemporary metaphors. The machine is rubbed, but it won't get hard, or won't get wet, or won't come. It's obviously in need of fixing/treatment. "It," the part, is not behaving in its "natural" way, as nature designed for it to behave, and as it would behave if there were not some obstacle in its way. This "essentialist" assumption, that there is some prior natural sexuality underneath all the culture, all the individual learning, all the social and religious values, is the root support for the DSM-III's authority and the authority of any medicalized model (Tiefer, 1987). By rejecting essentialist claims for sexuality, as we have for so many other aspects of life, feminists will seize the initiative to define and create a better world. As we've said all along, "The personal is political." Don't forget it.

NOTE

1. The Agenda has not been published, but copies are available from the author.

REFERENCES

American Psychiatric Association (1980). *Diagnostic and statistical manual of mental disorders*, 3rd ed. Washington, DC: American Psychiatric Association. [1st ed., 1952; 2nd ed., 1968.]

Bayer, R. (1981). *Homosexuality and American psychiatry*, New York, NY: Basic Books.

Cammaert, L.P. (1984). New sex therapies: Policy and practice. In Walker, L.E. (Ed.), *Women and health policy*. Beverly Hills, CA: Sage Publications.

Chester, R. & Walker, C. (1980). Sexual experience and attitudes of British women. In Armytage, W.H.G., Chester, R. & Peel, J. (Eds.), *Changing patterns of sexual behavior*. London: Academic Press.

Clark, A.L. & Wallin, P. (1965). Women's sexual responsiveness and the duration and quality of their marriages. *American Journal of Sociology, 71*, 187-196.

Fisher, S. (1973). *The female orgasm*. New York, NY: Basic Books.

Frank, E., Anderson, C., & Rubinstein, D. (1978). Frequency of sexual dysfunction in normal couples. *New England Journal of Medicine, 299*, 111-115.

Heiman, J.R., Gladue, B.A., Roberts, C.W. & LoPiccolo, J. (1986). Historical and current factors discriminating sexually functional from sexual dysfunctional married couples. *Journal of Marital and Family Therapy, 12*, 163-174.

Hite, S. (1976). *The Hite report*. New York: Macmillan.

Jayne, C. (1981). A two-dimensional model of female sexual response. *Journal of Sex and Marital Therapy, 7*, 3-30.

Kaplan, H.S. (1974). *The new sex therapy*. New York: Brunner/Mazel.

Kinsey, A.C., Pomeroy, W.B., Martin, C.E. & Gebhard, P.H. (1953). *Sexual behavior in the human female*. Philadelphia: W.B. Saunders, Co.

Masters, W.H. & Johnson, V.E. (1966). *Human sexual response*. Boston: Little, Brown.

Morgan, R. (Ed.) (1970). *Sisterhood is powerful: An anthology of writings from the women's liberation movement*. New York: Vintage Books.

Reissman, C. (1983). Women and medicalization: A new perspective. *Social Policy, 14*, 3-18.

Schmidt, G. (1983). Introduction: Sexuality and relationships. In G. Arentewicz & G. Schmidt, *The treatment of sexual disorders*. New York: Basic Books.

Shorter, E. (1982). *A history of women's bodies*. New York: Basic Books.

Smith-Rosenberg, C. (1985). *Disorderly conduct: Visions of gender in Victorian America*. New York: Oxford University Press.

Soble, A. (1987). Philosophy, medicine, and healthy sexuality. In E. E. Shelp

(Ed.), *Sexuality and medicine, Vol. I*. Dordrecht, Holland: D. Reidel. (Distributed by Kluwer Academic Publishers, Norwell, MA.)

Tavris, C. & Sadd, S. (1977). *The Redbook report on female sexuality*. New York: Delacorte Press.

Tiefer, L. (1986). In pursuit of the perfect penis: The medicalization of male sexuality. *American Behavioral Scientist, 29*, 579-599.

Tiefer, L. (1987). Social constructionism and the study of human sexuality. In P. Shaver & C. Hendrick (Eds.), *Sex and gender*, vol. 7 of the *Review of personality and social psychology*. Newbury Park, CA: Sage Publications.

Waterman, C.K. & Chiauzzi, E.J. (1982). The role of orgasm in male and female sexual enjoyment. *Journal of Sex Research, 18*, 146-159.

Weeks, J. (1981). *Sex, politics, and society: The regulation of sexuality since 1800*. London: Longman Group Ltd.

Propping Up the Phallocracy: A Feminist Critique of Sex Therapy and Research

Wendy Stock

As a feminist therapist specializing in the treatment of sexual dysfunctions, and as a sex researcher, I worked for two years (1984-1986) as a research scientist and project coordinator on a National Institute of Health-funded grant on diagnosis of erectile dysfunction in men with chronic illness. The principal investigator is a highly regarded and well-known sex researcher, and the grant represents a state-of-the-art, comprehensive approach to the problem of erectile dysfunction. The mission of this grant was to develop a cost-effective means of distinguishing organic from psychogenic determinants of erectile dysfunction. Three groups of men were compared, including a group of men with chronic illness frequently associated with erectile dysfunction (renal failure, diabetes, post-coronary males and males on antihypertensive medication); a second group of men with erectile dysfunction and no major organic predisposing factors; and a third group of men with no sexual dysfunctions, matched for age with the sexually dysfunctional subjects.

Data collection included an extensive physiological evaluation and clinical interview of the subject and his sexual partner, if one was available. Psychological assessment included individual and relationship history, current sexual functioning, and a number of questionnaires assessing psychopathology and sexual attitudes. The

Wendy Stock, PhD, is a feminist, a licensed psychologist, and co-founder of Brazos Counseling Associates: A Women's Resource Center, in College Station, TX. She is an assistant professor of psychology at Texas A&M University, specializing in research on sexuality, pornography, and women's issues.

physiological evaluation consisted of an extensive array of measures utilizing advanced technology to determine the presence of organic etiology of erectile dysfunction. Sophisticated medical devices were utilized to determine neurological or vascular impairment in the penis.

Subjects' erectile capabilities were assessed in waking and sleeping states, by means of a penile strain gauge, a thin piece of tubing worn around the penis which measures tumescence. Our subjects had agreed to be monitored in an even more direct manner, by having a video camera with a zoom lens trained on their penis to allow remote television observation of their penile changes by project staff. Subjects sat in a recliner chair to view four segments of sexually explicit material presented on a television monitor. They were directed to observe the material, and given the suggestion to masturbate if this would help them attain an erection. Only one subject out of ninety utilized this suggestion.

A description of the material presented follows: The first segment was a sex education film showing a heterosexual couple slowly and sensuously touching, engaging in manual and oral stimulation, and then in "simulated" intercourse (actual penetration not shown). Following this, a segment from the popular pornographic film *Debbie Does Dallas* was shown, in which a young female guest in her aunt's house of prostitution is bullied into sexual interaction by two of the house prostitutes, which includes penetration by a dildo. A sample from the film's dialogue follows:

> *Debbie*: Ever since I set foot in this town I've been raped, abused, humiliated and used.
> *Prostitute*: You must have made out pretty good this morning.

The final scene taken from mainstream video pornography featured two middle aged males taking turns receiving oral stimulation and penetrating a young woman in garter belt and stockings, who eventually manually stimulates them to orgasm, accompanied by a background of heavy metal rock music.

Following this, subjects were presented with a series of slides featuring women in swim attire taken from *Sports Illustrated* magazine, and photographs of women from *Penthouse* and *Playboy* magazines, affording them an opportunity to develop erections in response to static photographs.

The composition of this material was discussed at length among project staff, including myself and five males. The majority felt that a range of material should be presented, affording subjects every possible opportunity to demonstrate their erectile capabilities. As the objective of this assessment was to assess erectile functioning, the selection of material was based on empirical criteria, i.e., "whatever works." In this culture, many males do respond with erections to standard pornography, often characterized by objectification, degradation, and violence against women. I was quite opposed to the selection of this material, as the use of pornography in a research setting, particularly a government-funded grant, implies tacit approval and legitimization of this material. Unlike research which specifically examines pornography, no debriefing of subjects occurred following exposure to this material, which could have countered the acceptance implied by our experimental protocol. My objections were politely attended to, but I was simply outvoted on this decision. During the second year of research, I was able to substitute other pornographic material in our protocol, produced by women, and without the most obvious and blatant objectification, dehumanization and abuse depicted in the earlier choice of material. The new material, while sexually explicit, appeared to depict mutuality, affection, and respect of both partners. There are many other considerations for the use of pornographic material in sex research, some discussed below, and this new material merely reflected a compromise made within a system with a preexisting agenda.

The last component of data collection involved two consecutive nights of nocturnal penile tumescence monitoring (NPT), during which the subject slept in the laboratory. During either night of NPT monitoring, at the peak of the largest erection observed, a project staff member entered the subject's sleeping room, pulled away the covers to expose the subject's penis, and photographed the penis at close range using a polaroid flash camera. Based on this visual observation, penile rigidity was rated and assigned a numerical score.

As may be expected, serving in the role of project coordinator in the development and execution of this research protocol elicited some significant contradictions in the life of a feminist sex researcher and clinician, existing as it were in the belly of the beast of mainstream sex research. Such contradictions presented themselves to me as I dashed into a subject's sleep room at 3:00 AM, clad in a white laboratory coat to lend a professional image and an aura of scientific respectability, pulled the covers from a groggy middle-aged male's penis, focused a camera at very close range and snapped a polaroid photograph of an intimidated-looking and rapidly diminishing erection. Given how many hours are spent with male therapy clients deemphasizing the importance of erections and working to change sexual belief systems based on a nonproductive overfocusing on obtaining erections, certain aspects of the data collection process were jarring and inconsistent with my professional beliefs and identity.

A core contradiction arose over the paradox of my fascination with the type of data being collected, with the innovative and, in some areas, pioneering methodology employed. This fascination was contraposed by my discomfort with the extreme focus on erectile functioning, although not to the exclusion of psychological variables, which was nevertheless laden with the assumption of the primacy of erections over other sexual concerns. On one hand, the effort to develop a cost-effective index of factors which would ultimately facilitate accurate diagnosis and appropriate treatment seemed laudable. This index could and will hopefully help to avoid referral of undetected medical etiology for psychotherapy doomed to fail, or conversely, avoid medicalizing cases of erectile dysfunction with psychogenic etiology. On the other hand, the messages we were transmitting to clients by such intense scrutiny of their penises may have promoted or perpetuated an objectifying, segmented, potentially degrading and soulless message about sexuality. In the context of scientific and medical legitimacy, research subjects were not likely to question our authority or the intimidating armamentarium of technology used.

Although the subjective reactions of staff and subjects to the process of data collection were not systematically recorded, the following are several observations. Research subjects generally reacted well to the clinical interview, although many found specific questions concerning sexual functioning and behavior to be embarrassing. Subjects seemed to regard the physiological evaluation as a medical procedure, no more invasive than a physical examination.

Responses to the pornographic material varied. A majority of control subjects developed erections in response to the stimulus material, although a significant minority did not; among the dysfunctional group, erectile responses varied, as expected. Negative reactions to the "degrading" nature of the material were reported, distaste for the "lesbian" scene in one segment, and complaints about the artificiality of the segment which did not show penetration. Most of our research subjects were aged 40-60, from the southern United States, frequently fundamentalist and generally traditional in their attitudes toward sexuality and sex roles. Although most had been exposed to mainstream pornography magazines, many had not seen the fairly explicit pornographic video material of the type used in this research.

Although the subject's exposure to this material generally followed the medical evaluation and clinical interview, occasionally this order was reversed, and either I or the one female doctoral psychology student interviewed the subject immediately following the video exposure. Both of us felt uncomfortable interviewing and preparing subjects for sleep evaluation, who had so recently been presented with images of women in a degrading, demeaning, sexual context. I felt that this undermined our status as research psychologists, as well as dramatically contradicted the model of egalitarian and affectionate sexuality we encourage as therapists.

Another aspect of the research protocol which seemed potentially humiliating was the zoom lens video camera focused on the subject's penis during videotape exposure. Similarly, the polaroid photograph taken of subject's erections during the night is a procedure used by other sleep laboratories which monitor NPT. This was, subjectively, the most bizarre procedure, seemingly taken from a techno-science fiction fantasy. We did not ask our subjects how they construed these rather intrusive behaviors centered around their penis. Given that males are more desensitized to public display of their genitals, this procedure may have been justified in a similar fashion. Many subjects spontaneously indicated that they were willing to endure any procedure necessary in order to find out why they weren't obtaining erections and to change this. The research procedure was simply consistent with their preexisting attitudes. One can only hypothesize that on some intrapsychic level, it must be painful to equate self-worth with a flap of skin and cartilage hanging between one's legs, particularly when this appendage is not performing according to prescribed standards.

The treatment of choice for research subjects who exhibited no organic etiology for erectile dysfunction was sex therapy. Referrals were provided upon the request of the subject or his referring physician. Research subjects frequently expressed disappointment when no medical etiology had been detected, as if this implied greater inadequacy or personal failing. As Masters and Johnson (1970, pp. 187-188) noted, "Every sexually inadequate male lunges toward any potential physical excuse for sexual malfunction." Peplau and Gordon (1985), also cited in Tiefer (1986), noted in the same vein, "Medical treatments not only offer tangible evidence of nonblameworthiness, but they allow men to avoid psychological treatments such as sex or marital therapy, which threaten embarrassing self-disclosure and admissions of weakness men find aversive."

These findings are certainly consistent with the attitudes of subjects in the present study, who generally were quite invested in believing that their erectile dysfunction was a mechanical problem that had little or nothing to do with their behaviors or psychological factors. The penis was not regarded as having any connection with feelings, needs, or interactions with a spouse or partner.

One recommendation made frequently to such couples is the inclusion of more direct physical stimulation of the penis. The notion that "foreplay" might be necessary for erectile response was viewed as unmasculine and occasionally disgusting. Female partners were sometimes repulsed or threatened by this suggestion, as illustrated by one wife's response to this recommendation: "I've never touched that thing in thirty years of marriage, and I'm not about to begin now!" This response highlights the mixed feelings of many female partners in our sample. In some cases, female partners were sexually frustrated with the lack of erections, as this frequently led to a complete avoidance and absence of any sexual interaction in the relationship. Another type of response rejected the suggestion of becoming an active partner in the sexual interaction, which is inconsistent with the traditional female role. There are significant negative sanctions for traditional women who behave in a sexually assertive manner. In addition, many of the female partners had endured years of unsatisfying sexual relations, and viewed the male's erectile dysfunction as a welcome relief from such demands. In such cases, there was considerable secondary gain for the female partner, due to a cessation of non-arousing, uncomfortable and unwanted sexual activity. In this sense, phallically-oriented sexuality had led to an avoidance of all sexual activity, even when exploring alternatives to intercourse would be helpful for treatment of the erectile dysfunction, as well as potentially pleasurable for the female partner.

In some cases the quest for medical solutions raised some fundamental issues of value judgments in this area of therapy and research, as in the following case example:

> Mr. R. was a retired veteran in his mid-forties, of slightly sub-average intelligence, who had encountered no erectile problems in sexual relations with prostitutes in the service, but began to experience erectile difficulties during his first marriage, which continued during a second and third marriage. His sexual partners had occasionally been hostile and rejecting, ridiculing him for his erectile problems. Mr. R. felt that if he improved his erectile functioning that he would become an acceptable marital partner. Medically, Mr. R. presented with a neurological condition of unknown origin which included progressive deterioration of fine motor control (i.e., slurred speech), and diminishing control of larger muscle groups (he walked with a shuffling gait and had recently driven off the road into a parked automobile when he lost control of his vehicle). Mr. R. had been examined by several urologists, one of whom had referred him to our research project for further evaluation. His stated goal was to receive a recommendation for a penile prosthesis, from which other medical professionals had attempted to dissuade him without success. As indicated, Mr. R. had significant psychological problems including depression, low self-esteem, and a series of unsuccessful relationships with women. He also had a serious degenerative neurological condition only minimally controlled by medication,

> which was likely to result in complete physical incapacitation or death within the next year. Nevertheless, Mr. R.'s primary focus at that time was to obtain a penile implant. Having a rigid penis was viewed as equally important as walking, or more so. His sense of value as a male was deeply affected by his inability to produce erections. Although it was not considered likely that Mr. R. would ever use his penile prosthesis with a partner, it was decided by project staff that Mr. R. would probably experience improved psychological adjustment from this operation. Mr.R. received pre- and post-operative psychotherapy to ensure that he did not harbor any unrealistic expectations for the outcome of his surgery. He was seen for one month following his penile prosthesis surgery, and reported being pleased with the outcome, although this had not affected his current relationship status.

This case illustrates the extreme importance of having erections for a male with other serious medical problems; in this case, as with many others, having a hard penis was much more important than the uses to which it would be put. Examining Mr. R's "unrealistic expectations" included promoting his realization that his penile prosthesis would not guarantee that his woman friend would marry him; it did not succeed in convincing him that his value as a person did not depend on having an erection. (Therapists are often confounded by their inability to overcome a lifetime of social conditioning in a few sessions of psychotherapy.) In acting as an advocate for this operation, I was again in the role of supporting an assumptive system with which I disagree, but acting in a way that seemed sensitive to the client's concerns. On an individual level, I do not think the cause of sexual liberation and growth would have been served by depriving this rather pathetic man of having a penile prosthesis in what was likely to be his last few years of life.

By living and working in the belly of the beast, one tends to make decisions which support the dominant structure. By the very nature of our research methodology and by our participation in a system which assumes the primary importance of the erect penis, our actions may speak louder than the words we use in sex therapy to reassure our clients that erections aren't that important after all. The reason that erections have been studied so assiduously is embedded within a larger social context in which male power is defined symbolically and often enforced physically by the erect phallus. The technology that has developed around this has not grown in a vacuum of "pure science," although the scientists themselves often view it in this manner. The identification of "impotence" as a problem, its precise definition, and the methods of assessment and treatment are reflective of this cultural emphasis. As Tiefer (1986) points out, "The persistence and increased use of the stigmatizing and stress-inducing label of impotence reflects a significant social moment in the social construction of male sexuality." Tiefer observes that the first definitions dictionaries give for impotence do not mention sex but refer to a general loss of vigor, strength, or power. She argues that "potency" confirms gender: "The capacity for erection is an important sign element of masculinity and control" (Gagnon & Simon, 1973, p. 62).

In this culture, the inability of the male to have a cylindrical tube of flesh between the legs become sufficiently rigid to insert in a vagina or other body orifice is considered a major and incapacitating sexual dysfunction; the inability to be emotionally intimate or to communicate clearly with a sexual partner is not diagnosed as a sexual dysfunction, and is certainly not being researched as fanatically as erectile dysfunction.

The argument made here is not that therapists and researchers should cease their efforts to understand sexual function and dysfunction, but that we *must* be fully aware of how the social construction of sexuality shapes our methodology and determines our emphasis. Although the professional literature has focused on methods of differentiating between organic and nonorganic causes of erectile dysfunction, in many cases both organic and psychological factors may be significant (Lo Piccolo, 1985). A number of biomedical and mechanical solutions have been developed in the past decade to treat erectile dysfunction. As Tiefer (1986) notes, sexually dissatisfied men are increasingly willing to discuss their erectile problems with a physician (Bancroft, 1983), and to look for medical solutions. Penile implants have become increasingly popular, and have received generally positive publicity in medical journals and the media. Several studies have indicated moderate to high levels of patient satisfaction, although most studies to date have not employed adequate methodological control (Coleman et al., 1985; Collins & Kinder, 1984). Schover and vonEschenbach (1985) emphasize the use of pre-screening candidates for implants to rule out medical and psychological factors that are known to result in poor post-operative adjustment. Tiefer (1986) cites three recent urological papers reporting high rates of post-operative infection and mechanical failure of the inflatable prostheses, necessitating removal of the device (Apte, Gregory, & Purcell, 1984; Fallon, Rosenberg, & Culp, 1984; Joseph, Bruskewitz, & Benson, 1984). Our own research group heard many clinical anecdotes of patients who simply did not ever use their implants for purposes of sexual activity, suggesting that there are alternative reasons for many men undergoing these operations.

A relatively recent development in the medical treatment of erectile dysfunction is the use of papaverine, a drug substance which, when injected into the spongy tissues (corpora cavernosa) of the penis, result in an erection which lasts from thirty minutes to a number of hours. The papaverine may be injected by a physician or a partner, or self-injected. Few complications have been reported, although at least one case has been reported in which priapism occurred; the erection would not subside and medical intervention was required.

Another less invasive mechanical device now available is the Vacuum Constriction Device, consisting of a transparent acrylic cylinder to which a vacuum source, a piston syringe, is attached at one end. The instructions for use are as follow:

> The penis is placed in the cylinder, which is then pressed against the body with enough force to form an airtight seal. A vacuum of no more than 250 mmHg is applied, and the penis gradually fills with blood and becomes rigid, a process that takes two to seven minutes. The rubber bands are then pushed off the end of the cylinder to constrict the base of the penis, and the cylinder is removed. The resulting rigidity lasts until the bands are removed, which should be done within 30 minutes.

Nadig et al. (1984) claim that 96% of their sample of 95 men had been able to achieve an "erection-like state with rigidity sufficient for vaginal penetration." The Vacuum Constriction Device is expected to cost less than $500.00 and is commercially available through prescription, keeping this device under the control of medical professionals.

"The Strut" (TM) marketed by Integrated Medical Systems, Inc., is a mechanical device consisting of a loop, yoke, and silicone rods worn externally on the penis. The device holds the flaccid penis in an erect position to facilitate penetration. The description on the accompanying flyer proclaims under the heading "Positive Effects: The therapeutic effect of a successful sexual experience with the Strut is both reassuring and reinforcing even in the discouraged organically impotent. . . . Likewise, the psychogenic patient gains confidence, improved self-esteem, and feels like *a whole person* again [emphasis mine]." Under the heading "Women and the Strut," the flyer reads: "Use of the strut will facilitate the re-establishment of a healthy sexual relationship, and the woman will once again have a partner *capable of performing again* [emphasis mine]."

Finally, illustration of the popularity of medical solutions is seen in the marketing approach of Big-Ox vitamin mineral tablets. Excerpts from the Big-Ox promotional literature include the following:

> Hospital doctors in Michigan and Washington report vital health discovery for men—Weak Erections Rise Strong And Hard . . . Half-Mast Erections Rise Tall And Strong! . . . As a man grows older, one of the surest signs of sexual weakness is *puny ejaculation* . . . sperm that has *lost its potency and vigor* . . . half-dead climaxes that *can't make babies*! . . . Amazing Results With 70-Year-Old Men! . . . Short-Boned Boys Get A 'Tool Up' For Better Health . . .

As is clear from the promotional literature above, there is a blatant attempt to capitalize on the credibility of the medical profession. Although the two latter products above are not typically administered or endorsed by the sex research and therapy establishment, they are strongly evocative of the context in which we perform our work.

The dilemma discussed here is whether it is possible to conduct sex research in such a manner that our methodology and our questions are not shaped by, and do not reify, an inherently negative, segmented, destructive and iatrogenic construction of sexuality. Can we take the fascinating technology and methodology developed for diagnosing male sexual dysfunction, and with the same sophistication and precision, adapt it to the exploration of female sexuality, without also unwittingly being subverted into a mechanistic view of sexuality in which genital functioning becomes the primary focus? Is it absurd to attempt to conceive of sex therapy or research, or even sexuality itself, outside the cultural context? If so, what forms would sex therapy and research take?

Let us first examine the implications of abandoning a phallocentric model of sexuality, and the nature of resistance to such change. The symbolic meaning of erections to men goes far beyond that associated with self-esteem or confirmation of masculine identity, and concerns erections as a symbol of male power. The sex research and therapy establishment has not analyzed its own contribution to the maintenance of this model, and is largely unconscious and complacently liberal-sounding in its approach. As Jackson writes,

> Despite tokenistic denunciations of the "double standard," sex research has in fact been characterized by a profoundly anti-feminist stance. Masters and Johnson . . . are dedicated to the maintenance of marriage and heterosexuality. They have attacked feminism as a "fad" and declared: ". . . fulfillment for the overwhelming majority of women requires an enduring relationship with a man" (Masters and Johnson, 1975: 84) (Jackson, 1984)

Let us examine how males feel about erections and intercourse. According to Hite (1981), "For some men, part of this validation of themselves as men involves not only 'performing' intercourse but more importantly 'having' or 'conquering' the woman, feeling dominant, superior." The following are excerpts from Hite's data:

> "Intercourse give me physical pleasure, releases from sexual tensions, and perhaps a degree of possession (which I'm reluctant to admit). It's a sense of superiority."
>
> "I must admit that intercourse, to me, is tied in with a subsidiary feeling of power over the woman, like that of a master and slave; it means to me that I have conquered all of her resistance."
>
> "The penis has classically been viewed as a weapon and I must admit that I at times feel that I am wielding an instrument of destruction. . . . Power for power's sake but also a way of reasserting oneself to compete within and face the world."

The uses married men make of sexual intercourse with women in a small sample of fifteen men were studied by Hollerorth (1987). Six of these subjects openly acknowledged using sexual intercourse to dominate or have control over their partners. One man described his need to dominate and control in the following manner:

> "It's got to be that I want to be master and dominant and aggressive and controlling the situation and making somebody necessarily inferior. I'm gonna be the boss . . . I want the woman . . . to be below. I am over her. I'm superior. I'm controlling. I have the weapon . . . I'm fully equipped. . . . "

It seems likely that these examples represent a significant aspect of male sexual identity, although not always so blatantly expressed. In this view, being deprived of one's "equipment" means deprivation of male status as primary.

Littewa (1972) writes of the elements of socialized male sexuality and response as objectification, fixation, and conquest. Erections are generated by fixating on a female or parts of her body which become objectified. In sexual conquest, the male succeeds in reducing the female from a being into a thing and achieves some form of sexual gratification. Littewa cites the existence and effectiveness of pornography, both verbal and photographic, as expression of a male sexuality in which "responses have little (or nothing) to do with the specific female we are with at any given moment." An example from the Letter of the Month feature in *Forum* magazine illustrates Littewa's point. The author describes a personal technique for masturbating using a hollow cardboard roll lubricated with vaseline lotion: "Try it; you'll be happy you did. It's better than fucking a human and *there's no involvement* [emphasis mine]." According to Littewa (1972), "What pornography does is create a fertile environment that makes it 'natural' for the imagination to objectify, fixate on, and conquer a verbally or photographically depicted female." In a sense, the male becomes a "self-contained sexual system" which can then conquer imaginary or real women in order to maintain or experience power, all of which has little to do with a mutual, egalitarian sexual interaction, and a lot to do with rape.

Pornography has served as a mainstay of the phallocracy, bolstering it ideologically by defending the equation of erection = power = masculinity against the challenges of feminism. On the Editors' page of *Variations* magazine, a publication of *Penthouse* that boasts an editorial board of numerous prominent sex researchers and therapists, Philip Nobile, an editor of *Variations*, writes of his feminist opponents:

> What do women against pornography want? They say that they want to even the sexual score . . . Egalitarianism everywhere. That is what they want . . . What women against pornography really want, I am convinced, is to *feminize* [emphasis mine] sex. Erotically speaking, they wish men to think and act like women. Then what are we to make of Andrea Dworkin, the dark lady of the women against pornography who champions heterosex without erections? Dworkin *dares* [emphasis mine] to write:
>
>> For men I suspect that this transformation [of their violent sexuality] begins in the place they most dread—that is, in a limp penis. I think that men will have to give up their precious erections and begin to make love as women do together . . . men will have to renounce their phallocentric personalities, and the privileges and powers given to them at birth as a consequence of their anatomy, that they will have to excise everything in them that they now value as distinctively "male."

Nobile is quite accurate in naming what strikes fear in the gut of the phallocracy, and represents the type of resistance which has been encountered by those who have seriously questioned the male model of sexuality.

Stoltenberg (1984), in an article entitled "Refusing to Be a Man," writes of ejaculation as not being necessary for sexual satisfaction, and of learning other ways to experience multiple non-ejaculatory orgasms. With regard to erections, he writes:

> Similarly what's called "impotence" is another internalization of a perverse system of male-dominant cultural values. Men (and women) are taught to believe that a cock is either limp and dysfunctional or erect and functional, and anything in between doesn't have sense unless it's clearly on its way to erectness or legitimately on its way to limpness (a legitimacy which can be presumed only if ejaculation has been achieved) . . .

Stoltenberg brilliantly delineates the self-defeating aspects of overfocusing on erections, which may lead to a deadening of response and sensation for the male, in addition to difficulties generating erections for some men. The destructiveness of a sexuality which, extended beyond the self, implies eroticization of power and domination, has global implications as our nation arms itself with more nuclear missiles which rise automatically from the ground, and once fully erect, point toward people in other nations. The nuclear arms race and the impotence industry can be viewed as reciprocal metaphors, existing as macro- and microcosms of the same culture. In the words of one subject quoted above, "I have the weapon . . . I'm fully equipped."

What are the implications of this analysis on the practice of sex research and sex therapy? Dworkin (1983) speaks of the concept of sexual intelligence, defined as "a human capacity for discerning, manifesting, and constructing sexual integrity. Sexual intelligence could not be measured in numbers of orgasms, erections, or partners; nor could it show itself by posing painted clitoral lips in front of a camera; nor could one measure it by the number of children born; nor would it manifest as addiction."

Applying the model of sexual intelligence to the study of sexuality would require reconceptualizing erections and intercourse with awareness of their function in a phallocentric society. As Dworkin (1987) notes about intercourse:

> Most women do not experience orgasm from intercourse itself. When Shere Hite, in her groundbreaking study, asked women to report their own sexual experiences in detail and depth, she discovered that only three in ten women regularly experience orgasm from intercourse. The women's self-reports are not ideological.
>
> Intercourse occurs in a context of a power relation that is pervasive and incontrovertible. The context in which the act takes place, *whatever the meaning of the act in and of itself* [emphasis mine], is one in which men have social, economic, political, and physical power over women. (p. 125)

Dworkin (1979) wrote on this same theme: "Because women are exploited as a sex class for sex, it is impossible to talk about women's sexuality outside the context of forced sex or, at the least, without reference to forced sex" (p. 83).

Dworkin (1987), in her most recent book *Intercourse*, poses questions that we in the field of sexuality must consider in our formulations, our research, and our theory:

> Can intercourse exist without objectification? Would intercourse be a different phenomenon if it could, if it did? . . . Would intercourse without objectification, if it could exist, be compatible with women's equality—even an expression of it—or would it still be stubbornly antagonistic to it? Would intercourse cause orgasm in women if women were not objects for men before and during intercourse? (p. 141)

For the researcher or therapist in the area of sexuality, adoption of the sexual intelligence model does not mean that we must stop our research or deny our clients treatment. What it does mean is that we must not forget the phallocentric context in which we work, and choose our methodology and treatment with conscious awareness of our ability to either reify or challenge the dominant model. Reconsidering the case of Mr. R. presented earlier, I would not change my decision to support him in his quest for a penile implant. This person was a sexual version of the patient with metastatic cancer for whom anesthetic treatment is likely the most humane intervention.

As a sex researcher, I attempt to choose my methodology with awareness of how inadvertently negative messages about sexuality can be transmitted to experimental participants. I attempt to ask questions in my research which take nothing for granted about sexuality, to look with new eyes at the phenomena I wish to understand, and to know that what I observe has developed within a context of gender hierarchy. As a feminist sex therapist, I continue to treat individuals and couples with sexual concerns, with awareness of the power asymmetry within and outside relationships, and the effect of this on the sexual politics of relationships and on the individual psyche. This frequently involves restructuring the distribution of power and control in the relationship in areas beyond sexual interaction. Naturally, this occurs within a social structure that undermines gender equality.

As a psychologist specializing in the area of sexuality, I believe that we can use our energies in a far more creative and evolutionary way than to work in unconscious support of the phallocracy. It requires considerable energy to conceive of the questions posed by Dworkin (1979, 1987). It requires even more energy to maintain an awareness of an egalitarian model of sexuality while existing and working within a culture and social reality antithetical to gender equality. The consequences of supporting the phallocracy lead ultimately to the annihilation of self and quite possibly to the annihilation of all. Adoption of the model of sexual intelligence encourages the reconstruction of sexuality consistent with nonhierarchical gender relations.

Philip Nobile, the editor of *Variations* magazine, was entirely correct when he wrote that his opponents work for a transformation in which men will have to "give up their precious erections" [or at least their primary importance], learn to make love as women do together, and erotically, to feminize sex. Does it make sense to attempt to reconstruct sex within the patriarchy? The patriarchy has indeed attempted to define and control our sexuality. However, the fact that some of us are critical of phallocratic sexuality indicates its absence of complete control over our consciousness. We must not turn away from sexuality itself as if it were a patriarchal abomination. By nurturing a new model of sexuality with a critical feminist awareness, we can resist phallocratic sex and sustain a vision of what the erotic could be.

REFERENCES

Apte, S.M., Gregory, J.B., & Purcell, M.H. (1984). The inflatable penile prosthesis, reoperation and patient satisfaction: A comparison of statistics obtained from patient record review with statistics obtained from intensive follow-up search. *Journal of Urology, 131*, 894-895.

Bancroft, J. (1983). *Human sexuality and its problems*. Edinburgh: Churchill-Livingstone.

Brannon, R. (1976). The male sex role: Our culture's blueprint of manhood, and what it's done for us lately. In D. David & R. Brannon (Eds.), *The forty-nine percent majority: The male sex role*. Reading, MA: Addison-Wesley.

Coleman, E., Listiak, A., Braatz, G., & Lange, P. (1985). Effects of penile implant surgery on ejaculation and orgasm. *Journal of Sex and Marital Therapy, 11* (3), 199-205.

Collins, G.F., & Kinder, B.N. (1984). Adjustment following surgical implantation of a penile prosthesis: A critical overview. *Journal of Sex and Marital Therapy, 10*, 255-271.

Dworkin, A. (1983). *Right-wing women*. New York: Wideview/Perigee.

Dworkin, A. (1987). *Intercourse*. New York: The Free Press, Macmillan, Inc.

Fallon, B., Rosenberg, S., & Culp, D.A. (1984). Long-term follow-up in patients with an inflatable penile prosthesis. *Journal of Urology, 132*, 270-271.

Gagnon, J.H., & Simon, W. (1973). *Sexual conduct: The social sources of human sexuality*. Chicago: Aldine.

Hite, S. (1981). *The Hite report on male sexuality*. New York: Alfred A. Knopf.

Hite, S. (1976). *The Hite report*. New York: Macmillan Publishing Company.

Hollerorth, H.J. (1986). The uses men make of sexual intercourse with women. Round table presentation, the Annual Meeting of the Society for the Scientific Study of Sex, St. Louis, Nov. 1986.

Jackson, M. (1984). Sex research and the construction of sexuality: A tool of male supremacy? *Women's Studies International Forum, 7*(1), 43-51.

Joseph, D.B., Bruskewitz, R.C., & Benson, R.C. (1984). Long-term evaluation of the inflatable penile prosthesis. *Journal of Urology, 131*, 670-673.

Littewa, J. (1972). The socialized penis. *Liberation, 18*(7), 61-69.

LoPiccolo, J. (1985). Diagnosis and treatment of male sexual dysfunction. *Journal of Sex and Marital Therapy, 11*, 215-232.

Masters, W.H., & Johnson, V.E. (1975). *The pleasure bond*. Boston: Little, Brown.

Masters, W.H., & Johnson, V.E. (1970). *Human sexual inadequacy*. Boston: Little, Brown.

Nadig, P., Becker, R.A., Ware, C., & Blumoff, R. (1984). New vacuum device to treat impotence is said to be a safe and effective alternative to penile implants. *Diabetes Outlook, 19*(5), 5.

Nobile, P. (1985). Editor's page: Feminizing sex. *Forum*, July 1985, p. 3.

Peplau, L.A., & Gordon, S.L. (1985). Women and men in love: Gender differences in close heterosexual relationships. in V.E. O'Leary, R.K. Unger, & B.S. Wallston (Eds.), *Women, gender and social psychology*. Hillsdale, NJ: Lawrence Erlbaum.

Schover, L.R., & Von Eschenbach, A.C. (1985). Sex therapy and the penile prosthesis: A synthesis. *Journal of Sex and Marital Therapy, 11*, 57-66.

Stoltenberg, J. (1984). Refusing to be a man. *Women's Studies International Forum, 7*(1), 25-27.

Tiefer, L. (1986). In pursuit of the perfect penis: The medicalization of male sexuality. *American Behavioral Scientist, 29*(5), 579-599.

Women and Sexual Ecstasy: How Can Therapists Help?

Gina Ogden

> Real satisfaction is not enshrined in a tiny cluster of nerves but in the sexual involvement of the whole person. . . . Women must hold out not just for orgasm but for ecstasy.
>
> *Germaine Greer*

Why write about women and sexual ecstasy in the age of AIDS, the Meese Commission and skyrocketing statistics of incest, rape and other abuses of women's sexual selves? To affirm that even in the face of epidemic, there can be an approach to sexuality based on health and optimism rather than on disease and dread. To illustrate that sexuality includes emotional, intellectual and spiritual connection as well as physical contact. To propose a missing link in the widely accepted literature of sexuality: women's concerns; and to suggest some new parameters of sexual function and satisfaction for women.

This paper will briefly review how sex research and therapy traditionally set limits on women's expression of sexuality. It will then offer a feminist, holistic concept of sexual ecstasy, and suggest how therapists can help women open themselves to it and own their experiences of it.

Gina Ogden is in private practice in Sheffield, MA. She is co-author of *Safe Encounters: How Women Can Say Yes to Pleasure and No to Unsafe Sex* (McGraw-Hill, 1988), and is working on a manuscript, *The Ecstasy Connection*.

THE SEXUALITY LITERATURE AND FALSE PARAMETERS FOR WOMEN

Mainstream sex research suggests and creates false parameters for women. First of all, most sex researchers are men, whose traditions subordinate rather than empower women. Second, most of the research about women's sexual function and satisfaction—even research by women—is based on pathology, or on other research, and not on what sexually functional women say satisfies them. Third, in considering only what they can quantitatively measure, mainstream researchers leave out the emotional and spiritual dimensions of sexuality so crucial to women.

The result is a literature steeped in the assumption that women's sexual responses are like men's sexual responses and should therefore meet men's definitions. Because of this basic assumption, this literature actually sets proscriptive standards for sexual normality.

According to this literature, sexual normality depends on three interdependent factors. The first is the coitus standard: Normal women have the desire and ability to perform coitus. The coitus standard also assumes that normal women are heterosexual. A second is the orgasm standard: Normal women consider orgasm to be the goal of a successful sexual interaction. The third is the genital stimulation standard: Both the coitus and orgasm standards center like homing pigeons on the primacy of direct genital stimulation.

This assumption moves researchers into particular theories. Men's theories about effective genital stimulation for women's orgasms range from coitus to clitoral contact (e.g., Freud, 1905; Kinsey, 1953). From this literature, sex therapy developed its theories. For women in sex therapy, presupposed goals of therapy are the desire and ability to come to orgasm by coitus or some other kind of genital stimulation (e.g., Kaplan, 1974 and 1981; Masters & Johnson, 1970).

Research that specifically examines the sexual responses of women generally departs from coitus as a norm, but it continues to normalize for women a goal of orgasm by means of genital stimulation. A school of clitoral orgasm, based on research of Dickinson (1933), Kinsey (1953) and Masters and Johnson (1966), includes Sherfey (1966), Dodson (1974), Barbach (1975) and Hite (1976).

G-Spot research points to a double-reflex theory of orgasm involving vaginal stimulation (e.g., Addiego, 1981; Belzer, 1981; Hock, 1980; Ladas, Whipple & Perry, 1982; Perry & Whipple, 1981).

Even much of the lesbian sex literature reflects this same basic assumption by its goal-oriented focus on orgasm by genital stimulation (e.g., Dodson, 1974; Califia, 1981; The Nomadic Sisters, 1976), as does much of women's erotica (e.g., Barbach, 1984, 1986; Friday, 1973, 1975; Kensington Ladies' Erotica Society, 1984).

Parallelling gynomissions in other disciplines, the sexological literature lacks systematic research on extragenital stimulation and the range of women's possible responses to it. For instance, over the years only a handful of sexologists have mentioned that extragenital stimulation is an option, including Dickinson, 1933; Kinsey, 1953; Hite, 1976; Barbach, 1976 and 1980; and Money, 1980. But all of these reports still assume that the reason for sexual stimulation is orgasm. With the exception of Loulan (1984), who downplays orgasm's role in women's sexual satisfaction and stresses relationship issues, the emphasis of the current sexological literature is on orgasm – the goal-oriented, physical, time-limited set of responses defined by Masters and Johnson.

The sexological literature discounts much of women's experience and forces it into quantitative molds, setting limits on possibilities for women rather than opening up possibilities and expanding them. This leaves clinicians – as well as women and their partners – misinformed or uninformed about significant areas of women's sexual function and satisfaction.

SEXUAL ECSTASY: WHAT FUNCTIONAL WOMEN SAY

I set out to explore a number of discrepancies between what the literature was reporting about women's sexual response and what clients, colleagues and friends were telling me was true for them. My basic research question was: How do women experience sex – what does sexual function and satisfaction actually mean for women?

In an attempt to attain information about women through self-report rather than laboratory testing, and from a perspective of health rather than pathology, I interviewed 50 self-assessed easily orgasmic women. Although I had wished to avoid an orgasm bias, I chose "easily orgasmic" to satisfy the requirements of a dissertation committee which argued that orgasm was the major indicator of sexual health.

I addressed these women as experienced experts who valued their own sexuality, and asked them to fill in some omissions from the literature: What does "easily orgasmic" mean? Are there satisfying stimulations other than genital? Are there measures of satisfaction other than orgasm? Can sexual ecstasy be described? How is it different from pleasure and orgasm?

In this context, I asked each woman to remember a peak sexual experience with herself, with a man, with a woman, and with a group (as many of these categories as applied). Each woman answered at least 150 questions about genital and extragenital stimulation, and about her degree of response to them. Details of her responses to each peak experience were charted on a matrix showing 14 kinds of touch, and 46 parts of her body—genital and extragenital. Her emotional, intellectual and spiritual responses were also recorded as integral to each experience.

In the course of their individual, two-hour interviews, these women reported a range of sexual function and satisfaction far more extensive than the normality standards set by the literature. For instance, they reported a high degree of extragenital satisfaction—that is, satisfaction resulting from stimulation of other parts of their bodies, or emotions, spirit or intellect. And in reporting measures of satisfaction, the women described not only orgasm, but a holistic continuum that included pleasure, orgasm and ecstasy.

Moreover, interviews with these women helped me arrive at four major understandings about sexual ecstasy:

- Women have no written tradition of sexual ecstasy, and therefore no consistent language to describe it.
- Sexual ecstasy is more easily understood by its effects than by its differential characteristics; that is, women may know exactly how it makes them feel even though they may be unable to describe exactly what it is.

- –Once women experience and understand the effects of sexual ecstasy, their concept of sexuality changes permanently.
- –A conceptual framework for understanding sexual ecstasy could free our method of inquiry about sexuality, expand our norms and suggest an infinite variety of criteria for sexual satisfaction.

The following Ecstasy model of sexuality derives from seven principles extrapolated from the material these women reported:

1. *Sex opens connections between self and others*. The basis for this statement is the systems view that each person is made up of interdependent, self-organized parts. In disease, these parts are disconnected from one another so that they do not function smoothly together (the definition of dis-ease is that liver and kidney are out of tune with each other; the head doesn't know what the heart is doing). In health, these parts work in synchrony and harmony; the head bone's connected to the foot bone. Sexuality is one route to opening ourselves up and making those connections, both with our selves and with partners. The women interviewed felt this sense of connection was primary to their experience.

2. *Sex expands boundaries*. Here are some boundary-expanding figures from the interviews: 52% of the women said they were able to come to orgasm on extragenital stimulation alone, with no stimulation of the genitals, and 64% reported ability to come to orgasm spontaneously, with no physical stimulation at all. Why are these figures boundary-expanding? Because sexology has been so focused on the genitals that researchers have not explored the extragenital potential before, beyond giving it a cursory glance.

In the age of AIDS, where genital contact might actually be life-threatening, one of the tasks for both sex researchers and therapists is to explore the possibilities and implications of extragenital and spontaneous sexual satisfaction.

3. *Sex is personally empowering*. The women reported that sexual ecstasy included what they sensed in their whole bodies–fingers and toes and ears as well as clitoris and G Spot, and they expanded on that to say that what was often as important to them as the body was the mind's involvement, and the heart and the soul. Sometimes these were even more important than the body.

When sex includes what women are thinking about and feeling emotionally and intuiting spiritually, as well as their physical sensations, then they experience good sexual feelings throughout their entire beings. They experience what I call the ecstasy *connection* – a sense that women describe as pure, personal power. Not the kind of power that comes from the ego and wants to take over the world, but the kind of power that wants to share.

4. *Sex is potentially life-changing, transforming*. When the women interviewed experienced this ecstasy connection, they reported that something uncanny happened to them. Their self-image improved. They actually saw themselves differently when they looked in the mirror. They were able to know they deserved attention and pleasure. They were able to ask for what they wanted in a way that enabled them to get it. Family therapists call this kind of change a systems shift. In his theory of peak experiences, Maslow coined the term Self-Actualization to describe this kind of phenomenon.

5. *Sex involves individual responsibility*. This concept is central. All of the women interviewed had the ability to say Yes to what they wanted and No to what felt coercive or painful or boring. To experience the ecstasy connection requires taking charge in this way rather than blindly doing what others may think is right, whether these others are partners, clergy, doctors or sexologists.

6. *The roles of pleasure, orgasm and ecstasy fluctuate with the situation*. This, too, is a central concept. We can become so focused on the physiological signals of arousal and orgasm, that we let them overshadow everything else. But if we can free up our thinking about sex, we can see sex in three dimensions. We can imagine a continuum that includes ecstasy, pleasure and orgasm. Not a linear continuum with a beginning, middle and end, but one that constantly moves and changes. We can view orgasm, ecstasy and pleasure as interdependent elements that shift in size and shape and importance depending on the situation.

7. *Norms and goals of sex fluctuate with the situation*. The women interviewed did not always want the same experience during sex. Sometimes they wanted orgasm and sometimes not. What they craved most at certain times was romance and love, or tender nurturing, or intimacy rather than physical stimulation. Or some-

times they were excited and opened up by the idea of commitment. Some of the women said they could not have satisfying sex without commitment, some said they could not have satisfying sex with it. The important factors here are that the women were able to be clear about their own sexual norms and goals when they needed to be, and that they had a process for working out any conflicting norms and goals with their partners.

IMPLICATIONS FOR THERAPISTS

Clinical models for sex therapy all contain some version of the coitus, genital focus, orgasm construct of sexual normality. For instance, all the female dysfunctions outlined in the mainstream literature depend absolutely on this construct: anorgasmia, dyspareunia, vaginismus (e.g., Masters & Johnson, 1970), and even the relatively complex psycho-sexual dysfunction, disorders of desire (e.g., Kaplan, 1979 and 1983; Rosen & Lieblum, 1987). But by basing therapeutic attitudes, goals and interventions on how the literature says women are supposed to respond sexually, therapists may be exacerbating women's sexual problems rather than helping.

It is standard sex therapy to teach women how to "achieve" orgasm through at-home genital stimulation (e.g., Barbach, 1975 and 1981), how to "overcome" disorders of desire through behavior modification (e.g., Kaplan, 1979 and 1983) and how to open up penis-rejecting vaginas through hypnotherapy and graduated dilation (e.g., Hartmann & Fithian, 1974). Within all of these techniques, it is standard to try to render women sexually functional by teaching them how to disconnect themselves from their memories and their feelings, and how to alter their parasympathetic responses so that they can tolerate the kinds of stimulation and penetration that the literature labels sexual.

One problem with such a linear, goal-oriented approach is that it emphasizes the physical aspect of sex and may leave out the whole person. Another is that "adjustment" may be a Procrustean solution—altering the woman rather than extending the parameters of her experience. By aiding a woman's adjustment to a coitus, genital focus, orgasm standard, therapists may be acting out the male medical bias in the sexuality literature rather than acting in the best interests of the woman. They may even be playing into an unequal partner dynamic and, in some instances, might as well be suggesting that men remain on top of women, in perpetual missionary position.

The women's reports of their experiences of sexual ecstasy throw into question some popular notions of sexual normality for women, and the tenets upon which sex research and therapy are based. First, the findings extend the parameters of sexual behavior for women beyond an identifiable sex act and its genital concomitants. In reporting overwhelmingly positive responses to extragenital stimulation, and to the emotional and spiritual dimensions of their experiences, the sample suggests that we can broaden our view of what is sexual to include a variety of stimulations that evoke responses of satisfaction, whether or not the stimulations focus on the vulva or lead to coitus or orgasm.

Next, these reports extend parameters of sexual satisfaction. In reporting a holistic continuum of pleasure, orgasm and ecstasy, the sample points up that orgasm, as it is presently defined in the literature, is too narrow a concept to hold as the criterion, or even the major criterion, of women's sexual satisfaction. Reports on this sample suggest that we can broaden our definitions of orgasm, and also include pleasure and ecstasy as measures of satisfaction for women.

Third, they challenge the standards by which the clinical literature defines sexual function and dysfunction. With extended parameters of behavior and satisfaction, therapists can reframe what they mean by sexual function and dysfunction for women. For women with so-called sexual dysfunctions, and for their partners, and their therapists, the reports of the women in the study can help extend the possibilities of normality beyond the standards of coitus, genital stimulation and orgasm. In fact, sexually normal women can experience – and experience as ecstasy – a rich variety of behaviors and responses not yet seriously entertained in the sex literature. Such behaviors include a spectrum of extragenital stimulations, and such responses include emotional and spiritual satisfaction.

HOW CAN THERAPISTS HELP?

Research based on what self-assessed functional women say satisfies them suggests a method of therapy centered on health rather than on disease. It also suggests a feminist, holistic method that deals with more than a tiny cluster of nerves or a set of symptoms. It suggests a method that can encompass the complexity and ambiguity of sexuality – a whole-person therapy based on connection of body, mind, heart, and soul.

As a guide to practicing whole-person sex therapy, therapists can take cues from the seven principles of the Ecstasy model drawn from interviews with easily orgasmic women:

1. Sex opens connections between self and others. A systems view allows therapists working with women to move beyond the linear, goal-oriented standards of sexual normality outlined in the mainstream literature. It offers a conceptual framework to re-view sexual desires and actions as connected to mind and emotions and spirituality, and not as separated out into an act or an event or an isolated constellation of sensations. Its reframing processes can be useful in helping women connecting sexuality with the whole of health and the whole of life – self, relationships, society, karma.

As therapists look at the field of sexuality through a feminist and holistic lens – as they change their point of view just a few degrees from center – the whole picture changes, as if they had turned a kaleidoscope. They can see a new picture of women's selves, one that is freer and more powerful than the literature has defined and proscribed.

2. Sex expands boundaries. When a woman feels relaxed and open, how might she describe her experiences of sexual ecstasy? If she's anything like the women interviewed, she doesn't right off the bat talk about counting the spasms of her orgasms, or timing the intervals between them. Chances are, she talks about how safe she may have felt, or how passionate or elated. Or maybe she mentions the strength and tenderness of those moments, or the smells, or the way the light played across her partner's body, or the radiant expression on her partner's face.

I submit that these are all admissable as clinical evidence, and that they're just as important as numbers and physical measurements.

For instance, the technique of taking a sex history can be boundary-expanding if a therapist's approach is that of an explorer open to helping clients discover possibilities and implications of all kinds of sexual stimulation, genital and extragenital, emotional and spiritual. In this context a therapist can follow leads based on what she knows and what her clients tell her rather than confining herself to lines of questioning suggested in the literature. And she can use all her training and talents to gather information not only from what her clients say but from how they say it—metaphors, tones of voice, body language.

Here, also, is an important opportunity for a therapist to use an expanded view of sexuality in behalf of safer sex practices. By acknowledging stimulation beyond the usual homing sites, she can help clients understand that deleting unprotected intercourse or even genital focus from their encounters does not mean the end of sexual satisfaction.

3. Sex is personally empowering. A therapist able to understand that sexuality involves the whole person and not just the body can help clients see that sexual options are potentially limitless, and that sexual pleasure, orgasm and ecstasy—however these are personally perceived—are potentially limitless sources of energy.

Here is an opportunity to educate women and also their partners about the limitations set on women's power throughout history by social constructions of sex and proscriptions of sexual normality. She can point out that even if a woman has had a sexually "normal" life, she may experience sexual interactions negatively as a result of cultural proscriptions. Sex may feel like dis-ease to her, or dissatisfaction, duty, deprivation, or dis-orientation. And it may feel like outright exploitation.

The therapist's attitude may be political or general, as the situation indicates. The important factor is that she can honor each women's unique perception of her sexual self, and feed it back—reframing it positively, when possible without jeopardizing women's integrity. This is the ultimate gift of empowerment: encouraging women to be responsive to, and responsible for, their own sexuality.

4. Sex is potentially life-changing, transforming. Reports of the interview sample reveal that profound experiences of sexual connection can lead women to profound enhancement of self-image. This characteristic has a neurobiological base. Neuronal hookups between cerebellum, frontal-temporal lobe, and limbic system make women uniquely able to experience dimensions of sexuality that are beyond the physical and temporary, dimensions that are both integrative and transcendental (Prescott, 1984).

To affirm these positive systems shifts and help women believe in them, a therapist can stress the holistic aspect of sexuality; the notion that well-being and power are a natural result of fully flowing energy, and that dysfunction is a result of disconnection. For a woman to experience full personal power, the sexual part of her being requires some kind of satisfying expression.

5. *Sex involves individual responsibility*. The responses mentioned by the sample bespeak sexual self-evaluation and definition rather than evaluation and definition by others.

How can a therapist help? She can understand the power dynamics involved in women fully owning sexual feelings that encompass the whole person—body, mind, heart, and soul. She can take individual responsibility for breaking therapeutic rules that say women's responses are like men's responses and center on coitus, genital focus, and physiologic orgasm.

She can be outrageous, and encourage her clients to be outrageous.

6. *The roles of pleasure, orgasm and ecstasy fluctuate with the situation*.

> Sometimes a sexual experience is pure pleasure . . . touching and talking just for the comfort of it. And sometimes it's ecstasy, out there, on the far side, like when we called to each other by our Greek names. Other times it's as if orgasm takes over and decides to play flamboyant leading lady.

Reports like this, of the easily orgasmic women, remind therapists and their clients that there's nothing wrong with having orgasms or becoming orgasmic—but in the single-minded search for the signals of physiological orgasm, women can lose sight of factors that are deeply significant and empowering about sex.

7. *Norms and goals of sex fluctuate with the situation*. The therapist can use this final principle to stress sexual self-definition, based on the sum of a client's experience—negative as well as pleasur-

able. In particular, she can encourage women to develop their own sexual norms and goals, with the understanding that these may differ from those set by the literature or society or partners, and with the understanding that her norms and goals can fluctuate and change.

I like the story of the incested client who as an adult was unable to experience sex as pleasurable until she understood the seven principles of ecstasy, and especially the principle of fluctuating norms and goals. What finally shifted attitudes for her was to acknowledge that her sexual norm was neither pleasure nor orgasm, but terror of invasion, and that she was so successful in establishing this norm that terror was the result of every sexual interaction.

How did such an acknowledgment make a difference?

> I realized that every time I tried to make love in the present, I was really spacing back to being eight, when I couldn't control what was happening. All of a sudden it occurred to me I had a choice now. I could go on feeling scared and disgusted, or I could get a new concept of sex. I had power. I couldn't change the past, but I could do something about the present.
>
> I talked with my partner and we figured out a dozen ways of being together sexually that weren't so scary for me – talking about feelings, keeping the lights on. . . . I always initiated. We both knew that certain things were never going to be comfortable for me, like S/M or roughness or vaginal penetration.
>
> Gradually, I began to want to feel turned on instead of in control. When that happened, I knew that sex now was different than when I was eight. The person with the sexual problem was my father, not me. I began to connect with parts of myself I never knew existed.

In summary, the Ecstasy model of sexuality is a feminist, holistic, and positive approach that allows therapists and clients to review women's sexuality beyond the normality standards of coitus, genital stimulation and orgasm, and offers them a conceptual framework to expand their own attitudes and experience. Specifically, this approach can help therapists understand sexual interactions in systemic terms, entertain open-ended standards of sexual satisfaction, and base their interventions on sexual self-definition and individual ownership of sexuality.

REFERENCES

Addiego, F., et al. (1981, February). Female ejaculation: A case study. *The Journal of Sex Research, 17(1)*, 13-21.

Barbach, L. (Ed.). (1986). *Erotic interludes*. New York: Doubleday.

Barbach, L. (Ed.). (1984). *Pleasures: Women write erotica*. New York: Doubleday.

Barbach, L., & Levine, L. (1980). *Shared intimacies: Women's sexual experiences*. Garden City, NY: Anchor/Doubleday.

Barbach, L.G. (1975). *For yourself: The fulfillment of female sexuality*. New York: Signet.

Belzer, E.G., Jr. (1981, February). Orgasmic expulsions of women: A review and heuristic inquiry. *The Journal of Sex Research, 17(1)*, 1-12 (Abstract.)

Califia, P. (1980). *Sapphistry: The book of lesbian sexuality*. Tallahassee, FL: Naiad Press.

Dickinson, R.L. (1970, originally published, 1933). *Atlas of human sex anatomy*. Melbourne, FL: Krieger.

Dodson, B. (1974). *Liberating masturbation: A meditation on self love*. New York: Bodysex Designs.

Freud, S. (1938). [Three contributions to the theory of sex.] In A.A. Brill (Ed. and trans.), *The basic writings of Sigmund Freud*. New York: Random House.

Friday, N. (1975). *Forbidden flowers: More women's sexual fantasies*. New York: Pocket Books.

Friday, N. (1973). *My secret garden: Women's sexual fantasies*. New York: Pocket Books.

Hite, S. (1976). *The Hite report: A nationwide study of female sexuality*. New York: Macmillan.

Hoch, Z. (1980, Summer). The sensory arm of the female orgasmic reflex. *The Journal of Sex Education and Therapy, 6(1)*, 4-7.

Kaplan, H.S. (1974). *The new sex therapy: Active treatment of sexual dysfunctions*. New York: Brunner/Mazel.

Kaplan, H.S. (1979). *The new sex therapy: Vol. 2: Disorders of sexual desire*. New York: Brunner/Mazel.

Kensington Ladies' Erotica Society. (1984). *Ladies' home erotica*. Berkeley: Ten Speed Press.

Kinsey, A.C., et al. (1953). *Sexual behavior in the human female*. Philadelphia: W.B. Saunders.

Ladas, A.K., Whipple, B., & Perry, J.D. (1982). *The G spot and other recent discoveries about human sexuality*. New York: Holt.

Loulan, J. *Lesbian sex*. (1984). San Francisco: Spinsters Ink.

Maslow, A.H. (1968). *Toward a psychology of being* (2nd ed.). New York: D. Van Nostrand.

Masters, W.H., & Johnson, V. (1970). *Human sexual inadequacy*. Boston: Little, Brown.

Masters, W.H., & Johnson, V.E. (1966). *Human sexual response*. Boston: Little, Brown.

Money, J. (1980). *Love and love sickness: The science of sex, gender difference and pair bonding*. Baltimore: Johns Hopkins.

Nomadic Sisters, The. (1976). *Loving women* (2nd, rev ed.). Sonora, CA: Authors.

Ogden, G. (1981). *Perception of touch in easily orgasmic women during peak sexual experiences*. Unpublished doctoral dissertation, San Francisco: The Institute for Advanced Study of Human Sexuality.

Perry, J.D., & Whipple, B. (1981, February). Pelvic muscle strength of female ejaculators: Evidence in support of a new theory of orgasm. *The Journal of Sex Research, 17(1)*, 22-39.

Prescott, J.W. (1975, April). Body pleasure and the origins of violence. *The Futurist*, 64-74.

Rosen, E.C., & Lieblum, S.R. (1987, May). Current approaches to the evaluation of sexual desire disorders. *The Journal of Sex Research, 23(2)*, 141-162.

Sherfey, M.J. (1966). *The nature and evolution of female sexuality*. New York: Random House.

SECTION II: THEORETICAL CONSIDERATIONS

Sexual Socialization for Therapists: Applications for the Counseling/Psychotherapy of Women

Elizabeth Yarris
Elizabeth Rice Allgeier

The absence of rigorous education and socialization for responsible sexual expression and satisfying sexual experience, coupled with the numerous sexual myths that abound in our culture, leave many people vulnerable to a variety of sexual difficulties. Those who turn to mental health professionals to attempt to resolve their sexual problems, however, may discover that many of these profes-

---

Elizabeth Yarris obtained her PhD in counseling psychology with a minor in social psychology, and, as a therapist and a supervisor, deals regularly with sexual problems of college students in the counseling center in which she is employed and with members of the community in which she lives.

Elizabeth Rice Allgeier obtained her PhD in social psychology with a minor in clinical psychology, and has studied human sexual attitudes and behavior throughout her career. She teaches a course for clinical graduate students in her department called Clinical Aspects of Research on Human Sexuality.

sionals also lack basic knowledge about sexuality and may be uncomfortable and reluctant to encourage open discussion of clients' sexual concerns. There are a few doctoral training programs that focus specifically on the study of human sexuality such as those at New York University and the University of Pennsylvania in Philadelphia. Most of these programs, however, are embedded in Departments of Education and do not confer the doctorate in clinical or counseling psychology. Traditional graduate programs in psychology include very little coverage relevant to sexual functioning (Anderson, 1986). Although doctoral students in psychology may be required to study diagnostic assessment for several semesters, for example, courses on human sexuality may not be available or only offered as electives lasting one semester. Pope, Keith-Spiegel, and Tabachnick (1986) found that less than 10% of the 575 psychologists who responded to their survey believed that they had received adequate training or supervision regarding how to handle client-therapist sexual feelings.

The absence of training and supervision regarding sexual issues may leave therapists vulnerable to value conflicts, problematic therapist-client attraction, and inadequacies in providing knowledgeable, effective, and ethical service for clients who need help with sexuality-related issues. Those clients who suffer as a result are frequently women (Fitzgerald & Nutt, 1986). Many of the content areas recommended by Gilbert (1980) as important to treatment with women are sexual issues, including "rape, pregnancy, menopause, childbirth, body image, menstruation, issues of physical power, and sexual preference" (p. 248). To this, we would add sexual, reproductive, and contraceptive decision-making, sexual dysfunction, harassment, paraphiliac behaviors, and concerns about the normalcy of sexual feelings and behaviors. The issue of expectations about male and female roles, rights, and responsibilities is relevant to all of these topics. Ignorance in these areas is complicated by educators' modeling of inappropriate behavior between people who are not equal in power; e.g., sexual contacts between teachers and students, supervisors and supervisees, etc. The purpose of this article is to increase awareness of both content and process issues relevant to human sexuality, to emphasize the necessity for training and continuing education, and to provide suggestions for graduate and post-graduate training. We will also address conflicts between personal and professional sexual socialization both during the acquisition of relevant sexual knowledge and therapeutic techniques, and in response to clients' sexual difficulties and value conflicts.

SEXUAL CONTENT

The problem of ignorance about human sexual function actually exists at three levels. First, it is important to remember that research on human sexuality is still in its infancy, and the field of "sexual science," as some call it, has yet to develop a coherent body of theory or robust methodological approaches with demonstrated reliability and validity (Davis, 1983).

Second, a related, but more germane issue for the present article is the erroneous assumption that graduate students are aware of the body of knowledge that does exist vis-à-vis sexual attitudes and behavior. When one of us (ERA) first offered a course called "Clinical Applications of Research on Human Sexuality" to clinical graduate students several years ago, only 20% of the students had a sufficient background either through their own independent reading, or through enrollment in an undergraduate course on human sexuality. The other 80% were lacking basic information about normative behavior (e.g., "Is it normal for a 19-year old male to masturbate every other day or does frequent masturbation [per se] indicate that he's over-sexed?"), sexual orientation (e.g., "Is homosexuality caused by bad experiences with the other gender, or by 'too many' hormones, or the wrong hormones?"), and so on. Professional experience and empirical data suggest that doctoral students receive inadequate training, supervision, and consultation for sexual issues (Birk & Brooks, 1986; Bouhoutsos, 1985; Gartrell, Herman, Olarte, Feldstein, & Localio, 1986; Graham, Rawlings, Halpern, & Herns, 1984; Holroyd & Brodsky, 1977; Pope, Schover, & Levenson, 1980; Pope et al., 1986).

It is also important to be aware of the third level of problems of ignorance about human sexual functioning – the frequent controversies over the validity of conclusions appearing in the literature. As will be seen, scientific beliefs vary over relatively short periods of time, underscoring the need for training and continuing education. The following material is not meant to be exhaustive, but rather to illustrate the importance, in responding to clients, of a knowledge of sexual content as well as the areas for which there is little empirical support or considerable controversy. For example, students can benefit from an understanding of the historical connection between the status of women and the prevailing sexual scripts that are applied to their sexuality (Weinberg, Swensson, & Hammersmith, 1983). Beliefs about the nature of female sexuality may interact with therapists' responses and treatment recommendations for women clients who describe problems with sexual response. In the 19th century, marriage manuals described sex as "an unfortunately procreative necessity" (Gordon & Shankweiler, 1971, p. 460). They quoted the woman's role in coitus from a book on the physiology of women by Hayes (1869, p. 227):

> As a general rule, a modest woman seldom desires sexual gratification for herself. She submits to her husband, but only to please him; and but for the desire to maternity, would far rather be relieved from his attentions.

During the first half of the 20th century, marriage manuals began to demonstrate a more positive attitude toward sexuality (within marriage) for both husbands and wives (Gordon & Shankweiler, 1971). However, some 19th century assumptions were carried over. As Weinberg et al. (1983) point out, women's sexuality was assumed to be fundamentally different from that of men's. That is, women were assumed to be less experienced and knowledgeable about sex and to have weaker "sex drives." Further, it was assumed that women expressed their sexuality only within marriage.

Those who believe that the latter half of the 20th century has been characterized by a more enlightened view of women's potential for sexual pleasure may be surprised to discover that in the brief period from 1950 to 1980, views about women's sexuality have shifted several times. Weinberg et al. (1983) analyzed the approaches taken by 49 marriage and sex manuals published in the United States during those three decades. They characterized the manuals as reflecting one of three distinct models of female sexuality: different-and-unequal, humanistic sexuality, or sexual autonomy. The different-but-unequal model predominated in manuals published between 1950 and 1973, and Weinberg et al. suggest that they could have also called it the "sleeping beauty" model because of implicit assumptions of women's sexual dormancy and men's responsibility to awaken women's sexuality. The humanistic model of sexuality dominated sex manuals published in 1973 and 1974, portraying sexuality as a basic human quality that need not be restricted to the heterosexual marital relationship, thus the terms "husband" and "wife" were replaced by terms like "partner," "female," etc. An emphasis remained, however, on sexual expression in the context of a loving relationship. Finally, manuals published between 1975 and 1980 were characterized by Weinberg et al. as employing a sexual autonomy model in which women are portrayed as self-sufficient and in control of their own sexuality: "The fact that they place such strong emphasis on noncoital techniques renders the man dispensable. . . ." (Weinberg et al., 1983, p. 318).

Ellison (1984) has expressed concern that some therapists may have an implicit goal of getting their clients to learn to respond sexually in ways that are consistent with the model of sexual arousal to which the therapist subscribes. In working with a nonorgasmic female client, for instance, the therapist may prescribe masturbation training. If the client is comfortable which these exercises and develops increased knowledge about her own responsivity patterns, that is fine. But if the client believes that masturbation is bad or sinful, the therapist may label the client as rigid and as sabotaging therapy. Ellison suggests that clients' needs might be better served by tailoring the therapeutic approach to the needs and values of individual clients rather than by demanding that they adhere to a particular treatment approach. For example, the autonomy model may be maladaptive if applied too heavily to a woman who finds greater satisfaction and pleasure with arousal and orgasm in the context of an ongoing committed relationship than she does with solitary masturbation or with recreational sex. At a more fundamental level, controversies exist with respect to the diagnosis of various sexual dysfunctions. For example, see the discussion of logical and gender biases in Masters and Johnson's (1970) criteria for orgasmic dysfunction provided by Wakefield (1987).

In Graham et al.'s (1986) survey of therapists' knowledge, attitudes, concerns, and strategies in counseling lesbian women and gay men clients, the most common major concern reported by therapists involved issues related to bias, countertransference, and maintaining objectivity. The second major concern was lack of knowledge or understanding of homosexuality. Lack of knowledge about sexual orientation, of course, would increase the difficulty of maintaining objectivity. Again, in this area, controversies abound regarding the etiology of homosexual orientation and the appropriate therapeutic response to homosexual persons (De Cecco, 1987; Green, 1987; Meyer-Bahlburg, 1987; Perper, 1987). Therapists-in-training need to be aware of these controversies and to be given the opportunity to discuss their affective reactions to variations in sexual orientation, female sexual response, treatment strategies for sexual dysfunctions and the many other sexual issues that they are likely to encounter as practicing therapists.

PROCESSING SEXUAL ATTITUDES AND FEELINGS

The acknowledgment of the sexual nature of human beings is seen by many psychologists as basic to addressing any sexually-related content or process within therapy (Abramowitz, Abramowitz, Roback, Corney, & McKee, 1976; Marmor, 1976; Pope et al., 1986; Keith-Spiegel & Koocher, 1985; Schover, 1983; Taylor & Wagner, 1976). In discussing the design of his course on human sexuality for psychotherapists, Anderson (1986) maintains that graduate students in counseling and clinical psychology are uncomfortable with sexual concerns and must go through long-term, in-depth instruction and discussion to become comfortable with clients' sexual issues. Within the psychoanalytic tradition, it has been expected that clients will frequently experience attraction to the therapist due to the caring and intimate nature of the relationship and also due to the "transference" of feelings directed at others in the clients' lives onto the therapist (Durré, 1980; Holroyd, 1983). On the other hand, Helen Singer Kaplan (1977), writing on the training of sex therapists, noted that if one of their students reported an erotic response from a client more than once a year, "we assume that he is doing something seductive, something countertransferential that is outside of his awareness" (p. 186). Such an assumption might be expected to reduce the likelihood that students—once aware of that belief system on the part of their trainers—would seek appropriate consultation when working with clients who report erotic responses.

Early Freudian doctrine held that any erotic feelings that the therapist had toward the client were a "mistake," but Pope et al. (1986) have found that therapists, too, are vulnerable to normal sexual feelings and attractions and many therapists admit to these. In Pope et al.'s survey of 585 practicing therapists, only 77 reported never experiencing attraction to any client. When asked if their graduate programs or internships had provided courses or other structured education about sexual attraction to clients, 55% reported no such education, 24% had received "very little," 12% received "some" and only 9% believed that sexual attraction issues had been given adequate coverage (p. 154). As stated above, those therapists who had at least some graduate training about potential sexual attraction to clients were more likely to seek consultation when erotic attraction became an issue in therapy than were those with no such training (Pope et al., 1986).

The nature of some of the questions and comments of some of the graduate students taking the author's clinical applications course suggested negative attitudes toward sexual responsiveness except under very circumscribed conditions. For example, when they were told about the content of the LoPiccolo and Lobitz film, "Becoming Orgasmic," concern was expressed that the (male) undergraduate projectionist might become aroused while screening it for the class, the implication being that arousal, per se, was deleterious. (It should be noted that the projectionists are not required to remain in the room after starting films.) A related example occurred about half way into the semester, during discussion of erotic attraction between client and therapist. One very bright student acknowledged that he had seen sex as very compartmentalized and sexual attraction to a client as a non-issue, not because such feelings can be managed in a noninjurious manner, but because he didn't think that they would occur in that context.

As noted above, Graham et al. (1986) found that therapists were concerned with their own bias, countertransference and objectivity in working with gay clients. Questions were raised by their respondents concerning discomfort with same gender client attraction to the therapist and about the therapists' own sexuality. In general, reports indicate that trainees and practicing clinicians alike are not encouraged to be aware of their own sexual feelings in the professional setting although such reactions clearly exist (Bouhoutsos, 1985; Brodsky, 1980; Durré, 1980, Keith-Spiegel & Koocher, 1985; Marmor, 1976; Pope et al., 1986; Schover, 1983).

In summary, there is evidence that normal sexual feelings are denied, criticized, compartmentalized, and sometimes, result in discomfort when acknowledged. Inattention to normal and appropriate erotic feelings may lead to their inappropriate expression.

Inappropriate Sexual Relationships

When we entered graduate school in psychology in the 1970s, there was a common phrase heard among male faculty members. "The salary is lousy, but the fringe benefits are good." Among the "fringe benefits" referred to jokingly was the access to sexual favors from graduate and undergraduate females. Those students who engaged in sexual contact with their professors were subsequently described as getting their degrees "under" Dr. ______, the implication being that if they hadn't slept with their professor(s), they might not have obtained their advanced degrees. Both of us obtained our doctorates with the ethical and appropriate help of our major professors, but we have students, colleagues, and friends who experienced pressure for sexual relations during their training, or who, in some cases, initiated such relationships and received "favorable" responses to their initiations.

Earlier, we discussed the importance of being able to process issues relevant to sexual concerns and feelings during training and supervision and while dealing with clients' feelings. Such processing may be impeded when teachers, supervisors, or clinicians participate in sexual liaisons with students, supervisees or clients. Such inappropriate relationships contain a number of problems. One involves the issue of the importance of disinterest, from a personal standpoint. That is, when a teacher has a sexual relationship with a student, the teacher's judgment may be impaired regarding the student's level of mastery or what is in the student's best interest regarding educational or career development.

The second problem with such sexual relationships concerns unequal power between the participants. Increased awareness of sexual misconduct and its potential consequences may be part of a larger movement of concern over discriminatory unequal power relationships. Most victims of inappropriate therapist or educator sexual misconduct are younger females of lower status (Nathan, Thoreson, & Kilburg, 1983) or people in crisis following divorce or other problems (Zelen, 1985). However, educators, supervisors, or clinicians of either gender may harass students or clients of the same or other gender (Glaser & Thorpe, 1986; Robinson & Reid, 1985), and as Brodsky succinctly put it, "The major issue with seduction, of course, is not a sexual issue, but one of the abuse of power" (1980, p. 516). Nathan et al. (1983) conclude that there is an urgent need for the education of psychologists on the negative consequences of sexism, as well as consciousness-raising around the issues of power abuse and potential exploitation in the naturally unbalanced power relationship of psychologists with their students and clients (p. 32). Even if a student attempts to initiate the sexual relationship, the appropriate response of the educator is to help the student process his or her feelings and to point out the problems inherent in sexual relationships between people who are not equal in power, rather than to hop into bed with the student. Anxiety-produced heightened arousal is prevalent among graduate students and may, under certain conditions, be mislabeled as "erotic attraction" or "love" (Walster, 1971). Further, part of the students' attraction to a teacher is likely to stem from the teacher's greater power and, similar to transference in therapy, if the teacher is trying to help the student achieve his or her professional goals, the attraction may be enhanced. Such feelings are normal, but that does not mean that they should be carried out behaviorally.

The third problem is closely related to the first two: whose needs are being met? In all of these relationships (teacher-student, supervisor-supervisee, therapist-client), the first person in each of these pairs is in a position of authority over the second in which they are being trusted to act in a disinterested manner to help the second person attain personal or professional goals. When persons in authority choose to meet their intimacy and sexual needs using subordinate persons, the authority figures are violating the trust inherent in their position.

We have focused on the teacher-student relationship, because there is evidence that it is in this relationship that sexual harassment begins, and that students are confused about their inherently lesser status. Robinson and Reid (1985) found that younger women-in-training were more likely to experience seduction by educators than were older women. In the Glaser and Thorpe (1986) study, there was a higher rate of student-educator contact with students who were divorcing or separating during graduate training (34% vs. 22%). Robinson and Reid (1985) and Glaser and Thorpe (1986) also found that when surveyed at a later time in their lives, female psychologists who had been victims of some kind of sexual advance as students reported that as students, they had perceived the advances as less coercive, less of an ethical problem, and less hindrance to the working relationship than they now believed as professionals. Essentially, they reported that at the time of the advances, they believed that they were giving informed consent. When one person has evaluative, economic, or diagnostic power over another person, the likelihood that the other person can freely give informed consent is sharply reduced, however, and the likelihood of coercion is increased (Box, 1983).

In spite of the evidence, students have been prone to deny vulnerability. Some students object to being put on the same level with clients and being viewed as unstable, immature, with no rights to decision-making or respect for personal judgment (Gerard, 1981, as reported in Keith-Spiegel & Koocher, 1985). In support of this view, some feminist therapists believe that the counselor-client relationship is egalitarian (Gilbert, 1980). This belief system is in conflict with the premise that therapists and educators have inherent power over clients and students.

During the past decade, a number of researchers have examined the presence and sequelae of educator-student sexual relationships (Glaser & Thorpe, 1986; Pope, Levenson, & Schover, 1979; Robinson & Reid, 1985). For example, Pope et al. found that for females, sexual contact with educators when they were students was significantly related to the likelihood that later in professional positions, these females would engage in sexual contacts with students or clients.

Surveys of psychiatrists (Gartrell et al., 1986), licensed psychologists in California (Bouhoutsos, Holroyd, Lerman, Forer, & Greenberg, 1983), licensed PhD psychologists (Holroyd & Brodsky, 1977) and members of the Division of Private Practice of the APA (Pope et al., 1986) reveal that between .6 and 3.1 percent of female therapists and 4.8 to 9.4 percent of male therapists self-report sexual contact with clients. Many therapists who have sexual contact do so with more than one client (Gartrell et al., 1986; Holroyd & Brodsky, 1977). Legal and ethical complaints of sexual impropriety filed against psychologists have increased greatly, extending to violations which occurred after termination of the therapeutic relationship (Sell, Gottlieb, & Schoenfeld, 1986). In addition to concerns about sexual relationships with current students and clients, attention must be paid to such relationships after the educational or therapeutic relationship has been formally terminated. Ethical guidelines and most state laws do not address this issue, but reading of the legal claims by former clients might be enough to dissuade educators and therapists pursuing such relationships (Sell et al., 1986). Many hold the belief that the power differential between client and therapist can never be completely eliminated. If that is true, neither a social nor an erotic relationship can ever exist.

Sexual contact between therapist and client consistently has resulted in much more harm than benefit to the client (Grunebaum, 1986; Nathan et al., 1983; Taylor & Wagner, 1976; Zelen, 1985). Information reported by female clients who had been sexually involved with a previous therapist reveals difficulties with trust, self-concept, and expression of anger (Sonne, Meyer, Borys, & Marshall, 1985) and mistrust and anger at men along with increased psychological and psychosomatic problems (Feldman-Summers & Jones, 1984). Numerous other detrimental correlates are reported including subsequent hospitalizations and suicides (Bouhoutsos et al., 1983).

Therapist Vulnerabilities

Clearly there are harmful sequelae for clients who have sexual contact with their therapists. What are the correlates for therapists of engaging in sexual contact with their clients? The literature on sexual misconduct of therapists with clients provides us with a profile of the "typical" offending clinician (Keith-Spiegel & Koocher, 1985; Zelen, 1985), that is, the individual who was not able to manage erotic feelings appropriately in therapy. According to Keith-Spiegel and Koocher (1985), the most common offender was a male in his 40s or 50s. Typically there was more than one personal problem in his life such as fear of intimacy, marital crisis, feeling personally or professionally a failure, poor impulse control, isolation from peer support, and depression. There seem to be a tendency for therapists who have engaged in sexual contact with their clients to repress, minimize, or distort the potential for harm stemming from therapist-client sexual involvement. Specifically, Butler and Zelen (1977) found that the majority of therapists in their sample reported being unable to remember the details of their sexual contact with the client. Other studies have found therapists to minimize the impact of therapist-client sexual episodes (Gartrell et al., 1986) or to perceive a present client's sexual contact with a previous clinician as relatively harmless (Holroyd & Bouhoutsos, 1985). Therapists who become sexually involved with their clients, however, report a number of personal problems, discomfort, and guilt (Butler & Zelen, 1977; Keith-Spiegel & Koocher, 1985; Pope et al. 1986; Zelen, 1985). Unfortunately, these potential difficulties are not often addressed in graduate training programs (Pope et al., 1986), although attention to "sexual misconduct" (Nathan et al., 1983) of psychologists has increased within the last decade.

We are in agreement with the recommendation of Sell et al. (1986) who emphasize that clinical training programs must greatly increase attention to professional ethics and that faculty must act as appropriate models of social and sexual behavior. In addition, we recommend specific training in sexually related issues to be described below.

TRAINING

The consequences of inadequate knowledge, discomfort with, and repression of feelings around sexual issues, and ethical confusion results in value conflicts and deficient provision of effective and ethical services for clients. As a partial remedy, we have several broad suggestions and comments. To provide adequate training relevant to the variety of issues we have raised earlier in this article, therapists-in-training should be offered a year-long course in which they are exposed to the accumulated knowledge about human sexuality. Throughout the year, students should be given the opportunity to become aware of their affective reactions to the content, and to clarify both their personal and professional on sexually-related issues. They should be encouraged to consult with their supervisors or colleagues throughout their professional lives when sexual issues arise.

Ballou and Gabalac (1985) argue that traditional training methods cannot adequately meet the needs of women because the content is basically antifeminist and the structure is one of a power-based hierarchy. However, we believe that even within a more traditional training model, there is opportunity to confront stereotypes and to engage in productive self-assessment of sexuality-related issues. Brodsky (1980) recommended the use of group supervision as one way to accomplish this. The process that takes place in a sexuality class for graduate-level clinicians is similar to group supervision and provides an opportunity for changes in attitudes and values as well as the accumulation of knowledge about human sexual behavior.

Each student brings to the class his or her unique set of historical and current relationships. In a typical graduate student class, there is a range from the older-than-average student who is married or divorced, and who may or may not have children, to a 22-year-old fresh out of undergraduate school who has never had a sexual relationship. Some will be currently involved in an ongoing monogamous sexual relationship with a person of the same or other gender, some will be experimenting with numerous partners, and some may not be sexually active during their participation in the class. Some class members will be romantically and/or sexually involved with each other and some will be the recipients or perpetrators of sexual harassment or misconduct with peers, teachers, supervisors, or clients in practicum settings. Inevitably, there are lifestyle disagreements among members of the class.

The course instructor must be acutely aware of her/his position and responsibility to model appropriate behavior, including what is stated during a course (Glaser & Thorpe, 1986; Pope et al., 1986; Robinson & Reid, 1985). At the outset, both the syllabus and the instructor's verbal introduction to the course should contain enough description about the course to enable students to give informed consent. For example, some students will have seen movies or videos that are far more sexually explicit than are most audiovisual materials developed for sex education courses. Other students may never have seen another person of the same or other gender nude or, for those who have, they may believe that such viewing should only occur in the context of a marital relationship. Thus the instructor must be aware of, and respect, the value systems, vulnerability, and potential anxiety of the students. Some of the students may have been socialized in environments in which they have never heard the names of anatomical parts (e.g., penis, clitoris) spoken aloud, or in which the use of such terms is as unacceptable as the use of the kinds of four-letter words that are banned from prime-time television. It is likely that students raised in such environments will have also learned a strong association between sex, dirt, and sin. A period of desensitization may be necessary during which the students gradually become accustomed to, and comfortable with, hearing and using appropriate terminology in a gender-integrated classroom setting.

Another factor that is likely to interact with the process within a sexuality class is the relationship among the students themselves. The content, including films, may elicit a variety of responses, including sexual arousal that may or may not be appropriately directed toward one's classmates. The acknowledgment and negotiation of how to deal with the attraction or arousal can provide excellent modeling and practice for related concerns with clients or others.

We suggest holding class sessions once a week for two and a half to three hours each week to provide enough time to deal with the content of a particular topic and to discuss values and affective reactions to each topic. We are preparing a description of the contents of the course with specific suggestions for facilitating class discussion of their ethical and emotional responses to each of the issues. In particular, the instructor should be alert to unspoken difficulties that students may experience as they are exposed to the wide range of sexual topics about which therapists-in-training should be knowledgeable. Instructor sensitivity is especially needed before and after viewing films that are sexually explicit. Students can also be encouraged to discuss issues and concerns outside of class time.

A very important educational relationship for the trainee is with the clinical supervisor. Supervision provides a unique opportunity for the student to discuss sexual issues relevant to training and to work with clients. Those members of the sexuality class who have trusted supervisors will benefit from the freedom to consult concerning issues raised in class and with clients. Brodsky (1980) recommends that during training there be both same and other gender supervisors so that gender-role conflicts, biases, and erotic attraction can be experienced and processed to the benefit of all. Pope et al. (1986) found that practicing therapists were more likely to seek consultation when sexually attracted to their clients if sexual issues were discussed openly during graduate training.

SUMMARY AND CONCLUSIONS

The absence of education, training, and supervision of mental health professionals regarding sexual content, feelings, and interactions may leave therapists ill-prepared to respond to client needs and may increase the likelihood of inappropriate handling of therapist-client sexual attraction. Those therapists who had inappropriate sexual relations with their educators and supervisors while in training are more likely to engage in sexual contacts with their clients during their professional lives. However, those who receive training in sexual issues are more likely to seek consultation when needed. A year-long training model is suggested for students that would include exposure to sexual knowledge, processing of sexual feelings, and examining appropriate handling of those feelings. Students should be encouraged to process with their supervisors their concerns about sexual issues relevant to their training and work with clients. With the provision of sexual knowledge and the increase in conscious awareness of attitudes, values, and feelings relevant to sexuality, the ability of the therapist-in-training to provide accurate, ethical, and effective care for their clients should be enhanced. Women clients and students will benefit greatly from these improved training programs in sexuality. Women have suffered most from inappropriate sexual relations and many of the issues which bring women to therapy are a result of unequal power relationships and/or related to problems with various aspects of sexuality. We encourage all teachers, trainers, supervisors, and therapists to examine their knowledge, biases, and behavior when faced with the sexual and gender-role concerns of women.

REFERENCES

Abramowitz, S. I., Abramowitz, C. V., Roback, H. B., Corney, R. T., & McKee, W. (1976). Sex-role related countertransference in psychotherapy. *Archives of General Psychiatry*, 33, 71-73.

Anderson, W. (1986). Stages of therapist comfort with sexual concerns of clients. *Professional Psychology: Research and Practice*, 17, 352-356.

Ballou, M. & Gabalac, N. W. (1985). *A feminist position on mental health*. Springfield, IL: Charles C Thomas.

Birk, J. M. & Brooks, L. (1986). Required skills and training needs of recent counseling psychology graduates. *Journal of Counseling Psychology*, 33, 320-325.

Bouhoutsos, J. C. (1985). Therapist-client sexual involvement: A challenge for mental health professionals and educators. *American Journal of Orthopsychiatry*, 55, 177-182.

Bouhoutsos, J., Holroyd, J., Lerman, H., Forer, B., & Greenberg, M. (1983). Sexual intimacy between psychotherapists and patients. *Professional Psychology: Research and Practice*, 14, 185-196.

Box, S. (1983). *Power, crime, and mystification*. London: Tavistock Publications LTD.

Brodsky, A. M. (1980). Sex role issues in the supervision of therapy. In A. K.

Hess (Ed.), *Psychotherapy supervision. Theory, research, and practice* (pp. 509-522). New York: Wiley.

Butler, S. & Zelen, S. L. (1977). Sexual intimacies between therapists and patients. *Psychotherapy: Theory, Research, and Practice*, 14, 139-145.

Davis, C. M. (Ed.) (1983). *Challenges in sexual science: Current theoretical issues and research advances.* Lake Mills, IA: The Society for the Scientific Study of Sex, Inc.

De Cecco, J. P. (1987). Homosexuality's brief recovery: From sickness to health and back again. *The Journal of Sex Research*, 23, 106-114.

Durré, L. (1980). Comparing romantic and therapeutic relationships. In K. S. Pope (Ed.), *On love and loving: Psychological perspectives on the nature and experience of romantic love* (pp. 228-243). San Francisco: Jossey-Bass.

Ellison, C. R. (1984). Harmful beliefs affecting the practice of sex therapy with women. *Psychotherapy*, 21, 327-334.

Feldman-Summers, S., & Jones, G. (1984). Psychological impacts of sexual contact between therapists or other health care practitioners and their clients. *Journal of Consulting and Clinical Psychology*, 52, 1054-1061.

Fitzgerald, L. F., & Nutt, R. (1986). The division 17 principles concerning the counseling/psychotherapy of women: Rationale and implementation. *The Counseling Psychologist*, 14, 180-216.

Gartrell, N., Herman, J., Olarte, S., Feldstein, M., & Localio, R. (1986). Psychiatrist-patient sexual contact: Results of a national survey, I. Prevalence. *American Journal of Psychiatry*, 1986, 143, 1126-1131.

Gerard, S. (1981, April). Attitudes of students toward sexual relations between students and professor. Paper presented at the Western Psychological Association meeting, Los Angeles, CA (as reported in Keith-Spiegel & Koocher, 1983).

Gilbert, L. (1980). Feminist therapy. In A. Brodsky, & R. Hare-Mustin (Eds.), *Women and psychotherapy* (pp. 245-265). New York: Guilford.

Glaser, R. D., & Thorpe, J. S. (1986). Unethical intimacy: A survey of sexual contact and advances between psychology educators and female graduate students. *American Psychologist*, 41, 43-51.

Gordon, M. & Shankweiler, P. J. (1971). Different equals less: Female sexuality in recent marriage manuals. *Journal of Marriage and the Family*, 32, 665-674.

Graham, D. L. R., Rawlings, E. I., Halpern, H. S., & Hermes, J. (1984). Therapists' needs for training and counseling lesbians and gay men. *Professional Psychology: Research and Practice*, 15, 482-496.

Green, R. (1987). *The "sissy boy syndrome" and the development of homosexuality: A 15 year prospective study*. New Haven, CT: Yale University Press.

Grunebaum, H. (1986). Harmful psychotherapy experiences. *American Journal of Psychotherapy*, 40, 165-176.

Hayes, A. H. (1869). Physiology of woman and her diseases; or, Woman, treated physiologically, pathologically, and esthetically. Boston: Peabody Medical Institute (quoted in Gordon & Shankweiler, 1971).

Holroyd, J. (1983). Erotic contact as an instance of sex-biased therapy. In

J. Murray & P. R. Abramson (Eds.), *Bias in psychotherapy* (pp. 285-308). New York: Praeger.

Holroyd, J. & Bouhoutsos, J. C. (1985). Biased reporting of therapist-patient sexual intimacy. *Professional Psychology: Research and Practice*, 16, 701-709.

Holroyd, J. C., & Brodsky, A. M. (1977). Psychologists' attitudes and practices regarding erotic and nonerotic physical contact with patients. *American Psychologist*, 32, 843-849.

Kaplan, H. S. (1977). Training of sex therapists. In W. H. Masters, V. E. Johnson, & R. D. Kolodny (Eds.), *Ethical issues in sex therapy and research* (pp. 182-189). Boston: Little, Brown.

Keith-Spiegel, P. & Koocher, G. P. (1985). *Ethics in psychology: Standards and cases*. New York: Random House.

Marmor, J. (1976). Some psychodynamic aspects of the seduction of patients in psychotherapy. *American Journal of Psychoanalysis*, 36, 319-323.

Masters, W. H., & Johnson, V. E. (1970). *Human sexual inadequacy*. Boston: Little-Brown.

Meyer-Bahlburg, H. F. L. (1987). Psychoendocrine research and the societal status of homosexuals: A reply to De Cecco. *The Journal of Sex Research*, 23, 114-120.

Nathan, P., Thoreson, R., & Kilburg, R. (1983). Board of Professional Affairs Steering Committee on Distressed Psychologists: Draft Report. Washington, DC: American Psychological Association.

Perper, T. (1987). Enough is enough: Reflections on the views of De Cecco and Meyer-Bahlburg. *The Journal of Sex Research*, 23, 127-129.

Pope, K., Keith-Spiegel, P., & Tabachnick, B. G. (1986). Sexual attraction to clients: The human therapist and the (sometimes) inhuman training system. *American Psychologist*, 41, 147-158.

Pope, K. S., Levenson, H., & Schover, L. R. (1979). Sexual intimacy in psychology training: Results and implications of a national survey. *American Psychologist*, 34, 682-689.

Pope, K. S., Schover, L. R., & Levenson, H. (1980). Sexual behavior between clinical supervisors and trainees: Implications for professional standards. *Professional Psychology*, 11, 157-162.

Robinson, W. L., & Reid, P. T. (1985). Sexual intimacies in psychology revisited. *Professional Psychology: Research & Practice*, 16, 512-520.

Schover, L. R. (1983). Psychotherapists' responses to client sexuality: A source of bias in treatment? In J. Murray and P. R. Abramson (Eds.), *Bias in psychotherapy* (pp. 256-284). New York: Praeger.

Sell, J. M., Gottlieb, M. C., & Schoenfeld, L. (1986). Ethical considerations of social/romantic relationships with present and former clients. *Professional Psychology: Research and Practice*, 17, 504-508.

Sonne, J., Meyer, C. B., Borys, D., & Marshall, V. (1985). Clients' reactions to sexual intimacy in therapy. *American Journal of Orthopsychiatry*, 55, 183-189.

Taylor, B. J., & Wagner, N. N. (1976). Sex between therapists and clients: A review and analysis. *Professional Psychology*, 7, 593-601.

Wakefield, J. C. (1987). Sex bias in the diagnosis of primary orgasmic dysfunction. *American Psychologist*, 42, 464-471.

Walster, E. (1971). Passionate love. In B. I. Murstein (Ed.), *Theories of attraction and love*. New York: Springer.

Weinberg, M. S., Swensson, R. G., & Hammersmith, S. K. (1983). Sexual autonomy and the status of women: Models of female sexuality in U.S. sex manuals from 1950 to 1980. *Social Problems*, 30, 312-324.

Zelen, S. L. (1985). Sexualization of therapeutic relationships. The dual vulnerability of patient and therapist. *Psychotherapy*, 22, 178-185.

The Theory of Sexual Relativity: Female Reality/Male Myth

Gale Holtz Golden

After showing her boyfriend how to get rid of "ring around the collar," our "new age" woman settled in front of the T.V. with her "new age" boyfriend and grabbed the remote control out of his hand. She then turned off the T.V. and seductively demanded his attention (and his sexual favors, the commercial implies). While this 1987 commercial would have us subtly believe there is an end to the double standard in the sexual arena, that women can be sexually assertive, too, it appears that women have a long way to go in the laundry!

But is it desirable or realistic to do away with the double standard in the bedroom? What seems more realistic (indeed urgent) is a deeper understanding of the unique female and male sexual paradigms so that heterosexual couples are not handicapped in their push for equality in the logistics of sexual encounters. Masters and Johnson (1979) concluded that same-gender partners have less sexual dysfunction because they do not have to leap over their physiological differences in sexual situations. The body of the person they are making love to is like their own. Even if same-gender lovers fail to account for the unique psychological context of their partner, chances are they will do all right in applying their own experience to their partner's body, just because it is, at the very least, physiologically similar. For most same-gender partners, a few minor adjustments will probably facilitate a very satisfying sexual experi-

---

Gale Holtz Golden, MSW, CSW(R), is a clinical social worker in full-time private practice. She is Certified Sex Therapist and Clinical Assistant Professor of Psychiatry at the University of Vermont. This article is based on observations made during her clinical practice of twenty-two years.

ence. In a heterosexual experience, which will be the primary focus of this paper, the common physical and psychological bond is not likely to exist.

For roughly the past twenty years, researchers and writers in the field of human sexuality have focused on the similarities in female and male sexuality. For example, in 1975, Money and Tucker emphasized that there were only four distinct differences in reproductive biology between female and male: "only a man can impregnate, only a woman can menstruate, gestate, and lactate." Indeed, the female and male urogenital systems are homologous in most respects. Homologous structures arise from the same embryologic tissues but may develop into one kind of structure in the female and another, somewhat similar one, in the male. Sevely and Bennett (1978) developed a list of homologues in the female and male urogenital system which illustrates this point:

Female	Male
1. Ovary	1. Testis
2. Vagina	2. Vagina masculina
3. Uterus	3. Prostate utricle
4. Fallopian Tubes	4. Appendix Testis
5. Urethra	5. Prostatic Urethra
6. Labia minora	6. Urethral tube of penis
7. Labia majora	7. Scrotum
8. Clitoris	8. Penis
9. Bartholin glands	9. Bulbourethral glands
10. Prostate glands	10. Prostate glands

Given these similarities in the embryological origin of the female and male structures, it is not surprising that there are so many similarities in the physiological response of both genders to sexual stimulation. This was reinforced by Masters and Johnson (1966) in their study of the bodily responses to sexual stimulation. For example, both females and males experience orgasm when their urogenital systems spasm at .8 of a second intervals. Vaginal swelling, lubrication, and penile erections were seen as analogous responses to the adequate sexual stimulation. In 1981, I wrote:

> The only difference between these phenomena lies in the fact that the male vasocongestive response that produces an erection is more vulnerable to interruption than the female response. Therefore, men tend to experience much more difficulty with erectile capacity than females do with vaginal lubrication. (Gotwald and Golden, 1981)

This research was done in a political climate where the issues of doing away with the double standard seemed urgent. We were trying to bridge the gap between what appeared to be two highly polarized groups—we were trying to say: "there really are similarities between genders—men are okay, they respond like women. Women can respond like men and can be sexually free because the physiological responses are really similar." And while it still seems important to do away with the double standard, abolishing it in the bedroom can be highly dysfunctional, since many heterosexual couples use a male sexual model for the couple's sexual style. Unfortunately, there is often little or no appreciation or understanding of the female sexual paradigm. Furthermore, when trouble occurs in the marital dyad, both partners will often search the male model for solutions, rather than affirm each of their unique needs.

The prevalent model of sexuality in the American culture is a male one. Not only is it subtly taught through the media, but even in the present, supposedly enlightened, sexual climate, it is passed on from parents, peers, and teachers. And as careful as professionals try to be, it would be naive to believe that even they are totally free of a male model bias. It is so pervasive that most people are not usually aware they are being taught this information; they believe it is "natural" or "just the way it is." The popular male model is a genitally focused, orgasm oriented model. In this version penises are instantly ready for pleasure and become erect every time its owner wants it to! A female is expected to be instantly ready for intercourse when confronted with a "big enough" penis and be orgasmic merely because it is contained in her vagina. In addition, a vagina is supposed to be delighted to lend itself to the effort every time a penis needs to ejaculate. If the owner of that vagina is not instantly orgasmic with vaginal containment of the penis, something is surely wrong with her.

"Sexual relativity" refers to a situation in which one's sexuality is relative to or contingent upon the "other" or is defined by the "other." In a typical clinical situation, one person within the dyad will present her- or himself as "the one with the problem," although it is rarely as simple or as one-sided as that. It is essential to determine to what extent the person with the expressed sexual concern labels herself or himself dysfunctional relative to the partner's model of sexuality. Sexual relativity is clearly a major point to be explored in therapy. To what extent it is perpetuated in the dyad may be precisely what is dysfunctional. The following case may serve to illustrate the concept:

> Mr. and Mrs. J. had been married for nine months. It is a second marriage for each. Mrs. J. is 48 and Mr. J. is 54. Mr. J. is a heterosexual male who had been single for two years before re-marriage and had two sexual partners during that time. Mrs. J. is a heterosexual woman, two years post-hysterectomy, who had been single for almost ten years and had had several partners during that time. Mrs. J. presented with a complaint of secondary anorgasmia and lack of desire for intercourse. She was still desirous of affectional contact but rejected genitally focused sexual overtures. She and her new husband had labeled her the "patient."
>
> While Mrs. J. had labeled herself as anorgasmic and lacking in desire to have genital contact, it became clear that her labeling of her difficulties was really Mr. J.'s perception of the problem and not her own. Being in her first long-term stable relationship in several years, she quickly lost sight of her previously well-developed sense of sexuality. She began to try to be orgasmic in her husband's paradigm for orgasm—i.e., quickly and during vaginal containment of the penis. She had been reliably orgasmic with clitoral stimulation previous to their relationship but felt she should now be orgasmic with vaginal containment, giving up clitoral stimulation except for rare occasions when she secretly masturbated. She also expected to lubricate quickly and easily with a minimum of foreplay and to be ready for vaginal containment as soon as her husband was erect. Mr. J. had experienced secondary erectile

> problems during the end of his divorce and during his early days of being single. In the context of the marriage and emotional security, the erectile problems had been resolved but they left him with performance anxiety. As soon as he became aroused, he would need to ejaculate quickly, fearing he would lose his erection. When he lost erections he felt overwhelmed with inadequacy. He became so focused on his own processes and orgasmic release that he allowed himself to believe that vaginal containment and ejaculation was enough for both of them. He had no masculine model for sensuousness or for understanding the intrinsic value of touching. Therefore, affectional behaviors and foreplay became signals for getting erections which immediately had to be followed by intercourse to be satisfying. He had very little knowledge of the continuum of sexual behaviors and almost no knowledge of female sexuality. At the time I met them, they felt they had a good marriage, loved and respected one another, and had fairly good communication skills.

While both Mr. and Mrs. J. were essentially sexually functional as individuals, they had become dysfunctional as a couple. When Mrs. J. did not lubricate or have an orgasm in Mr. J.'s time frame or in his operational model, she was labeled dysfunctional. In fact, both of them had defined Mrs. J.'s sexuality according to the male paradigm for sexuality.

When making a diagnosis of sexual relativity, it is necessary to have a couple-specific diagnostic paradigm. In a previous publication (Gotwald and Golden, 1981), I discussed the concept of looking at diagnosis from a couple-specific point of view. Vaginismus, anorgasmia, ejaculatory and erectile problems, for example, can all be treated in couple's therapy or in individual therapy. But couple-specific diagnosis categories such as an unconsummated marriage or sexual relativity are intrinsically the *couple's* problem and must be viewed and treated as such. Using an individual treatment model would only serve to further polarize the couple, and underscore the mythology around female and male sexuality. If the diagnosis emphasizes the unique nature of each person's sexuality and helps them conceptualize the difficulty as one of relativity, then polarization and the dynamics of blaming and fault-finding are immediately diffused.

The seeds of sexual relativity are planted early in life and, like weeds in a garden, remain in spite of constant vigilance. There appear to be two major reasons for its development. In the first place, the blame for sexual problems in a marriage has been historically placed on the female. Non-consummation of a marriage, for example, was long considered the female's fault. This bias becomes evident when we scan the titles of some of the articles and monographs on the subject written in recent decades: "Virgin Wives" (Friedman, 1952) and "Wives Who Refuse Their Husbands" (Weiner, 1973)–to cite two. Husband were discussed only as valuable assets in treating their wives' problems. Traditionally, the same was true for infertility. Wives were blamed for childless marriages. In spite of our technology in this area, some cultures still hold the wife responsible for producing progeny.

Secondly, while it appears that the twentieth century unlocked the door of the Victorian era of sexual repression behaviorally, we still have many other doors to unlock. In her monograph on adolescent sex education, Michelle Fine (1987) discusses the concept of a "discourse of pleasure," which she observes is missing from curricula in sex education. She maintains that we teach children (particularly female children) a great deal about reproductive biology and the dangers of sexually transmitted diseases, but little about sex as an intrinsically pleasurable behavior. Indeed, it also appears to be missing from our overall consciousness when it comes to sexuality. Whether we have grown up in 1887 or 1987, women have largely missed a "discourse of pleasure" as part of our learning about sexuality. Even now, with the tyranny of sexually transmitted diseases, our adolescents are again missing that discourse because we are so concerned about teaching about protection and defensiveness in relationship to sexuality. Men are still being socialized differently when it comes to sex for the sake of pleasure. And women continue to be taught about their "duties" and "responsibilities" in bed. By the time women become sexually active, they have to overcome many years of negative training about their genitals and their sexuality. It may take years for the average woman to accomplish the very difficult task of developing a healthy and uniquely female sexual paradigm, an attempt that may be labeled as dysfunctional by both her and her male partner.

With a couple-specific concept in mind, a treatment paradigm almost becomes obvious. Since I am a solo-therapist, I usually see each person in the dyad separately once or twice to get a thorough individual history from each partner and to get a clear picture of each person's perceptions of the relationship. I also make a psychodynamic assessment to rule out gross psychopathology as well as an assessment to refer for medical examination if indicated. Then I see the couple together for feedback and for the opportunity to make decisions about treatment goals. I find that making the diagnosis of sexual relativity is intrinsically therapeutic. As I mentioned above, it effectively minimizes the dynamic of polarization that is often present in cases like this.

I usually start therapy by giving the couple some communication exercises that are done at home and reported back to me each week. These assignments set the stage for non-demand pleasuring exercises that will eventually be part of the therapy. The couple is instructed to set aside four half-hour sessions a week with one another to accomplish the "homework." We agree they will put their appointments with one another on their calendars and make a commitment to treating these dates as "top priority." This is often a very difficult task they have to accomplish. Learning how to set time aside for each other for communication, both sexual and conversational, is often the most difficult task in therapy. Couples naively believe that the opportunities for communication and sexual encounters will happen spontaneously. The required planning raises many issues that have been a block to intimacy in the past. The couple learns that their inability to set aside meaningful time for each other helps them avoid both emotional and sexual intimacy.

Human sexual arousal patterns and preferences are infinitely variable. But partners tend to apply their personal patterns and preferences to sexual encounters rather than finding out, specifically, what the other partner may like. A related goal of these early sessions is to help the partners see that they do not have to take responsibility for each other's feelings or preferences. All they have to do is try to understand them in a non-judgmental way. Once the skills of setting time aside for one another and of unconditional listening are established, I have them do some reading about male and female sexuality. (See list on reference page.)

I begin by having them read about their own gender and later share some of what they are reading in four or five structured sessions at home. In each of these structured sessions they share some of the reading they have found relevant or validating, and use the earlier communication techniques to give each other feedback. This gives them an opportunity to learn more about their own bodies as well as validate their personal attitudes and preferences. They also begin a dialogue about specific sexual behaviors in a non-threatening, structured manner that is very important to changing the dysfunctional pattern they have inadvertently created. To state it simply, using the reading as a point of reference, they can begin to talk about specific sexual behaviors which for most people is very difficult to begin to do. It also gives both partners an opportunity to re-examine, and perhaps change, many attitudes they have held for a long time. An atmosphere of acceptance and understanding of the differences intrinsic to each gender's sexuality can be developed in this way.

When their actual physical interludes begin, each has usually given up many well-entrenched attitudes about sexuality and is ready to learn to negotiate the differences in sexual preferences their partner may have. The sexual interludes, which are fairly similar to the original Masters and Johnson model of sex therapy steps, reinforce the prior learning that has taken place. Each new piece of "homework" builds upon the last one and incorporates and reinforces earlier learning. The interludes are structured to meet each couple's unique life styles, because it is within these varied frameworks that people have to function on a daily basis. In the case of Mr. and Mrs. J., since each of them functioned at a fairly high level psychodynamically, the systems/behavioral approach described above worked well and they were able to achieve their goals very quickly. On the other hand, there are cases where polarization around sexual issues has existed for many years. In these cases, it is often necessary to help the couple resolve some of the prior negative feelings in order to move ahead in therapy.

In conclusion, it seems important to develop a frame of reference that promulgates not only a salutogenic approach to sexuality and relationships, but one which promotes an appreciation of differences within individuals. Such an approach would promote an appreciation for what is unique in each gender, and support, preserve, and validate the dyad. We need to recognize that the mental health paradigm of diagnosis and treatment has traditionally mandated a pathogenic, individually oriented perspective on human sexual concerns. This particular frame of reference only serves to maintain a dysfunctional point of view of human sexual relationships. By enabling the persons in the dyad to preserve their sexual autonomy and to appreciate and understand each other's differences, we can empower them to be sexually satisfied and well-adjusted human beings.

REFERENCES

Fine, M. (1987). *Sexuality, schooling, and the adolescent female: The missing discourse of desire and the hegemonic discourse of victimization*. Unpublished monograph. Gradue School of Education, University of Pennsylvania.

Friedman, L.J. (1952). *Virgin wives: A study of unconsummated marriages*. England: Tavistock Publications.

Gotwald, W.H. & Golden, G.H. (1981). *Sexuality: The human experience*. New York: Macmillan.

Masters, W.H. & Johnson, V.E. (1966). *Human sexual response*. Boston: Little, Brown.

Masters, W.H. & Johnson, V.E. (1979). *Homosexuality in perspective*. Boston: Little, Brown.

Money, J. & Tucker, P. (1975). *Sexual signatures: On being a man or a woman.* Boston: Little, Brown.

Sevely, J.L. & Bennett, W. (1978). Concerning female ejaculation and the female prostate. *Journal of Sex research, 14*, 1-20.

Weiner, M.F. (1973). Wives who refuse their husbands. *Psychosomatics, 14*, 277-282.

RECOMMENDED READING

Barbach, L.G. (1976). *For yourself: The fulfillment of female sexuality*. New York: Doubleday.

Barbach, L.G. & Levine, L. (1980). *Shared intimacies*. New York: Anchor Press.

Barbach, L.G. (1982). *For each other: Sharing sexual intimacy*. New York: Signet Press.

Zilbergeld, B. (1978). *Male sexuality*. Boston: Little, Brown.

Reporting Colleagues Who Are Sexually Intimate with Clients: It's Time to Talk

Margery M. Noel

Has it happened to you yet? Has a client revealed that she was sexually exploited by a former therapist? Have you ever become aware that a colleague was sexually intimate with a client? What did you do? Did you receive support from your peers or your professional organizations? If you chose to report, how do you now feel about the process you experienced while reporting a colleague?

If you have not yet had to face the difficult issues raised by these questions, you cannot rest easy. Most of us will, at some time in our professional lives, treat clients who have been sexually abused by a therapist or know of a colleague who is said to have sexual contact with clients. There are very serious problems with the currently available reporting processes, and it will take a concerted and cooperative effort to change them so that whistleblowers are not abused again by the very systems they turn to for help. Before anything can change, however, therapists in all disciplines must acknowledge the problems and begin to talk plainly about sexual exploitation of clients by therapists.

No one should imagine that the problem of sexual misconduct by a therapist will be easy to resolve, for it is rooted in long-held societal attitudes and practices regarding the socialization of men and women, access to power, and protection of peers. Professional associations have been reluctant to move beyond denial to the consid-

---

Margery M. Noel, PsyD, is a certified sex therapist and psychologist in private practice in Falmouth, ME. She would welcome an exchange of ideas with readers concerned about reporting sexual exploitation of clients.

eration of sexual misconduct as an issue of profound importance to every clinician, every training program, and every ethics or licensing board. Documentation of the extent and impact of this problem is very difficult to find. Research regarding sexual intimacy within the therapeutic relationship faces serious methodological problems. How could researchers ever have access to each client who has experienced a therapist as sexually abusive? The sexual misconduct has taken place within the context of a private and deeply valued relationship. It is unlikely that persons in the role of client often feel sufficiently empowered to publicly confront a trusted therapist. Occasionally, clients have come forth when the media reports charges brought against a therapist. The silence is broken, a client now knows she is not alone, and it becomes possible to join others in speaking of the unspeakable. The silence is not often broken by professionals who know about colleagues who are or have been sexually intimate with clients. Ethical codes stressing confidentiality currently prohibit many professionals from reporting or confronting allegedly unethical colleagues without the permission of the involved client. Few offending therapists volunteer public descriptions of their sexual contacts with clients. The few existing studies probably describe only the tip of the iceberg, and we may never have a scientifically reliable account of the full dimensions of this problem. How many more trusting clients will be hurt while we wait for the perfect empirical studies to convince us of the need for change?

Let us begin by considering some of what is known:

–*Sexual intimacy with clients does occur, and with distressing frequency*. In the most recently published report, Gartrell et al. (1987) report that 65% of psychiatrists studied had treated patients reporting sexual contact with a previous therapist. In a 1986 study (Noel) of 371 clinical psychologists, 84% knew of colleagues reported to have been sexually intimate with clients. A study by the California Psychological Association (Bouhoutsos, Holroyd, Lerman, Forer, & Greenburg, 1983) reveals that over 50% of practicing clinical psychologists had received reports of therapist-client sexual activity either from clients or from colleagues. Holroyd and Brodsky (1977) reported that 7% of male psychologists and .5% of female psychologists responding to their study acknowledged having sexual intercourse with a client or clients. "It is not likely that subjects over-claimed erotic contact with patients, so the obtained results may be taken as conservative estimates" (Holroyd & Brodsky, 1977, p. 848). The first published empirical study of erotic practices in treatment showed that 10% of male psychiatrists surveyed had engaged in erotic contact with patients (Kardener, Fuller, & Mensh, 1973). In 1974, Masters and Johnson stated, " . . . time and time again, year in and year out, male and female patients have reported sexual experiences with their therapists. Even if only 25% of these specific reports were correct, there still would be an overwhelming issue confronting . . . professionals" (pp. 390-394). Thirteen years later, that issue still confronts us, and we are doing little to ensure that it will not still be with us into the twenty-first century!

–*Sexual contact with a therapist is usually harmful to a client*. A recent description of symptoms commonly found in adult incest survivors (Gelinas, 1983) is remarkably similar to the common client reactions to sexual exploitation by therapists (Schoener, Milgram & Gonsiorek, 1984). Both incest survivors and clients sexually involved with therapists may evidence symptoms of guilt and shame, depression, loss of self-esteem, grief, fear, and massive distrust. A survey of psychologists (Bouhoutsos et al., 1983) indicated that negative effects were suffered by 90% of clients who had been sexually intimate with a previous therapist.

–*Erotic touching of a client is* ***never*** *sex therapy*. No body of literature exists which would advocate such behavior as an effective technique for treating sexual dysfunctions. It is unfortunate that some offenders have offered the explanation that they were treating a sexual dysfunction by engaging in sexual intercourse with the client. While there might be a small number of specific clinical situations in which a well-trained sex therapist could consider the supervised short-term use of a sexual surrogate, the therapist could never ethically (or effectively) function as the surrogate. No ethical sex therapist would create or condone a treatment plan which prescribed a sexual relationship between the therapist and the client. Sex therapy offers far more effective remedies – none of which involve erotic stimulation of a client by the therapist.

–*Sexual misconduct by a therapist is seldom reported*. Only 8%

of the psychiatrists who had treated clients who had been sexually involved with a therapist had ever filed a report to a professional board (Gartrell et al., 1987). In a study of clinical psychologists (Noel, 1986), less than 20% of the sample had ever utilized the first step suggested in the Code of Ethics of the American Psychological Association – confrontation of the allegedly unethical colleague in person or by mail. Only 35% had ever encouraged a client to file a complaint about sexual misconduct with an ethics committee, and less than 10% had assisted a client in filing such a report. The proportion of psychologists encouraging (9%) or assisting (4%) a client in the use of the legal system to prosecute the accused psychologist is even lower. The literature provides no information about the number of legal cases brought or prosecuted.

– Reporting sexual misconduct by a therapist is a frustrating and often painful process. Current disciplinary structures may act to benefit the perpetrator, not the victim. Professional ethics committees have not been especially effective in processing clients' complaints about sexual misconduct by therapists. "Nothing happened" was the report of fifty-five percent of the clients who filed formal complaints against a therapist for sexual intimacy in one study (Bouhoutsos et al., 1983). It took nearly four years for an ethics committee to resolve the charge of sexual misconduct by a psychiatric resident against her psychiatrist, and the victim finally felt that she "would never refer a patient of mine to the ethics committee because the process was so traumatic to me, and because ultimately I was not believed or the abuse was seen as insignificant, worthy only of a one-year suspension" (Gartrell et al., p. 291). It is not difficult to imagine the costs of such an experience – even to someone who is familiar with the system and could expect to use it effectively. For the client who feels less powerful than her therapist to begin with may not yet have told anyone about the sexual abuse at the hands of her trusted therapist, and has little idea of the structure of the therapist's professional hierarchies, it is hard to know where to begin in the search for justice. It is harder still to sustain a strong sense of self through the maze of professional committees, feeling shame as the story is told and re-told to strangers over months and perhaps years. Surely we have a responsibility to care for the victims better than this!

Knowing that sexual misconduct by therapists exists, is harmful, and is not often or easily reported, what can we do? We can teach therapists to understand their own sexual values and attitudes, and to creatively manage the inevitable instances of sexual attraction to a client. We can all learn to talk more comfortably and directly about sexuality. We can train all therapists to understand the real-life complexities of professional ethics. We can create a climate in which clients expect ethical treatment by therapists, and understand that erotic stimulation by a therapist is never acceptable. We can re-write our ethical codes and legal statutes to specifically prohibit defined sexual contacts with current clients. We can work to humanize the reporting procedures so that clients are not re-abused by our system while we protect the rights of the accused therapist. We can develop treatment programs for impaired therapists. If we do not first heal ourselves, how can we be trusted to create healing relationships?

RECOMMENDATIONS

1. Professional disciplines must create careful, complete, and explicit descriptions of the behaviors involved in terms such as "sexual intimacy." While it may seem at first that we must already have a shared understanding of such apparently obvious words or phrases, we do not. We must be able to say, for example, that it is no more acceptable to engage in manual erotic stimulation with a client than to have intercourse with her. It is time to move beyond your own inhibitions and limitations and engage in plain talk, so that no one can question whether kissing a client or touching her breasts or genitals is within the limits, or whether mutual erotic touching is ever acceptable within the therapeutic relationship. How can we effectively prohibit behaviors we have not defined or will not describe?
2. The complex and difficult question—"Is a client always a client?"—must be resolved within each discipline. The answer to this question is critical to the development of specific ethical prohibitions. While most clinicians could probably agree that sexual intercourse in the office during a therapy session with a

current client is unethical, it becomes more difficult to achieve such agreement when the sexual contact occurs with a former client or when the therapist and client have "fallen in love." Since clinicians vary widely in their theoretical orientations, there will be differing understandings of the meanings and importance of such concepts as transference, countertransference, relationships of "permanent inequality" or "temporary inequality" (Miller, 1976), power, termination, etc. This task will call for great empathy and cooperation, rather than the competition which often surfaces when clinicians discuss the relative merits of their personal approaches to therapy.

3. It seems clear that our society is still permeated with pain and misunderstanding about sexuality, and that many therapists have not been offered adequate professional opportunities to reconsider old personal attitudes and values in this area. It is difficult to imagine how a therapist could avoid communicating such attitudes to clients, especially when a sexual experience such as incest, rape, or sexual exploitation by a therapist is the central focus of the work. Formal coursework in human sexuality should become a part of the basic curriculum of *every* graduate program training mental health professionals. Furthermore, any clinician wishing to work with couples, families, adolescents, incest survivors, physically disabled individuals, the mentally retarded, those who are chronically mentally ill, or persons at high risk for AIDS should seek advanced coursework in sexuality education and the basic theories and principles of sex therapy.
4. Every graduate program needs to offer specific training in the real-life ethical problems which will face mental health professionals, especially in regard to feeling sexual attraction to a client, receiving a client's report that she or he has been sexually exploited by a therapist, or reporting unethical colleagues. Each of us *will* experience these problems during our professional life, and we must be better prepared to manage our own responses to them rather than continue to accept denial and dissociation as coping strategies.
5. When an offender holds no license or certification, and thus

cannot be disciplined effectively through a professional organization, a legal remedy is needed. Clients will often need assistance to use the court system to prosecute offenders. Professionals could form local multidisciplinary work groups to create safe and workable reporting systems which protect the rights of both the client and the offender.

6. Treatment programs for impaired clinicians are essential, and should be accessible in every region. More violations may be reported when adequate treatment is available for offenders.

Hopefully, these recommendations will stimulate clinicians to begin the many conversations which will be needed to produce new approaches to the old problem of sexual exploitation of clients. There are many appropriate forums in which we could begin to address the difficult issues—training programs for new clinicians, local and national professional association meetings, peer supervision groups, and lunchtime with a colleague. As women, we can and must provide special leadership to see that sexual exploitation of clients no longer goes unnoticed. No one source will provide all the answers, but together we are resourceful enough to raise consciousness and create new structures. It's time to talk!

REFERENCES

Bouhoutsos, J., Holroyd, J., Lerman, H., Forer, B.R., & Greenburg, H. (1983). Sexual intimacy between psychotherapists and patients. *Professional Psychology: Research and Practice, 14*(2), 185-196.

Gartrell, N., Herman, J., Olarte, S., Feldstein, M., & Localio, R. (1987). Reporting practices of psychiatrists who knew of sexual misconduct by colleagues. *American Journal of Orthopsychiatry, 57*(2), 287-295.

Gelinas, D. (1983). The persisting negative effects of incest. *Psychiatry, 46*, 312-330.

Holroyd, J., & Brodsky, A. (1977). Psychologists' attitudes and practices regarding erotic and non-erotic physical contact with patients. *American Psychologist, 32*, 850-856.

Kardener, S.H., Fuller, M., & Mensh, I. (1973). A survey of physicians' attitudes and practices regarding erotic and non-erotic contact with patients. *American Journal of Psychiatry, 130*(10), 1077-1081.

Masters, W., & Johnson, V. (1974). *Human sexual inadequacy*. Boston: Little, Brown & Co.

Miller, J.B. (1976). *Toward a new psychology of women*. Boston: Beacon Press.

Noel, M.M. (1986). Sexual misconduct by psychologists: Who reports it? Unpublished doctoral dissertation, Antioch-New England Graduate School, Keene, NH.

Schoener, G., Milgram, & Gonsiorek (1984). Sexual exploitation of clients by therapists. *Women and Therapy 3*(3/4), 63-69.

"Nice Women" Don't Say Yes and "Real Men" Don't Say No: How Miscommunication and the Double Standard Can Cause Sexual Problems

Charlene L. Muehlenhard

Imagine that a man is with a woman and he wants to have sex with her (or he feels he should try to have sex with her, so that he can avoid the stigma of being sexually inexperienced). He does not attempt to discuss their sexual desires; instead, he tries to interpret her behaviors. She is wearing tight jeans and a low-cut blouse, and she is willing to go to his apartment to listen to records. He interprets these behaviors to mean that she is interested in sex. He begins to make advances. She says no. He assumes that she is merely offering token resistance to sex so as not to appear promiscuous—and, even if she does mean no, why was she "leading him on" with her "suggestive" clothing and behavior? He thinks of jokes he has heard about unmasculine men who stop their advances after being told no, he thinks of movies in which the woman first resists the man's advances but soon becomes overwhelmed with desire, and he thinks of his male friends who all have sexual stories to tell. He has sex with her in spite of her protests.

Women and men often communicate indirectly when initiating

Charlene L. Muehlenhard received her PhD in clinical psychology from the University of Wisconsin—Madison. She is currently affiliated with the Department of Psychology, University of Kansas, Lawrence, KS. She does research on the causes and prevention of rape, communication and miscommunication about sex, social skills, and women's and men's issues.

sexual relationships. They often observe the other person's behavior and make inferences as to whether that person is interested in a sexual relationship. This can cause problems, however, because women and men often make different inferences about the same behaviors. In addition, there continues to be a sexual double standard that women and men are expected to follow. All these factors contribute to miscommunication about sex.

This paper discusses the sexual problems that can result from the sexual double standard and women's and men's discrepant interpretations of social behaviors. These issues are especially important for heterosexual women. These issues can be problematic for all women, however, because miscommunication and the double standard can contribute to rape, and all women are vulnerable to rape. Some of the information presented in this paper is addressed to women. Some of the information is addressed to men, especially information about rape, because the burden of reducing rape rests on their shoulders.

DISCREPANCIES BETWEEN WOMEN'S AND MEN'S SEXUAL INTERPRETATIONS OF BEHAVIORS

One problem with indirect sexual signaling is that women and men often interpret behaviors differently. Men are generally more likely than women to interpret a variety of behaviors as signals that the other person is interested in sex.

In one study, for example, high school girls and boys were asked how much they thought various types of clothing, dating activities, and dating behaviors were signals for sex (Zellman, Johnson, Giarrusso, & Goodchilds, 1979). Boys interpreted almost everything they were asked about more sexually than did girls. In another study, I asked women and men to read scenarios describing what two people did on a date and asked them how much they thought the woman wanted to have sexual intercourse (Muehlenhard, in press). Both women and men clearly made sexual attributions regarding the couple's dating behaviors: They rated the woman as more willing to have sex when she asked the man out rather than hinting or waiting for him to ask her out, when the couple went to the man's apartment rather than to a movie, and when the man paid for the woman's concert ticket rather than splitting the cost of the tickets. There were discrepancies between women's and men's interpretations, however: No matter who initiated or who paid or where the couple went, men's mean ratings of how much the woman wanted sex were higher than women's.

As a result of such discrepancies in women's and men's interpretations, a man is likely to overestimate a woman's desire for sex. This could cause problems if he makes a sexual advance which she refuses. He might feel that she has been "leading him on" by behaving in ways that he has interpreted as "suggestive." Many people believe that a woman who "leads a man on" deserves it if the man forces her to have sex (Burt, 1980; Giarrusso, Johnson, Goodchilds, & Zellman, 1979; Muehlenhard & Felts, 1987; Muehlenhard & MacNaughton, in press). Thus, men's and women's discrepant interpretations could result in men's feeling that rape is justified.

Another possible consequence of miscommunication is that a man might not believe a woman when she says no to sex. He might assume that she is merely acting according to the sexual double standard dictating that it is acceptable for men but not for women to be sexually active. According to this double standard, unless women are in committed relationships, they cannot acknowledge that they want to engage in sex for fear of appearing promiscuous; hence, even when a woman wants to engage in sex, she has to say no. According to the sexual script dictated by this double standard, when a man makes a sexual advance and the woman refuses, he can ignore her refusal, assuming it is merely token. In fact, according to this script, not only can he ignore her refusal, he should ignore her refusal, because a man who stops when a woman says no is not sufficiently masculine (Check & Malamuth, 1983; Laws & Schwartz, 1977; Zilbergeld, 1978).

Is there really a sexual double standard dictating that it is unacceptable for women to be sexually active outside of a committed relationship, whereas for men, it is not only acceptable, it is expected? Do men really believe that women's refusals are merely token? Do women ever offer token resistance to sex because of the sexual double standard? Do men ever have unwanted sex because the double standard dictates that they should be sexually experienced and should not refuse sex? If the answer to any of these questions is yes, does this cause sexual problems? Let us look at the research on these questions.

THE SEXUAL DOUBLE STANDARD

Society's attitudes regarding acceptable sexual behaviors for women and men are captured by the words that exist to describe sexually active men and women: "Studs" are men; "sluts," "tramps," "pushovers," and "nymphomaniacs" are women. In a study of college men, Komarovsky (1976) found that "outright defense of the double standard was rare. . . . But [men's] sentiments did not always harmonize with their ideal principles" (p. 89). The double standard was evident in three areas: The men expected sexual fidelity from women but not from men; they tolerated sex without affection for men but not for women; and they disapproved of women, but not men, initiating sex.

Whereas the double standard censures sexually active women, it demands that men be sexually active. Komarovsky found that male virgins were consistently more anxious and self-critical and had less self-confidence than did nonvirgins. She concluded that the male virgin had "failed to live up to his own and his peers' ideal of masculinity" (1976, p. 126).

Do Men Believe It When Women Say No to Sex?

There is evidence that they do not. My student Albert Felts and I asked men to read scenarios about two people who go on a date (Muehlenhard & Felts, 1987). In one of these scenarios, the woman engaged in numerous behaviors that previous research suggested would signal a lack of sexual interest: for example, she dressed modestly in a blouse with a bow at the collar, a pleated woolen skirt, and penny loafers; she drank iced tea rather than alcohol; she never kissed the man voluntarily. When the man made sexual advances, she said no three times and tried to move away. When men read this scenario and rated how much they thought she wanted to have sex, their mean rating was almost at the middle of the scale ($M = 4.50$ on a scale where 1 = *she did not want to at all* and 9 = *she wanted to very much*). In another scenario in which the woman wore a miniskirt, drank alcohol, and voluntarily kissed the man, men were even less likely to believe it when she said no (M = 6.72). In another study, even when the woman in the scenario began protesting early during foreplay, the man used force to obtain sex, and the woman used force to try to resist, men's ratings of how much she wanted to have sex were still greater than the lowest possible rating (Shotland & Goodstein, 1983).

Do Women Ever Offer Token Resistance to Sex?

We have just seen that at least some men think that women's refusals are insincere. Is this belief founded in fact? A recent study suggests that sometimes, some women do say no to sex when they mean yes. My student Lisa Hollabaugh and I asked 610 college women if they had ever been with a man "who had wanted to engage in sexual intercourse and you wanted to also, but for some reason you indicated that you didn't want to, although *you had every intention to and were willing to engage in sexual intercourse?* In other words, you indicated 'No' and you meant 'Yes'" (Muehlenhard & Hollabaugh, 1987). If they had ever engaged in this behavior, we asked them to rate the importance of 26 possible reasons, obtained from a pilot study.

We found that 39.3% of the women reported that they had said no to sexual intercourse when they had meant yes. Of these women, 32.5% reported engaging in this behavior only once; 45.6% reported 2 to 5 times; 19.0% reported 6 to 20 times; only 2.9% reported more than 20 times.

To investigate women's reasons for engaging in token resistance to sex, we first factor analyzed the women's ratings of the 26 possible reasons for this behavior. The results of this factor analysis were used to group the possible reasons into 11 more general reasons; a second-order factor analysis was used to group these 11 reasons into three categories. One of these categories included reasons such as not wanting to appear promiscuous and uncertainty about her partner's feelings. We labeled this category "practical reasons" because, given the sanctions against women who violate the sexual double standard, offering token resistance to sex might be a rational behavior for women to engage in (although, as will be discussed, this behavior is not without its negative consequences). Of the women who had said no when they meant yes, almost all (98.1%) indicated that this category of reasons was at least somewhat important; 23.3% indicated that it was moderately to very important; 49.0% specifically indicated that not wanting to appear promiscuous was a moderately to very important reason.[1]

We can draw several conclusions from this study. First, society's double standard seems to have had an effect on women's behavior, making them concerned about not appearing to be too sexually active. Second, there appears to be a kernel of truth to the myth that women say no to sex when they mean yes. Yet, it should be emphasized that most women had never engaged in token resistance to sex, and even among those who had, most had done so five or fewer times. Thus, this clearly is not a behavior that all, or even most, women engage in. Still, it does happen occasionally. If a woman refuses sex, a man might not know if her refusal is serious or token (which, of course, does not justify his ignoring her refusal, but it does help explain why this sometimes occurs). Token resistance—perpetuated in part by society's restrictive double standard—contributes to miscommunication about sex.

Does the Double Standard Affect Men's Sexual Behavior?

Do men ever have sex when they do not want to in order to uphold the image of being sexually experienced and not turning down opportunities for sex? My student Stephen Cook and I investigated the prevalence of men and women engaging in unwanted sexual activity (Muehlenhard & Cook, in press). More men (62.7%) than women (46.3%) reported engaging in sexual intercourse when they did not want to.[2] We compared the percentages of men and women who reported engaging in unwanted sexual intercourse for various reasons. There were several reasons for unwanted sexual intercourse that men cited more often than women, most of which related to the sexual double standard. More men (57.4%) than women (38.7%) reported that they had engaged in unwanted sexual intercourse due to being enticed—that is, the woman made an advance that the man had difficulty refusing. This might be related to the double standard dictating that "real men" do not refuse opportunities for sex. More men (33.5%) than women (11.9%) had unwanted sexual intercourse because they wanted to get sexual experience, wanted something to talk about, or wanted to build up their confidence. Gender role concerns, such as not wanting to appear to be homosexual, shy or afraid, unmasculine (for men) or unfeminine (for women), or inexperienced, were cited as reasons for unwanted sexual intercourse by more men (18.4%) than women (4.5%). Peer pressure was a motive for 10.9% of the men but only 0.6% of the women. Thus, the sexual double standard relates to numerous reasons for men engaging in unwanted sexual intercourse, and it further impedes openness between women and men about their sexual desires.

MISCOMMUNICATION, THE DOUBLE STANDARD, AND SEXUAL PROBLEMS

The patterns of miscommunication just documented can cause sexual problems. Awareness of these patterns can lessen these problems.

Discrepancies Between Women's and Men's Interpretations of Behavior

1. Men need to be aware that if a man interprets a woman's behavior as signalling interest in sex but she refuses, this does not mean that she has been "leading him on." Instead, it is likely to be a misunderstanding due to differences in how women and men interpret behavior. Men also need to take women's refusals seriously and not assume that their interpretations of women's behavior are necessarily correct.
2. It would also be useful for women to be aware of this problem. This does not mean that women need to restrict their behavior, dress modestly, abstain from alcohol, and only go to public places on dates. Direct, open communication might help reduce misinterpretation while preserving women's freedom to behave as they want. To study this, my student Sandy An-

drews and I made videotapes depicting a couple going on a date (Muehlenhard & Andrews, 1985). The woman in the tape engaged in numerous behaviors that increase men's ratings of how much a woman wants sex and how justifiable it would be for a man to have sex with her against her will—she asked him out, wore a low-cut top and tight pants, drank alcohol, went to the man's apartment, and kissed him voluntarily. In some versions of the tape, she openly communicated what she wanted: "I hope you don't misinterpret my going to your apartment on the first date, but seriously, I don't want to do anything more than kiss tonight." When she told him this early during the date, compared with when she waited to say no until he had already made an advance, men rated her as less likely to want to pet or have sexual intercourse, they rated her as "leading the man on" less, and they tended to rate it as less justifiable for the man to engage in petting after she said no. Men also rated this approach as appropriate, and most said they would feel positive toward a woman who took such an approach. Thus, open communication seems to be a reasonable way for women to deal with the problem of misinterpretation.

"Nice Women" Don't Say Yes

1. The double standard dictating that women should not initiate sex could make it difficult for women to become sexually aroused. Women might find it difficult to become aroused if they have sex only when their partners desire it, rather than when they desire it.
2. The double standard perpetuates traditional gender-role stereotypes. It dictates that women should be passive and submissive, whereas men should be active and dominant; women should be indirect and manipulative, whereas men should be direct. Both women and men rate the feminine pole of these traits as less desirable than the masculine pole (Broverman, Vogel, Broverman, Clarkson, & Rosenkrantz, 1972). Thus, adhering to the double standard could lower women's self-esteem as well as lowering men's opinions of women.

3. Adhering to externally-imposed standards injects dishonesty and game-playing into intimate relationships. Intimate relationships could be among the most honest and open relationships that people have. This becomes impossible, however, when they are acting out roles to conform to the double standard.
4. A woman who engages in token resistance to sex could be disappointed if the man believes her refusal and stops his advances.
5. The myth that women typically engage in token resistance to sex could be a factor in rape. Most women do not engage in this behavior, but this myth is perpetuated by pornography, jokes, movies, and so forth (Malamuth & Check, 1981; Smith, 1976; Zilbergeld, 1978). A typical scenario portrays a woman who at first refuses a man's advances but who soon becomes passionately aroused when he forces her to engage in sex. A man's acceptance of this myth could be reinforced if he has sex with a woman who says no and there are no negative consequences; he might decide that this will be the case for all women.[3]

The solution to this problem, of course, is for men to believe women's refusals and stop their sexual advances. Even if a man thinks that a woman is not serious when she refuses sex, if she is serious and he has sex with her despite her protests, it is rape.

Ideally, a woman's refusal should be sufficient to cause a man to stop his advances. Unfortunately, this is not always the case. About 15% of all college women have been raped (Koss, Gidycz & Wisniewski, 1987; Muehlenhard & Linton, 1987; Wilson & Durrenberger, 1982). Russell (1984) concluded that there is about a 26% probability that any given woman will be a victim of rape during her lifetime. What can a woman do if a man disregards her refusals?

Shotland and Goodstein (1983) found that people are more likely to believe a woman's refusals if she protests not only verbally, but also physically, such as by pushing, slapping, biting, and hitting the man. There is also evidence that physical force is effective in stopping sexual aggression. Bart and O'Brien (1985) compared the type of resistance used by rape victims with that used by women who had thwarted rape attempts. They found that the most successful strategy was using physical force, accompanied by screaming and yelling and fleeing or trying to flee. My student Ginna Beal and I gave questionnaires to men, asking them to rate how likely they would be to continue making sexual advances if a woman responded in various ways (Beal & Muehlenhard, 1987). We were especially interested in the responses of men who reported that they had engaged in sexual coercion and could imagine themselves continuing to be physically aggressive even after a woman said no. These men reported being most likely to stop their advances if the woman was physically forceful (such as kneeing, biting, slugging, kicking, or clawing him) or being verbally forceful (such as screaming or saying, "This is rape and I'm calling the cops"). This information could help women deal with sexual aggression.[4]

"Real Men" Don't Say No

1. If a man believes that he should always be able to engage in sexual intercourse, he will eventually fall short of his expectations. If a man worries that he is "impotent" because he is not able to meet his own impossible standards, his concerns could become a self-fulfilling prophecy. Male clients having problems with "impotence" should be advised to have sex only when they feel aroused and comfortable with the situation (Zilbergeld, 1978).
2. Pressure for men to have sex could lead to sexual aggression against women. If men feel that they must obtain sex because of peer pressure or to affirm their masculinity, they might feel pressure to have sex regardless of the willingness of their partners. Kanin (1967) found that sexually aggressive men reported considerably more peer pressure to have new sexual experiences than did nonaggressive men. We found that men who reported engaging in sex when they did not want to tended to believe that women often say no to sex when they actually mean yes (Muehlenhard & Cook, in press). Perhaps these men believe that everyone behaves according to the double standard—that is, just as they are acting out their part of

the sexual script by engaging in sex when they do not want to, they think that women are acting out their part of the sexual script by offering token resistance to sex. This belief could increase the probability that these men will ignore women's refusals and commit rape.

3. Even men are sometimes coerced into having sex. Sometimes men are coerced verbally by their partners or their peers (Muehlenhard & Cook, in press; Struckman-Johnson, 1987). Sometimes men are coerced physically by other men (Davis, 1968; Groth & Burgess, 1980; Kaufman, DiVasto, Jackson, Voorhees, & Christy, 1980; Sagarin, 1976) or by women (Muehlenhard & Cook, in press; Sarrel & Masters, 1982; Struckman-Johnson, 1987). Men appear to be more reluctant than women to report being forced to have sex, and sometimes therapists do not believe men's reports of forced sex (Kaufman et al., 1980; Sarrel & Masters, 1982). Men's reluctance to report forced sex and therapists' incredulity probably relate to the myths that men should always be sexually dominant, that men always want sex, and that therefore men's reports of unwanted sex are either trivial or untrue (especially if the unwanted sex was with a woman). The women's movement has made therapists, police officers, and the public more aware of the sexist myths surrounding female rape victims. A similar awareness of myths surrounding male sexuality can help therapists deal with men more sensitively and can help therapists challenge destructive myths men have about themselves.

CONCLUSION

Socialization of women and men according to gender-role stereotypes and the sexual double standard can take its toll on both women and men. It can inhibit honest communication, interfere with sexual arousal, and even contribute to rape. Therapists can make clients aware of the sources of these problems and help clients overcome these difficulties and achieve greater sexual satisfaction.

NOTES

1. There were two other categories of reasons for saying no when meaning yes. One we labeled "inhibition-related reasons." This included emotional, religious, or moral reasons; fear of physical discomfort; and embarrassment about her body. Of the women who had engaged in token resistance to sex, 19.0% indicated that these reasons were moderately to very important.

A third category we labeled "manipulative reasons": for example, game-playing reasons (wanting to get the man more sexually aroused by making him wait, wanting him to talk her into it, or wanting him to be more physically aggressive); being angry with her partner and wanting to "get back at him"; and wanting to be the one in control. Of the women who had engaged in token resistance, 22.9% indicated that these reasons were moderately to very important.

2. Note that "unwanted" does not mean "unavoidable." Most of the unwanted sex that men and women reported was avoidable. They engaged in unwanted sex because they felt some pressure to do so. Sometimes this pressure came from their sexual partner, sometimes it came from their peers, and sometimes it came from their own internalized standards. Research is currently underway to assess the prevalence of unavoidable sex among women and men.

3. I am not suggesting that rape is women's fault because some women engage in token resistance to sex. Women face a double bind due to society's constraints on their behavior, and token resistance is one way some women try to deal with these constraints. In addition, I am not suggesting that all rape results from miscommunication. Many factors contribute to rape, including a power differential between women and men, men's hostility toward women, men's espousing traditional gender-role stereotypes, and men's feelings of sexual dominance over women (Check & Malamuth, 1983; Malamuth, 1986; Muehlenhard, in press; Muehlenhard & Falcon, 1987; Muehlenhard, Friedman & Thomas, 1985; Muehlenhard & Linton, 1987; Russell, 1984).

4. No strategy is always effective, and rape victims should never be made to feel they are at fault for not using a more effective strategy. If they survived, they did the right thing.

REFERENCES

Bart, P. B., & O'Brien, P. H. (1985). *Stopping rape: Successful survival strategies*. New York: Pergamon.

Beal, G. K., & Muehlenhard, C. L. (1987, April). *Decreasing miscommunication about sex: Approaches for getting men to stop their sexual advances*. Presented at the annual Midcontinent meeting of the Society for the Scientific Study of Sex, Bloomington, IN.

Broverman, I., Vogel, S. R., Broverman, S. M., Clarkson, F. E., & Rosenkrantz, P. S. (1972). Sex role stereotypes: A current appraisal. *Journal of Social Issues, 28*, 59-78.

Burt, M. R. (1980). Cultural myths and supports for rape. *Journal of Personality and Social Psychology, 38*, 217-230.

Check, J. V. P., & Malamuth, N. M. (1983). Sex role stereotyping and reactions to depictions of stranger versus acquaintance rape. *Journal of Personality and Social Psychology, 45*, 344-356.

Davis, A. J. (1968). Sexual assault in the Philadelphia prison system and sheriff's vans. *Trans-action, 6*, 8-16.

Giarrusso, R., Johnson, P., Goodchilds, J., & Zellman, G. (1979, April). Adolescents' cues and signals: Sex and assault. In P. Johnson (Chair), *Acquaintance rape and adolescent sexuality*. Symposium conducted at the meeting of the Western Psychological Association, San Diego.

Groth, N., & Burgess, A. W. (1980). Male rape: Offenders and victims. *American Journal of Psychiatry, 137*, 806-810.

Kanin, E. J. (1967). An examination of sexual aggression as a response to sexual frustration. *Journal of Marriage and the Family, 29*, 428-433.

Kaufman, A., DiVasto, P., Jackson, R., Voorhees, D., & Christy, J. (1980). Male rape victims: Noninstitutionalized assault. *American Journal of Psychiatry, 137*, 221-228.

Komarovsky, M. (1976). *Dilemmas of masculinity: A study of college youth*. New York: W. W. Norton.

Koss, M. P., Gidycz, C. A., & Wisniewski, N. (1987). The scope of rape: Incidence and prevalence of sexual aggression and victimization in a national sample of higher education students. *Journal of Consulting and Clinical Psychology, 53*, 162-170.

Laws, J. L., & Schwartz, P. (1977). *Sexual scripts: The social construction of female sexuality*. Washington, DC: University Press of America.

Malamuth, N. M. (1986). Predictors of naturalistic sexual aggression. *Journal of Personality and Social Psychology, 50*, 953-962.

Malamuth, N. M., & Check, J. V. P. (1981). The effects of mass media exposure on acceptance of violence against women: A field experiment. *Journal of Research in Personality, 15*, 436-446.

Muehlenhard, C. L. (in press). Misinterpreted dating behaviors and the risk of date rape. *Journal of Social and Clinical Psychology*.

Muehlenhard, C. L., & Andrews, S. L. (1985, November). *Open communication about sex: Will it reduce risk factors related to date rape*? Presented at the annual meeting of the Association for Advancement of Behavior Therapy, Houston.

Muehlenhard, C. L., & Cook, S. W. (in press). Men's reports of unwanted sexual activity. *Journal of Sex Research*.

Muehlenhard, C. L., & Falcon, P. L. (1987). *Social skills and attitudes of nonincarcerated forceful rapists*. Manuscript submitted for publication.

Muehlenhard, C. L., & Felts, A. S. (1987). [An analysis of causal factors for men's attitudes about the justifiability of date rape]. Unpublished raw data.

Muehlenhard, C. L., Friedman, D. E., & Thomas, C. M. (1985). Is date rape justifiable? The effects of dating activity, who initiated, who paid, and men's attitudes toward women. *Psychology of Women Quarterly, 9*, 297-310.

Muehlenhard, C. L., & Hollabaugh, L. C. (1987). *Why a woman would say no when she meant yes: The incidence and correlates of women's token resistance to sex*. Manuscript submitted for publication.

Muehlenhard, C. L., & Linton, M. A. (1987). Date rape and sexual aggression in dating situations: Incidence and risk factors. *Journal of Counseling Psychology, 34*, 186-196.

Muehlenhard, C. L., & MacNaughton, J. S. (in press). Women's attitudes toward women who "lead men on." *Journal of Social and Clinical Psychology*.

Russell, D. E. H. (1984). *Sexual exploitation: Rape, child sexual abuse, and workplace harassment*. Beverly Hills: Sage.

Sagarin, E. (1976). Prison homosexuality and its effect on post-prison sexual behavior. *Psychiatry, 39*, 245-257.

Sarrel, P. M., & Masters, W. H. (1982). Sexual molestation of men by women. *Archives of Sexual Behavior, 11*, 117-131.

Shotland, R. L., & Goodstein, L. (1983). Just because she doesn't want to doesn't mean it's rape: An experimentally based causal model of the perception of rape in a dating situation. *Social Psychology Quarterly, 46*, 220-232.

Smith, D. D. (1976). The social content of pornography. *Journal of Communication, 26*, 16-24.

Struckman-Johnson, C. (1987). *Forced sex on dates: It happens to men, too*. Manuscript submitted for publication.

Wilson, W., & Durrenberger, R. (1982). Comparison of rape and attempted rape victims. *Psychological Reports, 50*, 198.

Zellman, G. L., Johnson, P. B., Giarrusso, R. & Goodchilds, J. D. (1979, September). *Adolescent expectations for dating relationships: Consensus and conflict between the sexes*. Paper presented at the meetings of the American Psychological Association, New York, NY.

Zilbergeld, B. (1978). *Male sexuality: A guide to sexual fulfillment*. New York: Bantam.

SECTION III: PHYSIOLOGICAL CONDITIONS AND ISSUES

Sexual Difficulties Experienced by Women with Interstitial Cystitis

Naomi B. McCormick
Robert K. Vinson

Interstitial cystitis (IC) is an uncommon but by no means rare syndrome characterized by bladder pain, urgency, and an increased frequency of urination (Messing, 1987; Messing & Stamey, 1978). There is considerable variation among individuals, but many IC patients complain about genital pain, dyspareunia, and sleep difficulties as the discomfort and urgency associated with this disease may interfere with both daytime and nighttime activities. Patients

---

Naomi B. McCormick, PhD, Fellow of the Institute of Rational-Emotive Therapy, is Associate Professor of Psychology at the State University of New York College at Plattsburgh. Robert K. Vinson, MD, is Clinical Associate Professor of Surgery, Department of Urology, at the Medical Center Hospital of Vermont in Burlington.

We wish to thank L. Shaffer, W. Dryden, and E. R. Allgeier for their support and inspiration and dedicate this article to patients with interstitial cystitis and the friends, family members, and health professionals who care about them.

are usually female, ranging from 20 to 70 years of age (Messing, 1986, 1987; Messing & Stamey, 1978).

Symptoms can be present for many years and range in severity from mild to extreme cases (Oravisto, 1975). For example, one woman with a mild case of IC said that she experienced no pain although she was obliged to visit the bathroom every two hours. Other women with mild symptoms described having no difficulty falling asleep and little likelihood of waking up as a result of the disease. In contrast, a woman with a more severe case of IC described feeling like her bladder was "on fire" or filled with some "caustic poison" and noted that she could easily visit the bathroom every fifteen minutes if she let herself. Another woman with more severe symptoms described spending much of the night in the lavatory, desperately trying to get some relief.

Unlike common cystitis in women, which is usually caused by bacterial infection, IC patients usually have sterile urine. The diagnosis of interstitial cystitis is confirmed when the bladder is hydrodistended under anesthesia; most patients are administered a spinal for this purpose. Patients with the disease exhibit characteristic multiple pin-point hemorrhagic areas within the bladder lining. Depending on the duration of symptoms and the severity of the disease, bladder capacity under anesthesia may vary from normal to a markedly small contracted bladder holding only several ounces of fluid. Bladder biopsy may be obtained which will show nonspecific inflammation in the bladder wall, but this is important to rule out occult bladder cancer.

The etiology of IC remains obscure. Areas of current interest and research relate to vascular/lymph obstruction, autoimmunity, deficiency in bladder mucosal lining, and the presence of toxins in the urine (Holm-Bentzen & Lose, 1987).

A myriad of treatment regimens have been reported but most have been of limited value. The most effective and time proven have been periodic hydrodistention of the bladder and bladder instillation of Dimethyl Sulfoxide (DMSO), an anti-inflammatory agent. Both of these treatments are usually performed in an outpatient setting under local anesthetic. Although complete cure is unusual, a supportive physician who administers these treatment modalities on a continuing basis can usually lessen the patient's symptoms. One of the problems with judging various treatment regimens is that IC may be characterized by periods of acute distress followed by partial spontaneous remissions, making it difficult to state whether improvement is the result of a particular treatment or just the natural course of the disease.

An increased awareness of IC has been recently noted in the lay literature as well as by patient advocate groups (Brody, 1984; Interstitial Cystitis Association, 1986). In addition, the National Institute of Health has demonstrated an increased interest in interstitial cystitis research and dissemination of information (Rodgers & Striker, 1987).

It should come as no surprise that IC is associated with sexual difficulties as confirmed in our study of nine women patients, ages 22 through 69 (median age = 36). Six of the women we interviewed and distributed questionnaires to (66% of our sample) indicated that IC definitely interfered with some aspect of their sexuality in contrast with two women (22%) who were uncertain and only one woman (11%) who experienced no sexual difficulties at all. Typically, women with severe IC symptoms were more likely than those with milder symptoms to describe having sexual difficulties. However, one remarkable woman noted that the disease "did not interfere a whole lot" with her sexuality despite chronic, severe pain because sex was a high priority in her life, more powerful than her experience of the disease. Other women expressed uncertainty about the disease's impact because they did not have a current sexual partner, suffered from numerous other health problems which might impair sexual functioning, or had blamed arousal problems on themselves and not their medical condition.

Most women were convinced that IC harmed some aspect of their sexuality. For example, some single women developed anticipatory anxiety about sex. Although they still desired sex strongly, they worried that their constant need to go to the bathroom would get in the way of romantic feelings should they find a suitable, new partner. As one woman described it, intimacy is a delicate process. If her disease continues to be active, she is afraid that "the moment will be killed" such that she and her partner will no longer want to have sex. Other women noted that pain and a constant urge to urinate contributed to embarrassment with or rejection by a partner. "I don't feel clean any more," one woman explained, noting how her frequent visits to the bathroom caused her to develop an image of herself as a sexless, unattractive person.

Interstitial cystitis does more than contribute to anxiety about sex and lowered sexual self-esteem. The disease also disrupts sexual arousal. Chronic and severe pain in the genital area associated with the acute phase of this disease may be experienced as a cruel parody of the first two stages of the sexual response cycle, mainly excitement (or sensations from initial blood engorgement and muscle tension throughout the body) and the plateau period (the time of maximal sexual responsiveness preceding orgasm) (Masters & Johnson, 1966). As a result, the patient may come to associate sexual arousal with pain and thereby develop a pattern of avoiding sexual feelings and interactions. As one woman indicated, she didn't want anyone to touch her when the disease first struck, giving her relentless pain and desire to urinate. Another woman described disliking the sensation of feeling like she has to urinate a lot during sexual arousal even though she has recently emptied her bladder, adding "it takes a lot to turn me on." A third woman said that sexual arousal was impaired even when she was free of pain because she felt anxious about when the pain might return and ruin her experience.

Interstitial cystitis can also impair the healthy partner's sexual arousal. As one woman noted, "At times when I am ready for sex, my partner gets so worried about hurting me that he has a hard time maintaining an erection. This is especially true since he uses a condom which decreases sensitivity. The end result is that we either don't have sex or sexual intercourse takes too long and irritates my bladder. Ironically, we wouldn't have these problems if I had a less caring partner."

It is well documented that painful intercourse or sharp pains in the vagina during penetration, alleviated only temporarily during orgasm, are common among heterosexual IC patients (Gillespie, 1986). This debilitating symptom can lead to two unadaptive responses: rejecting all of a partner's sexual advances which contributes to anger and disharmony in the intimate relationship or being a martyr and having sex even when it hurts which increases the woman's repugnance for sex and depression. This process was eloquently described by a married woman who noted that she had passively complied with her husband's requests for sexual intercourse when initially struck with the disease. "He would stop and ask if I was okay and I would say yes even if this was not true." Naturally, this patient became resentful and her marital relationship deteriorated until she learned to communicate her true desires and feelings. Without benefit of formal psychotherapy but with the support of her physician and loving family members, this woman was able to grow from her experience of the disease, becoming assertive and frank about what she wanted from others for the first time in her life. Presently, she experiences her husband as very sensitive to her feelings and health status, and their sexual relationship has improved as a result.

For some individuals, interstitial cystitis may contribute to guilt about interfering with the partner's sexual pleasure. After noting how compassionate and sensitive their sexual partners were, three women described a variety of emotions. On the positive side, they were happily surprised that they could have such solid relationships despite suffering from a disease that greatly lessened the frequency with which they could have sex. On the negative side, they felt guilty for denying sex to committed lovers when their symptoms were active, worrying that their partners might feel rejected or hopelessly frustrated.

Interstitial cystitis patients could benefit greatly from the services of feminist therapists who have familiarized themselves with the medical problems they face. Ideally, the psychotherapist should consult with the woman's urologist so that both can come up with a coordinated treatment plan. Each patient will present unique assets and problems. Obviously, there is no single, correct procedure for handling sexual difficulties associated with the disease. The following five considerations are important, however.

First, the therapist will want to inquire about the extent to which the patient blames herself for IC symptoms. Knowledge of the disease will help the therapist explain that IC, not psychopathology, is responsible for sexual difficulties. With this in mind, the patient will be better able to cope with the possibility of making the best of her sexuality despite interference from her disease. If necessary, the therapist might want to dispute or argue against guilt, anxiety, and anger-creating beliefs which diminish sexual pleasure still further, e.g., "I owe it to my partner to have sex, regardless of how I feel"; "This disease makes me an undesirable lover"; "I can't stand this disease."

Second, it is valuable to assess how the partner reacts to the impact that IC has had on the woman's experience of sexuality. Couple counseling can be directed towards increasing the partner's empathy for the patient's situation and appreciation for the fact that difficulties with sex and frequent urination are not symptomatic of sexual dysfunction or partner rejection. Furthermore, especially compassionate partners can be taught to control anxiety about causing pain to the IC patient during sex when she reassures them otherwise.

Lesbian couples may achieve an easier sexual adjustment than heterosexuals because they already engage in a greater variety of sensual activities (cf. Bell & Weinberg, 1978). In contrast, alternatives to traditional sexual intercourse will need to be explored with heterosexuals such as the IC patient's willingness to bring a partner to orgasm, manually or orally, when pain is too severe or persistent to make sexual intercourse desirable. As with any handicapped person and most able-bodied individuals, it is useful for the therapist to dispute the belief that coitus is the only proper or normal way to enjoy sex (cf. McCormick & Jordan, 1986). Sensual, mutual massage, enjoying one another's nude bodies, intimate conversation, sharing sexual fantasies, and mutual bathing are a sample of a variety of ways couples can enjoy one another even when sexual intercourse is not practical.

Third, if sexual intercourse is not painful but the main problem is that sensations of genital pain and bladder urgency mask excitement, various techniques can be employed to bring the IC patient to orgasm rapidly. The powerful sensation of orgasm overrides pain. Therefore, a partner can stimulate the IC patient's clitoris in a direct and efficient manner, helping her to achieve orgasm more rapidly than she might through a combination of foreplay and intercourse. An electric vibrator, in combination with various lubricants, can be effective for this purpose. Relevant to this, one woman with IC noted that she sometimes preferred masturbating alone to having sex with her partner because she could feel certain to pick a time when she was relatively free of pain and felt greater control over her sexuality. In addition, a number of women indicated the importance of sexual fantasies in overcoming pain and experiencing sexual excitement. Powerful fantasies, in combination with reassuring cognition like "I don't have to have sex unless I want it" and "My partner loves me and will be sensitive to what I want" have helped some women with active IC symptoms achieve normal levels of arousal.

Interstitial cystitis patients might want to observe patterns in their symptoms. For instance, they may find that they are relatively free of symptoms during particular times of the day but are worse at other times. These observations can be taken into consideration when planning sexual activities. Two women in our study indicated that they usually had little or no pain in the morning but were "in bad shape" at night. Instead of having sex at night as is traditional for many couples, these women might negotiate to have sex as soon as they wake up in the morning.

Consideration of our interview data suggests that those women with high frustration tolerance or a willingness to work hard to overcome the barriers to sexual excitement presented by their disease were most likely to achieve a satisfactory sexual adjustment. However arousal is achieved and no matter how long it takes, sexual intercourse should be delayed by heterosexual couples until the woman begins to achieve orgasm. It is probably not wise for a couple to strive for an athletic form of sex with the goal of multiple orgasms for the woman regardless of the woman's symptoms.

Fourth, heterosexuals benefit from learning that there is no "should" or "must" for having frequent sexual intercourse. It simply may not be the best way of an IC patient to enjoy sex. However, there are several techniques for reducing the pain that might be associated with sexual intercourse developed by Gillespie (1986) and her associates who offer brief courses on sex therapy for IC patients. Specifically, the couple should experiment with coital positions which minimize the possibility of the penis stimulating the base of the bladder. For example, the woman can get on top of the man so as to control the angle of her partner's penis through her own position. Alternatively, the woman can rest on her hands and knees with her partner entering her vagina from behind. Another relatively pain-free position involves the man sitting on the edge of a bed or chair with the woman sitting on top and the couple rocking so that the penis rests against the cervix rather than the woman's bladder. Pain management techniques taught in hypnosis, biofeedback, and natural childbirth classes may be helpful. In addition, urologists recommend that women with IC and other bladder disorders avoid the diaphragm as a contraceptive method as it may prove to be an irritant.

Fifth, the therapist should not be too quick to recommend relaxation training unless there is clear evidence that anxiety about the disease is contributing to sexual difficulties. Gillespie (1986), Reid (1985), and others working with IC patients advocate relaxation training to increase coping and alleviate pain associated with sex and other activities. In our experience, however, relaxation training may be counterproductive as most IC patients feel worse when they are relaxed or unoccupied than when they are busy with multiple activities. Distraction appears to be one of the most powerful ways of reducing the sensation of bladder pain and this is best achieved by introducing powerful, alternative stimuli to the situation. Generalizing these observations to sexual interactions, we suggest that the IC patient and her partner experiment with a variety of distracting stimuli during sex such as loud music and hot baths before and after orgasm. Heat provides pain relief for some patients in any event (cf. Gillespie, 1986), and can be used as a sensual adjunct to the couple's sexual routine. In addition, since sexual fantasies help many women with IC overcome pain and experience arousal, couples may want to experiment with various erotic stimuli including videotapes and audiotapes with powerful and appealing sexual imagery.

A number of women we interviewed indicated that particular positions such as spreading their legs far apart or elevating their knees while reclining on their backs were helpful for reducing pain. Experimentation with such positions is advisable before and after sexual activity.

IC is a painful, frustrating disease which can seriously impair sexual functioning and the pleasure patients take in living. Therefore, sexual therapy alone may be insufficient for helping patients and their partners make the best of their lives and sexual relationships. In some instances, therapists will need to work on helping patients increase their sense of self worth by pointing out how the disease does not diminish their physical or psychological attractiveness. Frustration tolerance should be increased because the demand that sex should be easy appears to play an etiological role in many sexual problems (Jordan & McCormick, in press). It is true that IC makes sex difficult. However, the belief that sex and erotic pleasure are impossible should be disputed. Rather, the symptoms of IC challenge the patient to come up with alternative ways to be a sexual person. Experimenting with this challenge, especially when there is a supportive partner available, can enhance sexual functioning and psychological adjustment.

Many IC patients will benefit from joining support groups composed of individuals with similar difficulties. Active participation in such groups will help patients dispute unadaptive beliefs such as the convictions that they suffer alone or have a psychiatric rather than a medical problem (cf. Ratner, 1985). In addition, feedback from group members may increase the IC patient's sense of mastery over her situation and provide ideas as to how others make the most of their sexuality despite the disease. The Interstitial Cystitis Association (ICA) is a national, nonprofit organization which refers women to support groups and serves numerous other purposes. Interested IC patients and their families and therapists can request additional information by writing to: The ICA, P.O. Box 1553, Madison Square Station, New York, NY 10159.

As a final note, the first author would like to point out that she is an interstitial cystitis patient as well as being a clinical psychologist. Personal knowledge of Rational-Emotive and feminist therapy techniques have helped her adjust to the sexual and other debilitating symptoms of the disease. In fact, collaborating on this and other articles with her urologist, to help other patients and the clinicians and family members who care about them, has been therapeutic in itself.

Our insight as authors is that it is critical for the IC patient to take an active role in coping with the disease. The worst thing for a woman to do is to assume the sick or victim role, resting too much, isolating herself, and resigning herself to doing nothing. With few exceptions, IC doesn't go away except for brief periods of remission; its symptoms may be intractable for some individuals. Nonetheless, a patient's attitude towards the disease can be controlled.

One can be a fighter instead of a victim as espoused by Johnson (1981) who wrote an inspiring book describing his own battle to overcome the devastating sexual and physical impairment caused by scleroderma. With grace and insight, some of the IC patients we talked to described psychological growth as a result of the disease in terms of increased appreciation of their own strength and improved communication and intimacy with others. Self education about the disease, political activism in the ICA and other organizations, involvement in self-help groups composed of other IC patients, and the firm decision to make the best of a bad situation are positive steps towards the management of sexual and other life difficulties associated with this chronic disease.

REFERENCES

Brody, J. E. (1984, December 5). Obscure bladder ailment that tries physicians as well as its victims. *The New York Times*.

Gillespie, L. (1986). *You don't have to live with cystitis!* New York: Rawson Associates.

Holm-Bentzen, M., & Lose, G. (1987). Pathology and pathogenesis of interstitial cystitis. *Urology Supplement, 29*, 8-13.

Interstitial Cystitis Association (1986, September 20). *Transcript: Second annual meeting*. New York: Interstitial Cystitis Association. [Available from Interstitial Cystitis Association, P. O. Box 1553, Madison Square Station, New York, NY 10159].

Johnson, J. (1985, September 11). The PMS of the 80s. *Washington Post*.

Johnson, W. R. (1981). *So desperate the fight: An innovative approach to chronic disease*. New York: Institute for Rational Living.

Jordan, T. J., & McCormick, N. B. (in press). Sexual irrationality questionnaire (SIQ). In: C. Davis & W. Yarber (Eds.) *Sexuality related measures: A compendium*. Lake Mills, Iowa: Graphic Publishing Company. (Copyright held by the Editors.)

Masters, W. H., & Johnson, V. E. (1966). *Human sexual response*. Boston: Little, Brown.

McCormick, N. B., & Jordan, T. J. (1986). Thoughts that destroy intimacy: Irrational beliefs about relationships and sexuality. In W. Dryden & P. Trower (Eds.) *Rational-Emotive Therapy: Recent developments in theory and practice*, pp. 47-62. Bristol: Institute for RET (UK).

Messing, E. M. (1986). Interstitial cystitis and related syndromes. In P. C. Walsh, R. F. Gittes, A. D. Perlmutter, & T. A. Stamey (Eds.) *Campbell's Urology, Fifth Edition*, pp. 1070-1092. Philadelphia: W. B. Saunders.

Messing, E. M. (1987). The diagnosis of interstitial cystitis. *Urology Supplement, 29*, 4-7.

Messing, E. M., & Stamey, T. A. (1978). Interstitial cystitis: Early diagnosis, pathology, and treatment. *Urology, 12*, 381-392.

Oravisto, K. J. (1975). Epidemiology of interstitial cystitis. *Annales Chirurgiae et Gynaecologiae Fenniae, 64*, 75-77.

Ratner, V. (1985). Interstitial cystitis. *Progress in Clinical and Biological Research, 197*, 163-168.

Reid, J. S. (1985). The other cystitis: Interstitial cystitis. *Journal of Nephrology Nursing, 2*, 294-296.

Rodgers, C. H., & Striker, G. E. (1987). Interstitial cystitis: The NIH perspective. *Urology Supplement, 29*, 43.

Disorders of Desire: Women, Sex, and Food

Nechama Liss-Levinson

There is a profound relationship for women between sex and food. When it comes right down to it, women are not supposed to like food or sex very much. At the same time, there is a role requirement to provide both sustenance and sexual pleasure to others.

Of course, expectations have changed over the past twenty years or so. We can now enjoy less food, and perhaps, more sex. Although women have been exhorted to enjoy the pleasures of sex, with some caveats most recently due to the AIDS crisis, mixed messages about women's participation in sex have continued. In addition, the idealized women's body size continues to be shrinking each year. We have trained women to be afraid of both sex and food. Or more precisely, we have trained them to be afraid of their hungers, of their desires, for either one.

The emphasis of clinical work in sex therapy for this past decade has been on "desire disorders," also known as "inhibited sexual desire"(ISD), or "desire discrepancy disorders." This problem is marked by a lack of sexual desire, or a sexual desire which is problematically less than that of the partner. As Kaplan (1979) notes, these problems seem particularly difficult to treat, and constitute the bulk of treatment failures for the short-term behaviorally oriented sex therapies.

These past ten years have also seen the explosive rise to prominence of eating disorders, both in sheer numbers of patients, and in attention in the professional and popular literature and media. The eating disorders include anorexia (refusal to eat, or self-starvation),

---

Nechama Liss-Levinson, PhD, is a psychologist in private practice in Great Neck, NY. She is affiliated with the Human Sexuality Service at Long Island Jewish-Hillside Medical Center, as well as the Eating Disorders Center of the National Institute for the Psychotherapies.

bulimia (binging and purging), and compulsive overeating. In a sense, these three also constitute desire disorders, in that the individual is alienated from her own sense of hunger and satiation. Clinical impressions also suggest that these patients do not typically respond to simple behavioral interventions (Thompson & Gans, 1985).

Females are disproportionately represented among the eating disorder patient population (over 90% of anorexics and bulimics are women or girls). Common cultural stereotyping would indicate that ISD is also a "women's problem." Although professional literature considers sexual desire disorders in the domain of both men and women, in Kaplan's book (1979) 19 of 22 cases portray the woman as the one with low desire or phobic avoidance. Clearly, it is the "she" whom is designated as the partner with a desire disorder.

The purpose of this article is to explore the linkages between the metaphors being expressed by women with disorders of desire in the realms of sexuality and eating. In both of these areas, roles and expectations have changed over time. Both areas encompass issues of power and powerlessness, nurturance and pleasure, anger and assertiveness, and entitlement and cultural scripts. Both are deeply linked to a woman's developing sense of self within her family and society. In both areas, women ask themselves about how much one can want, and what it would be like to be out of control, and desire too much. Both areas can be used as powerful weapons against one's intimates, and against one's self. Both involve the issue of desire and hunger.

Much has been written about the possible causative factors for both inhibited sexual desire and eating disorders. For both problems, it is clear that the aetiology is multi-leveled including intrapsychic, systems, family, and sociocultural factors. In this article, I wish to examine some of the causative factors in which there is an interfacing around the issue of desire.

DESIRE, HUNGER, AND THE BODY

Desire disorders imply that something has gone awry with our desires. And indeed, this is the case. We have been cut off from our desires, and from knowing our hungers. With both areas, there is an anesthetizing of the self. The woman does not, cannot know what she would like, whether in the form of nourishment and sustenance, or in the form of pleasure and sensuality. With eating disorders, she is out of sync with her self. With the sexual disorder, she is out of sync with her self in relation to another.

Women are afraid to "give in" to their hunger, whether for food or for sex. We learn to stop paying attention to our desires and lose contact with them.

> If I eat when I'm hungry, I'll eat all the time . . . There is always the body that is crying our for more food and the mind that is crying out for more weight loss. We learn to treat our bodies like naughty children whose wishes are absolutely out of the question. We learn to judge them, ignore them, ridicule them, torture them. (Roth, 1984)

Sherfey (1973) suggests that society suppresses women's sexual desires, knowing that beneath the surface there is an insatiable lusting. And women seem to fear this themselves, in regard to both food and sexuality. What if she craves donuts, chocolates, and ice cream? What if she wants to be touched again, and again? What if she takes too long? Or wants too much?

The message is that her body is untrustworthy. One cannot trust one's bodily sensations, whether it hungers for food or sexual encounter. There is an ultimate paradox. Her body is her most important asset. She must spend hours taking care of it, paying attention to it, and making it pleasing. And yet, at the same time, she must disparage it, ignore it, and ignore it's messages.

In describing the anorexic, Orbach writes,

> She turns to her body which becomes the arena for struggle. Treating it as an enemy, she wrestles with it, trying to dominate it by denying its needs. She puts all of her energy into trying to conquer her body, control it, and have it submit to her will. (Orbach, 1985a, p. 133)

Her obsession with denying herself her physical desires also allows her not to be aware of her emotional hungers which might conflict with those around her.

> I'm afraid to let myself get hungry; I feel so empty. . . . If we are fearful of allowing ourselves to need, if we fear that those needs, if expressed, might never be met, the sensation of hunger can evoke the emotion of hunger. Because it is an emotion that is repressed, we push it away; we don't want to be reminded of it. When physical hunger activates our yearning or wanting or aching, we feel frightened. (Roth, 1984, p. 18)

NURTURANCE

Early feminist therapists noted the paradoxical relationship between women and nurturance. Women, the mothers and caregivers, who nourish and nurture, receive little nourishment for themselves or from themselves. Women, however, are called on to provide both physical and emotional sustenance to their families.

At a centennial celebration for a school of professional nursing, there was a sticker which read, "One hundred years of nursing makes your breasts dry." Perhaps women with ISD are suffering from a complicated case of dry breasts. As Barbach notes,

> Placing the needs of others before our own and barely considering our own at all can greatly interfere with attaining sexual satisfaction. Many of us expend our energy on making our partner happy during lovemaking. We may concentrate on being a good lover for our partner's enjoyment. However, while we may be good at pleasing our partner, we may not be obtaining sufficient pleasure for ourselves. (Barbach, 1983, p. 25)

The lack of self-nurturance is evidenced also in all of the eating disorders. The compulsive overeater enacts the stereotype of the woman nurturer, "in this case the all-giving, nurturing, reliable, loving, caring earth mother who excels in feminine skills of caretaking, food preparation and sensual hugs" (Orbach, 1978, p. 170). The anorexic woman cannot be nourished; she cannot allow the food in. The bulimic woman binges, but does not nourish herself. She purges the food, and heaps herself with shameful self-accusations. None of these women feel entitled to the nourishment.

Related to the issue of nurturance is pleasure. The infant who sucks receives pleasure along with the nourishment. As the child develops, however, pleasures are restricted, whether the pleasures of food and sweets, the pleasure of oneness with one's parents, or the sexual self-pleasuring of one's body.

> The consequences of these requirements are that by denying themselves, women are unable to develop an authentic sense of their needs or a feeling of entitlement for their desires. Women become dependent on the approval of those to whom they give, preoccupied with others' experience, and unfamiliar with their own needs. The imperative of affiliation means that many aspects of the self are underdeveloped, producing insecurity and a shaky sense of self. Under the competent care giver lives a hungry, deprived, and needy little girl who is unsure and ashamed of her desires and wants. (Orbach, 1985b, p. 84)

POWER STRUGGLE/ANGER

I remember arguing with my mother about wearing a sweater. I knew that I did not feel cold. But she did. Our struggle was intense. I often lost, losing some of myself in the process.

For the anorexic, the struggle is one of life and death. Orbach (1985a) suggests the anorexic is engaged in a hunger strike, protesting against the societal norms about what it means to be a woman. Or perhaps she is engaged in a struggle for individuation.

> In a mixture of rage and demureness, the adolescent girl gags on the first mouthful or is full after a few bites. She is rejecting what her mother gives and hurting her in the most powerful way she knows how while simultaneously carrying out what she imagines to be her mother's wish, which is for her to disappear. (Orbach, 1978, p. 175)

Or perhaps the struggle is to gain control of the adolescent body which is growing and changing in unpredictable and seemingly uncontrollable ways. The struggle for the anorexic is painfully obvious as the family tries to get her to eat, similar to trying to force a toddler to defecate in the toilet – usually to no avail.

For the compulsive overeater, there is also a power struggle, and there is also unarticulated anger. In her adolescent years, she struggles with her parents, who try to get her to eat less, to diet, to deny herself, and her desires. For the adult woman, she continues her struggle with a spouse, or a boyfriend, or society, all telling her not to want so much, all telling her how to make her body more acceptable.

The power struggle within a relationship and the unexpressed anger are often cited as underlying causes of inhibited sexual desire (Kaplan, 1979). He may want a car, and she may want a vacation. She wants attention, and he wants respect. The struggle moves to the bedroom, where he wants sex, and she doesn't.

> If we have been trained not to rock the boat, not to express our anger, not to threaten the only security we have, we may be afraid to confront our partner directly. If our partner were to leave us, we might be left helpless and alone in the world. Therefore, the only power we may feel we have is the power of withholding–particularly withholding our sexuality. Some of us get headaches when it comes to lovemaking. Others of us, while submitting, may express our ire indirectly by not feeling excited, by not responding orgasmically, or by trying to get sex over with as quickly as possible. This negative withholding is powerful. (Barbach, 1983, p. 24)

In the classic Greek play, Lysistrata, the women of the city unite to engage in sexual abstinence until their husbands agree to end the war they are waging. This is the only power they have.

Both eating and sexual disorders involve bodily functions. In a passage describing the strategy of the compulsive overeater, Roth described the dilemma for all women with desire disorder: "They use their bodies as their battlegrounds; they know that in our culture, women's voices may not be heard, but their bodies will still (and always) be noticed" (Roth, 1984, p. 213).

SEXUAL DESIRE DIFFICULTIES FOR THE WOMAN WITH EATING DESIRE PROBLEMS

The main focus for the woman with an eating disorder is on her eating behavior. The symptom is a metaphor to express the conflicts in her life. Therapeutic exploration often reveals that the sexual behavior of the eating disordered patient may also be metaphorical, serving as an expression of the same characterological issues (Hirsch, 1986).

Many writers, including Bruch (1985) and Orbach (1978), have noticed the apparent lack of sexual desire or activity for the anorexic girl or woman. She seems as terrified of her sexuality as she is of eating. The reasons proferred for this aversion vary according to the theoretical perspective of the author.

The bulimic woman is noted to be more active sexually. To some, it may seem like she is "binging" on sex, in a manner not dissimilar to her binging on food. She may date or sleep with many men, having difficulty distinguishing one from another, or fully savoring any of the experiences. The relationships may tend toward the superficial, with each man "thrown up" as a new one enters the scene.

The compulsive overeater may feel that she is putting herself out of the sexual arena by her overweight body. She considers herself sexually unavailable. She may engage in a lot of sexual fantasy, but it is amorphous, and dreamy. She may feel that food, not sex, is her pleasure. Unfortunately, the food is often not fully enjoyed, but rather eaten without awareness, or with much guilt.

Roth (1984) describes an eating binge shared by two teen-age girls. The description sounds vaguely sensual. There is something illicit about the activity. There is a build up of excitement, and there is a sense of release and exhaustion at the end. The two girls never talk about it, at the time, or in the future. It is cloaked in secrecy and shame. This atmosphere, heavy with guilt, shame, and secrecy speaks to the sexual experiences of many young women, whether in masturbation, or a shared sexual encounter.

This trio of feelings are particularly salient for women who have been abused sexually, including childhood molestations, incest, and rape. Kaplan (1979) and Barbach (1983) both refer to numerous cases of sexual inhibitions which stem from episodes of such abuse. What is becoming evident from clinical material and discussion is that a subgroup of women with eating disorders have also been victims of sexual abuse. The metaphor is clear and apt. The girl or woman needs to control what she takes in to her body, and what she keeps out. Since the sexual abuse may be only a vague memory, or deeply hidden in shame, it is important for the therapist to keep in mind this historic possibility when working with the woman with a desire disorder.

Women, sex, and food are the royal triumvirate which populate the pages of women's magazines, whether it be diet desserts, sexual exhortations, or more ways to please the one you love. Szasz notes,

> Eating and copulation have always been of interest to people and are likely to remain so. Each of these behaviors satisfies a basic biological need – eating, the survival of the individual; copulation, the survival of the species. Each may be a rich source of pleasure through gratification of desire – or a rich source of pain, for many reasons . . . (Szasz, 1980, p. xiii)

The goal of the therapy for the woman with a desire disorder is that she learn to love and trust her body, her self, and her desires.

> I'm not frightened anymore. I've learned that kisses, like cold brussel sprouts, don't taste very good when you don't want them. I don't kiss when I don't want to kiss, just as I don't eat when I don't want to eat. I respect my appetites for food, and for sex, and trust that if I say no today, there will be either kisses or cookies tomorrow.
>
> Spend your hunger for touch the way you spend your hunger for food: on only that, and with only those, who nourish you. (Roth, 1984, p. 222)

REFERENCES

Barbach, L. (1983). *For each other: Sharing sexual intimacy*. New York: Anchor Books.

Bruch, H. (1985). Four decades of eating disorders. In D. Garner and P. Garfinkel (Eds.), *Handbook of therapy for anorexia nervosa and bulimia*. New York: Guilford Press.

Hirsch, I. (1986). Sexual disorders: A perspective. *American Journal of Psychoanalysis, 46:3*, 239-248.

Kaplan, H.S. (1979). *Disorders of sexual desire*. New York: Simon and Schuster.

Orbach, S. (1978). *Fat is a feminist issue*. New York: Paddington Press.

Orbach, S. (1985a). Visibility/invisibility: Social considerations in anorexia nervosa – a feminist perspective. In S.W. Emmett (Ed.), *Theory and treatment of anorexia nervosa and bulimia*. New York: Brunner/Mazel.

Orbach, S. (1985b). Accepting the symptom: A feminist psychoanalytic treatment of anorexia nervosa. In D. Garner & P. Garfinkel (Eds.), *Handbook of therapy for anorexia nervosa and bulimia*. New York: Guilford Press.

Roth, G. (1984). *Breaking free from compulsive eating*. New York: New American Library.

Sherfey, M.J. (1973). *The nature and evolution of female sexuality*. New York: Vintage Books.

Szasz, T. (1980). *Sex by prescription*. New York: Anchor Books.

Thompson, M., & Gans, M. (1985). Do anorexics and bulimics get well? In S.W. Emmett (Ed.), *Theory and treatment of anorexia nervosa and bulimia*. New York: Brunner/Mazel.

Intimacy and the New Reproductive Options

Sandra R. Leiblum

Infertility is a devastating blow to the woman who longs for a biological child. Often, women practice conscientious and responsible birth control for many years before deciding that the time is ripe for having a child. To discover, after months or years of first trying to avoid pregnancy and then trying unsuccessfully to conceive, that an infertility problem exists in either herself or her partner, or involves both of them together, is bitterly ironic and greatly distressing. Typically, women pass through a series of phases in eventually adapting to the unwelcome "crisis of infertility" (Leiblum, 1987; Menning, 1980), although some women experience long-term grief reactions.

To be infertile at this particular point in history is unique in many ways since there has been an unprecedented technological explosion in new methods for achieving pregnancy. Weil and Walters (1986), for example, have tabulated over sixteen alternative reproductive possibilities where variations exist in the source of gametes (e.g., husband, wife, surrogate), site of fertilization (e.g., wife, surrogate, laboratory), and site of pregnancy (e.g., wife, surrogate). The new reproductive options include a variety of artificial insemination procedures relying on either husband or donor semen, in vitro fertilization procedures which require either the husband's

---

Sandra R. Leiblum, PhD, is Co Director of the Sexual Counseling Service and Associate Professor of Clinical Psychiatry at UMDNJ-Robert Wood Johnson Medical School, Piscataway, NJ. She is the co-editor of several books on sexual dysfunction including *Principles and Practice of Sex Therapy* and *Sexual Desire: Clinical Perspectives*. Her research interests center on women's reproductive health, with special emphasis on infertility and menopause.

sperm and wife's ovum or donated sperm, donation of eggs or even both eggs and sperm donation, and surrogate mothers, in addition to variations on these methods. In recent years, there has been increasing reliance on gonatropic stimulation in order to produce more than one viable ovum for fertilization and transfer (e.g., Jewelewicz, 1975). Many of these ovulation stimulation methods have unexpected (and unwanted) side effects (Leiblum, Kemmann, & Lane, 1987).

The plethora of new reproductive options boggles the imagination and creates a host of thorny dilemmas ranging from moral, legal, and economic considerations, to political, medical, and personal ones (Singer & Wells, 1984). Feminists have mixed reactions to these new noncoital reproductive techniques. While they permit many infertile women to achieve a biological pregnancy, they may lead to the economic exploitation of certain groups of women, such a would-be surrogate mothers or gamete donors. Some feminists feel that this new "medicalization" of reproduction is yet another example of male domination of women via control over her reproductive capacity. Some feminists believe that the quest for new reproductive options reinforces the notion that the only acceptable role for women is motherhood and that women who voluntarily opt for child-free lives are either selfish or deficient in their womanhood. These feminists suggest that women are being discouraged from finding nongenetic routes to motherhood (e.g., adoption) by men and furthermore that women are being coerced into fulfilling traditional and restrictive societal expectations of marriage and maternity. Other feminists feel grateful about the current availability of noncoital reproductive options for single and lesbian women as well as infertile women generally.

While the political, medical, legal, and moral implications of the new reproductive options merit careful analysis, a meaningful discussion of them is beyond the scope of the current chapter. Rather, we will be considering the impact of these new reproductive options on women's psychological well-being and experience of intimacy. For it is certainly the case that conflict, frustration, and keen disappointment may characterize a woman's (and her partner's) experience with an experimental or relatively new reproductive program. Generally, many months elapse between the diagnosis of infertility and the decision to undertake one of the new infertility programs and then additional time is spent giving a particular technique a "fair" trial. Often, women and their partners feel as though they have stumbled onto an emotional roller coaster, as they initially enter a new program with high hopes and bright expectations, only to meet unforeseen obstacles, disappointments, and often, reproductive failure.

This paper will consider some of the conflicts and dilemmas created by the new reproductive technologies and the threats they pose to couple intimacy. General issues will be highlighted and these will be illustrated with actual case examples.

PARTICIPATION IN THE NEW REPRODUCTIVE OPTIONS EXTENDS THE DURATION OF THE "CRISIS OF INFERTILITY"

Prior to the advent of the new reproductive technologies, a woman who learned that she was infertile grieved over the loss of the biological child she would never have and then, since there were no other biological options available, came to accept this reality. In time, she might eventually decide to remain child-free or, alternatively, to apply for adoption.

To some extent this is still true. In a follow-up study of the sequelae of unsuccessful in vitro fertilization, we found that eight or more months following the last in vitro fertilization attempt, 33% of couples had applied for adoption and 11% had secured an adoptive child (Leiblum, Kemmann, Colburn, Pasquale, & DeLisi, 1987). Further, more than half of the couples contacted indicated that they had abandoned biological attempts to conceive and 52% felt as though they had "resolved" the infertility crisis. Nevertheless, 93% of respondents indicated that they would, in fact, participate in any new reproductive option that promised to enhance their likelihood of achieving a biological pregnancy! Therein lies the potential problem.

The seemingly endless supply of new or potentially available reproductive options currently suggests to women and their partners that if one procedure or technique does not work, the next one is just around the corner. Sometimes, couples move from one procedure to another, in part because of their own strong desire to have a genetic child, and in part because medical professionals suggest alternative options. Each attempt leads to the resurrection of hope and positive expectation, only to be followed, for many, with frustration and failure. For it must be recalled that the success rate of many of the new reproductive procedures varies considerably, and disappointment, rather than pregnancy, may be the net result.

ENHANCED SEXUAL PRESSURE

Unwanted infertility is not conducive to good sex (Leiblum, 1987). Sex dictated by the calendar diminishes ardor and leads to enhanced performance pressure for both men and women. Ovulatory sex typically lacks spontaneity and imagination. The goal becomes one of achieving a successful ejaculation within the vagina rather than discovering new and exciting ways to pleasure one another. The situation becomes worse when the woman is placed on ovulation stimulation medication. Women taking Pergonal (human menopausal gonadotropins [hMg]), for example, must submit to daily and often uncomfortable injections of medication and frequent blood tests as well as endure the side effects that often accompany the medication, such as fatigue, moodiness, weight gain, headaches, etc. (Leiblum, Kemmann, & Lane, 1987). They are understandably intent on having coitus at the requisite time with a receptive and cooperative mate. Having a spouse display ambivalence or worse, performance difficulties at the time of ovulation is extremely distressing. Consequently, most women feel the burden of encouraging and stimulating their male partners into a state of sexual readiness while generating sexual arousal themselves. This is not always readily accomplished, particularly after many frustrating months of unsuccessful efforts to conceive. Sexual desire typically diminishes or vanishes altogether, eliminating a significant source of couple intimacy. Compounding the problem is the fact that many reproductive options (e.g., artificial insemination with husband semen [AIH], in vitro fertilization [IVF], intrauterine insemination [IUI]), etc.) require the male to supply a semen specimen on demand and everyone, from the technician to the physician, knows how well he is doing. So, while the drama of ovulatory sex is initially private, it becomes a semi-public event and both partners feel the demand characteristics of this situation.

Such sexual problems are not peculiar to heterosexual couples. Lesbian couples also may suffer sexual side-effects from infertility work-ups and procedures. Preoccupation with ovulation is distracting and can lead to sexual disinterest. Sexual intimacy with a lover may be seen as less important than achieving conception. The partner who is not committed to experiencing a pregnancy (or becoming a parent) may feel ignored, unloved, and sexually deprived. The partner who is intent on becoming pregnant feels sad, discouraged, and often emotionally unavailable with the unwelcome arrival each month of menses and may become even less sexually enthusiastic and receptive.

Finally, the fact that infertility work-ups and procedures typically last for many months and even years compounds the sexual problems for both hetero- and homosexual couples.

Case Example

Ms. J., a 42-year-old woman who desperately wanted to become a biological mother, was unable to reach the stage of ovulation retrieval on two earlier IVF trials. Now, at last, all signs appeared perfect. Not wanting to place any undue performance pressure on her 59-year-old husband, she waited until 5 a.m. of the morning of the scheduled laparoscopy to inform her husband that he needed to produce a semen specimen – immediately! Her husband became extremely agitated and screamed, "I'm nothing but a semen machine for you! You use me for your own ends! All you care about is my sperm, not me! At times, I feel so depressed about our relationship that I don't even feel like waking up in the morning." Ms. J. became equally upset since she felt her husband had contributed little physically or emotionally to their reproductive attempts. Now that ovum retrieval was finally scheduled after months of past disappointments, her husband was balking! In frustration, she shouted, "You've made a deal and you better make good on it! If you don't give me the semen, I'll get inseminated with donor sperm!" Her husband retorted, "If you do that, I'm walking out of this door and never returning!"

It is obvious that the impact of the prior unsuccessful fertilization attempts coupled with the current demand to perform exacerbated an already stressed marital relationship. Ejaculating on demand—whether at home or in a doctors office—is not easy to do, particularly for a 59-year-old man. Having frozen sperm available might have avoided the performance obligation, but would not have eliminated the problem of cumulative years of tension surrounding conception. In this example, which is not atypical, the wife felt she was disproportionately shouldering the burdens of becoming pregnant. It was she who had to submit her body to daily injections and medical scrutiny. Now, when it was finally her husband's turn to actively participate, he was protesting. In such instances, it is not surprising that couples feel stressed. Regrettably, words cried out in anger can never be revoked. While the immediate crisis was resolved, there were long-term relationship consequences for this couple.

THE NEW REPRODUCTIVE OPTIONS MAY LEAD TO INSTANCES OF COERCION

The use of coercion, whether subtle or overt, may result when one partner is consumed with the wish to become pregnant or have a child, and senses hesitation in a mate. For example, despite discussion, couples may still not totally agree on which reproductive options are acceptable and which are not. Donor insemination, for instance, is often viewed skeptically by the infertile male. He worries that any child resulting from such a procedure will psychologically as well as genetically "belong" more to his wife than to himself. He may be concerned that he will be unable to attach to a child who is not his own biologically. Sometimes, a man admits that he will feel as though his wife has been "unfaithful" by carrying the fetus fertilized with another man's sperm. Women worry about "protecting" the secret of their husband's infertility and are concerned about his feeling excluded from or resentful about any resulting pregnancy.

On the other hand, men sometimes pressure their wives into accepting a surrogate because they are unwilling to father any child that does not bear their genetic "stamp." While most women believe they could become attached to any child they parent, men often wonder whether they can love an adoptive child. The fact that so many women feel "guilty" if they are infertile leads them, at times, to consent to reproductive options they are uncomfortable with. For example, it is not uncommon to find a woman who has had biological children in a former marriage, and has had a voluntary tubal ligation, to attempt to become pregnant with a new husband because he is insistent on "having a child of his own" even though she is disinterested in having additional children.

Case Example 1

Ms. S., an Indian woman, sought IVF, because of secondary infertility. She already had one biological child but was unable to conceive a second child, despite months of medical consultations and ovulation stimulation. At the insistence of her husband, who was unwilling to come to the clinic for the initial consultation, Ms. S. requested IVF. Interviewing revealed that her husband was committed to the idea of having a second son. Even though adoption of an Indian child could readily be arranged, he was unwilling to even consider raising a nonbiological child. Despite the wife's concerns about the physical discomfort and likely disappointment associated with IVF, she felt constrained to give it "one shot" in order to satisfy her husband.

This case is a striking illustration of how women feel responsible for "fulfilling" traditional sex role demands and "supplying" their spouses with a child. In cultures where having children is considered both the birthright and duty of women, resisting either societal or spousal pressure to conceive is difficult. Without adequate assessment of the motivations for pursuing pregnancy and an endorsement by medical personnel of child-free living as a viable life option, undue pressure can be exerted on women.

Case Example 2

After being married for seven years and unsuccessfully attempting conception for two, Mr. Z. learned that his sperm were deficient in quantity and form. He felt devastated by this news. Augmenting his despair was his wife's open and unrestrained expressions of anger and disappointment. While he attempted to mollify her by showering her with gifts and attention, she remained committed to the idea of having a biological child. One day, she announced her decision to undergo donor insemination. When he protested, she declared that if he would not consent to this procedure, she would leave the marriage. Mr. Z. reluctantly agreed. His wife became pregnant following the first donor insemination and Mr. Z found himself withdrawing from her. Following the birth of a healthy son, he continued to avoid interaction with both his wife and the infant. It was only following a medical crisis in which his son's life was endangered that Mr. Z. was able to identify strong feelings of love and responsibility toward the child.

Case Example 3

Sharon and Ruth were a lesbian couple who had lived together for 13 years in a committed, monogamous relationship. When Sharon turned 38, she decided she wanted a child although Ruth was ambivalent. After months of discussing this issue without agreeing on a course of action, Sharon independently decided to go ahead with donor insemination. After becoming pregnant, she told Ruth that she expected her to participate in the financial and parenting responsibilities. Because Ruth was a highly responsible and committed individual, she reluctantly agreed, although she had had earlier thoughts of leaving the relationship for another woman.

In these examples, one partner is committed to the idea of having a child, despite the reluctance or ambivalence of another. Because parenthood is generally overvalued in this society, women are easily made to feel that they "ought" to have children and/or support partners who want them. The variety and availability of new reproductive technologies for overcoming infertility makes it difficult to abandon pregnancy attempts even though there are difficulties in conceiving and ambivalence about parenthood altogether. It is the responsibility of infertility counselors to ensure that women are freely electing a reproductive method and that, moreover, the costs – financial, physical and psychological – are carefully explained. Moreover, sufficient encouragement must be offered for child-free life options.

The following case example illustrates how readily a woman may feel coerced into submitting to infertility procedures for which she has little intrinsic motivation.

Case Example 4

Gwen, a 39-year-old manager, had an 11-year-old daughter from her first marriage. Her present, never-married, 34-year-old husband, urged her to have a child with him. After 3 years of unsuccessfully trying to conceive, Gwen's endometriosis was diagnosed and successfully treated. She then started taking ovulation medication and became pregnant after 3 months. To her husband's chagrin, she refused to undergo aminocentriosis, indicating that she wanted this child despite any possible birth defects. Her husband was upset, saying he did not want a "damaged" child. This remark greatly distressed her since she worked with handicapped children and she knew that the health and well-being of a newborn could not be guaranteed. However, the immediate crisis was by-passed since she had a miscarriage. Gwen was reluctant to resume pregnancy attempts immediately, but her husband pressured her, saying "time is running out." He alluded to her age and to the fact that if she did not become pregnant, he might leave the marriage.

While it is obvious that this marriage might have been doomed without the availability of methods designed to overcome ovulatory problems or to detect genetic defects, it is also obvious that having these options available exacerbated pre-existing relationship tensions and spotlighted individual conflicts that might otherwise have been circumvented.

OBSESSIVE PREOCCUPATION WITH ACHIEVING A PREGNANCY LEADS TO INCREASED COUPLE CONFLICT

Motherhood is rarely viewed neutrally. Many religious groups consider procreation to be the sole justification for sexual intimacy and, indeed, as the major goal of marriage. In some societies, having children is presented as a patriotic duty. For many years, analysts and other members of the medical profession considered childbirth the quintessential task of women and viewed maternal disinterest as a sign of psychopathology. Little girls are still repeatedly reminded of their future roles as mothers, as witnessed by the unending supply of baby dolls and other paraphernalia of motherhood sold in toy stores and marketed by the media. Many women have been raised to believe that no career other than that of wife and mother is important, while others feel that they will feel incomplete or frustrated if they do not have children. It is not surprising, then, that many women become seriously depressed when they have difficulty conceiving or have repeated miscarriages. Not only do they feel betrayed by their bodies but seriously deficient as women.

Tragically, some women become obsessed with trying to achieve a pregnancy, even though their lives and their marriages may be jeopardized. Some women forget that relationships, even stable long-standing ones, require nurturance. They become increasingly consumed with the endless round of infertility treatments, support groups, and indecision about which reproductive option to attempt next. Their partners – male and female – come to feel increasingly resentful, neglected and unappreciated. At times, of course, it is men who express the stronger desire to have a biological child and who impose their demands on women. As indicated earlier, women often receive little support from friends or relatives for resisting this pressure. Moreover, men rarely define their entire self-worth in terms of their ability to bear a child. Regrettably, it is more often the infertile women who is reared to believe that her self-worth is centered in her procreativity and who thinks that a successful pregnancy and delivery will put to rest any doubts about her womanliness.

Case Example

Susan, a 34-year-old teacher, has been trying to become pregnant for 4 years. Robert is ambivalent and worried about the financial burdens of parenthood, particularly in light of his recent job lay-off. Nevertheless, he is reasonably supportive of Susan during her reproductive attempts. He is angry, though, about the deteriorating quality of their sexual life. He complains that Susan has become so obsessed with becoming pregnant that she displays little interest in him, either in or out of bed. Sex has become a sterile, mechanical activity designed strictly for procreation and occurring almost exclusively at the time of ovulation. The couple have few intimate discussions on any topic other than their infertility experiences and options. Susan indicates that she understands Robert's feelings but rejects the notion that she should simply submit to Robert's sexual demands. She believes that Robert relies on sex as the sole means of reassurance about his masculine adequacy. She complains that Robert rarely expresses genuine empathy regarding her grief and distress about the infertility difficulty and does not provide adequate affection and support for her plight. Needless to say, both partners feel misunderstood and lonely.

INCREASED CONFLICT OVER ALLOTMENT OF COUPLE FINANCES

Couples usually have limited finances. Many of the new technologically sophisticated reproductive methods are expensive and are not covered by insurance. If one partner is ambivalent about a reproductive option, it often takes the form of bickering about whether or not it is worth the money given the small likelihood of success. As one husband put it, "I'd rather blow my savings on a fabulous vacation in the South Pacific than on one unsuccessful cycle of in vitro fertilization!"

His wife did not share this sentiment, particularly since she felt he was responsible for her undergoing an abortion some years earlier which resulted in their current infertility problems! Since he controlled their finances, she felt powerless and resentful.

In this case, as in many others, women feel castrated because of their economic dependence on their partner as well as by the power imbalance in the relationship. The conflict about infertility options serves to highlight more basic obstacles to couple intimacy.

DELETERIOUS IMPACT OF SECRECY REGARDING REPRODUCTIVE DECISIONS AND ITS IMPACT ON INTIMACY

The insidious impact of secrecy of any sort on relationships is well-documented (Scharff, 1978, Imber-Black, 1987). At times, one spouse attempts to keep a "secret" from the other, ostensibly to "protect the partner" but often to satisfy her own wish for a biological child when the partner is unenthusiastic or unwilling.

Case Example 1

Caroline does not want the administrator of the pergonal program to tell her husband, who has ejaculation difficulties, that she is starting gonadotropic stimulation because she fears he will be unable to ejaculate at the proper time. In fact, she requests intrauterine insemination in order to avoid the problem of intercourse on demand.

Case Example 2

Mary wants to tell her parents and sister that she and Robert have decided on donor insemination as a reproductive choice because of Robert's low sperm count. Robert is adamant that she keep his infertility secret. She feels he is depriving her of family support; he feels she would be betraying him if she tells. The conflict around whether or not to tell family members precipitates considerable marital strife.

While "secrets" between partners or between partners and family members do not necessarily cause problems, they do erode couple intimacy since they stifle spontaneous and total communication. They lead to self-monitoring and hesitation, which can interfere with couple intimacy. Further, by avoiding some more basic issues, the significant problems in a relationship may not get addressed, e.g., a partner's ambivalence about becoming a parent, the sexual difficulty of a individual, etc. If infertility program personnel agree to maintain a secret and "collude" with one partner or another, they become part of the problem rather than part of the solution. In such instances, their behavior is ethically questionable.

This paper has highlighted some of the potential pitfalls of the new reproductive options. Because it is women, rather than men, who are the primary focus of the new reproductive choices and because it is their bodies rather than their partners that are probed, pricked, and otherwise penetrated, it is women who usually bear the physical and emotional costs of the new reproductive technologies; but both men and women are vulnerable to the threat these options pose to couple intimacy. On the other hand, it is equally as clear that the new reproductive technologies may enhance as well as diminish intimacy. Surviving the fears and difficulties associated with overcoming infertility can lead to increased sensitivity, empathy, and closeness. Success in becoming pregnant or having a child enables many couples to share the tremendous and unique joy associated with conception, pregnancy, delivery, and parenthood.

REFERENCES

Imber-Black, E. (January 9, 1987). Working with secrets in marital and family therapy. Workshop presented at Robert Wood Johnson Medical School.

Leiblum, S.R. (1987). Infertility. In E. Blechman & K. Brownell (Eds.) *Behavioral medicine for women*. New York: Pergamon Press.

Leiblum, S.R., Kemmann, E., & Lane, M.K. (1987). The psychological concomitants of in vitro fertilization. *Journal of Psychosomatic Obstetrics and Gynecology*, 6, 165-178.

Leiblum, S.R., Kemmann, E., Colburn, D., Pasquale, S., & DeLisi, A.M. (1987). Unsuccessful in vitro fertilization: A follow-up study. *Journal of In Vitro Fertilization and Embryo Transfer*, 4, 46-50.

Menning, B. (1978). The emotional needs of infertile couples. *Fertility and Sterility*, 34, 313-319.

Scharff, D. (1978). Truth and consequences in sex and marital therapy: The revelation of secrets in the therapeutic setting. *Journal of Sex and Marital Therapy*, 4, 1, 35-49.

Singer, P. & Wells, D. (1984). *Making babies: The new science and ethics of conception*. New York: Charles Scribner's Sons.

Weil, B. & Walters, L. (1986). In ethics and the new reproductive options. *Fertility and Sterility*, 46, 3, 16S-20S.

When Abortion Is a Blessing

Lynn Leight

Two weeks after a first trimester abortion, Jayne is referred to my office for counseling. My cheerful greeting contrasts with the mournful aura that seems to envelop this 21-year-old, single, Anglo-American woman.

Jayne has been in therapy for three years. The brief history provided by her therapist reveals that she has resolved the psychopathological behavior of self-deprivation that characterized her original presenting diagnosis of anorexia nervosa. Since adolescence Jayne had been unable to accept her physically maturing body. Jayne was born to parents who shared with her their belief that sex was meant for beauty queens. She became obsessed with fear that her beauty demanded she become a sex-object. The more emaciated she became the less threatened she felt by her emerging sexuality. The less she valued herself the more she distanced herself from social interactions. While Jayne craved the warmth of intimacy, she feared rejection and her ability to sustain an emotional or physical relationship.

With the nurturant yet firm direction of her skilled therapist, Jayne has learned to appreciate her natural beauty. She no longer deprives herself of food as a means of controlling her sexuality. The assertiveness skills that she has developed enable her to accept and reject overtures of affection without feeling inadequate or threatened. And since Jayne began dancing and playing to her androgynous spirit, she has experienced the joy of sexual unfolding. It was during this period of transformation that Jayne met Bruce; the first

---

Lynn Leight, RN, is the founder/director of Sex, Health, Education (SHE) Centers nationwide, and the author of *Better Let Them Know Before You Let Them Go: Parents Guide to Raising Sexually Healthy Children*.

man who had the sensitivity and alchemy to sexually arouse her. Jayne explained that on one glorious night when she was feeling particularly sexual and desirable she engaged in intercourse without giving contraception a second thought.

Jayne did not want to become a mother. She wasn't ready to assume the responsibility for another human being; after all, she was just learning to love and trust herself. Jayne explained that she was testing her "equipment" and she was ecstatic to discover that she was, as she put it, a "female female." Jayne chose to abandon precaution. It is now two weeks after the abortion. Jayne had elected to terminate the pregnancy after weighing the alternatives. And, now that the experience is yesterday's news, the expectation would be that Jayne is pleased she exercised her freedom to choose. Why then does she appear troubled and depressed?

"How was it for you?" I gently ask. "It was OK" she answers in a monotone. "Was it as you expected?" "Yes," she replies, "it wasn't any better or worse than I anticipated." "So, how are you feeling now?" I pursue. "I'm feeling blue – I'm feeling heavy-hearted. I know having an abortion is no big deal, millions of people have had one. I truly believe in what I did. But, I just feel depressed." "With whom have you shared this experience?" I ask. "No one – it's no big deal!" she insists. "I didn't have to burden anyone with my problem." "So," I continue, "no one accompanied you to the Center. No one held your hand on the way home. For the past two weeks no one has inquired about how you are feeling and if they did, you guarded your response."

Jayne explains, "I was going to tell Bruce but then I decided against it. After all, it was my problem not his. Besides, I didn't want to scare him away. I was also going to tell my sister but decided the disclosure would be too stressful for me as well as her. You know, she still lives at home with my parents and I couldn't chance their finding out. I had enough to do taking care of myself. I didn't want to be burdened with their disappointment or fear for my safety."

Abortion isn't pleasant, even when the decision is rational, mature and loving. Under the best of circumstances, it may be considered a minor medical procedure, but in all instances it is a major emotional event. It is one thing to objectively intellectualize the virtues of freedom of choice, but quite a different story when you are faced with the dilemma personally. My sixteen years of experience in this field have convinced me that even the strongest and the boldest of women fare better with the assistance of an empathetic friend.

"So, you think you're some kind of a big shot," I teasingly retort. "I bet you are the kind of super-woman who competently shoulders your everyday problems and all those that are dropped on your doorstep. You know," I continue, "in reaching out to others, you will not be losing control, you'll only be gaining a friend." She tentatively considers my advice. "I bet I know what you can use." I motion to Jayne to stand and when she does I give her a hug. She weeps quietly and finally sobs. "It feels so good to be hugged. It feels good to share a secret with someone who cares."

Finally, Jayne gains her composure. I turn on a mood relaxing audio tape and silently wait for the metaphorical clouds to lift. Jayne breaks the silence. "It really wasn't bad," she muses. "Although at times I feel guilty that I don't feel guilty and society expects and wants me to feel guilty." The statement may sound convoluted, but I understand what Jayne is saying. It is not easy to feel good about yourself when there are strident voices denouncing those who select an opposing belief. Their counsel is repentance to rid oneself of guilt and shame. The assumption is that the consequences of abortion are always negative.

"Tell me, Jayne, what did you most like about the abortion?" Jayne looks startled. "Like!" she entones, "what was there to like?" "Well," I continue, "I believe there are no mistakes in life. Every situation is a lesson from which we learn valuable principles about ourselves. From these lessons we grow wiser, stronger and more insightful. In time something of value emerges, even from our darkest moments."

With this philosophy in mind I ask Jayne to tell me what she has learned and what she most values from the experience. After some deliberation Jayne timidly admits that she feels a great sense of relief. "In fact, I feel liberated." Jayne begins to sit taller and express herself more confidently as she reveals for the first time her thoughts about giving and taking control. "In having sex with Bruce I relinquished my control but I made a conscious decision to do so—and that's good. In choosing not to prepare for the occasion with birth control, I learned that I alone must face the consequences—and that's both good and bad. In having made an unwise decision about birth control I accepted my right to control my future—and that feels very good." Jayne pauses and then reflects, "I can be feminine and powerful. I can be self-directed and submissive." Jayne smiles, nods her head affirmatively and continues without taking a breath. "I'm an independent, assertive, self-sufficient human being. I'm not ready to be a mother yet, but it's reassuring to know that I'm capable of motherhood when the time is right." Jayne begins to laugh. "I no longer doubt my ability to be sexually aroused. I am grateful I met Bruce. I feel lucky in making this private decision without the medical risks that women once endured. It's great to feel physically well and healthy! I really feel fortunate that I'm getting to know myself in such an intimate way. You know what?" Jayne exclaims. "I really like myself!!" The tears of sorrow are replaced with tears of joy as Jayne embraces her torso. With another surge of enthusiasm she exclaims, "It's hard to believe that such a negative experience can be viewed as a personal blessing."

The concept of abortion as a blessing is not a new one in my life. In June of 1972 (eight months before the Roe v. Wade Supreme Court decision legalizing abortion) the celebrated rabbit sacrificed its life to reveal that I was pregnant. My response to this report was less than gleeful. I had neither the desire to become pregnant nor the wish to mother another child. The "natural" maternal urge about which books are written had already been satisfied with the birth of three wonderful children. Each planned pregnancy had been heralded with joy; a team of wild horses could not have persuaded me to choose abortion.

But this time it was different. I had changed since the birth of our oldest, thirteen years ago. The days of PTA, scout meetings and car pools no longer symbolized the measure of my competence. The drive to resume my nursing career was not only desirable but urgent in light of our financial reverses. But, more important, I had developed a chronic systemic disease which was physically debilitating and emotionally stressful. We were advised to consider adoption if we chose to increase our family; another pregnancy was contraindicated. I was to have had my tubes tied but postponed the operation for lack of funds. And now it was too late. Somehow one tenacious sperm escaped the well intended barrier of birth control. I felt victimized: by my husband, my body, the contraceptive manufacturer, a society that glorifies and glamorizes motherhood, and by nameless, faceless government officials who control the sanctions of reproductive options.

My husband and I were frantic at the prospect of bearing an unwanted child. We considered counseling but were too embarrassed to go to our conservative religious leader, too skeptical about the cost of therapy, and expertise of a therapist in dealing with this kind of a problem. We finally learned of a free peer counseling clinic located in the basement of a Lutheran prayer center. Desperate for some assistance, we passed through the beaded curtains and sat on the floor pillows as we shared our crisis with two recovering drug abusers. They prefaced their remarks with "Hey man" (the jargon of the early 70s) and advised us to "go with the flow." The encounter was depressing. We felt ourselves party to an amoral social underground conspiracy. The "counselors" did however give us the names and telephone numbers of compassionate doctors who have been known to assist "women in distress."

The next day we visited the (in)famous Dr. Greene, renowned obstetrician of upper middle class society and celebrated gynecologist to the unintended pregnant. Dr. Greene was warm and empathetic. After the examination he assured us that my medical history would justify a legal abortion at the major private community hospital at which he was a chief of staff. The abortion was scheduled for the following week. Seven sleepless nights later we arrived at the hospital at the appointed time and date, never suspecting that the medical board would decline my request for an abortion. The Board decided that I or the child might be at risk but they were not satisfied that I might die. My request was therefore tabled until Dr. Greene could provide definitive data as to the gravity of my disease.

My husband and I were incensed. My life literally hung in the balance. I had to provide the hospital with hard, factual evidence that I would die or be sentenced to the risks of a compulsory and potentially dangerous pregnancy. For three weeks the debate ensued. Dr. Greene produced supporting evidence and the board deliberated. With each passing week the emotional tension grew more exquisite. With each passing week my options decreased. Finally, as the tenth week of the pregnancy approached we decided that I would take the 1,000 mile air journey to New York, the closest city to Miami, Florida that had enacted Freedom to Choose legislation. (New York, Alaska, Hawaii, and Washington were the only states that had passed statutes allowing abortion on request).

We searched the portfolio of abortion brochures Dr. Greene had collected from facilities throughout the United States. The literature read like travel ads with glamorous renderings of a wonderful trip to New York coupled with quality medical care at affordable prices. We finally chose a facility that was near the airport with medically qualified gynecologists. The complete package fee of $450.00 included transportation. Such a bargain could hardly be resisted. Besides, the italicized endorsements of women from all over the United States read like acceptance speeches at an Academy Award presentation.

Somehow, we managed to raise the money. And on a sunshiny Monday morning I kissed our three children goodbye without an explanation of where I was going for the day. My husband and I silently drove to the airport each consumed by our own thoughts. "What an injustice to be forced to seek medical services 1,000 miles away from those you love." "I hope I'll be safe." "I wish we could be together to support one another." "I feel guilty, angry, isolated, scared and terribly alone." "I wonder what the children would think if they knew?" "I wonder what my parents would say?" "I wonder what God is thinking?" We hugged, kissed and wept as I boarded the airplane, exiled, banished to another state.

Four hours later, I was waiting my turn to be discharged back into society as a non-pregnant citizen. I had filled out the medical forms and provided blood and urine samples to the laboratory. I was given a number and I sat in the waiting room with twelve or fourteen other women who busied themselves with magazines as they too clung to their assigned number. I wondered about the counseling but soon learned it consisted of an office worker reading with you the medical consent form for minor surgery and then asking to sign on the dotted line. I also learned that this "counseling session" meant that my number was the next to be called. The tiny surgical cubicle just accommodated the doctor, a medical assistant and the procedure table. Conversation was kept to a minimum as I was directed to remove my clothing from the waist down and scoot up on the table. I was reminded to take a few deep breaths as the doctor dilated my cervix, inserted the narrow plastic cannula, switched on the vacuum aspiration machine and swept this unplanned/unwanted pregnancy from my body. Within ten minutes the task was done. Ten weeks of anguish were resolved. I was overcome with tears of relief mixed with those unexplainable, inappropriate giggles that frequently accompany moments of high anxiety or distress. The $450.00 packaged abortion was certainly efficient but it was a far cry from what I had anticipated. I was reduced to a chart, a urine bottle, and a number on the assembly line of abortion services.

The sun had just set as I arrived at the airport to catch the return flight to Miami. In flight I was glad to be alone to collect my thoughts. I closed my eyes to the world and pondered the magnitude of the day's events. Like Jayne, I asked myself what I had learned. I learned that freedom of choice didn't necessarily mean dignified health care. I learned that even though abortion is a legal health service in New York, it was not a health care option that I chose to disclose to anyone I knew. I learned and relearned that my marriage is stable and can withstand a crisis. I relearned that my husband was my strongest and most loving ally. I learned that there is a copable solution for every life circumstance. I, too, like Jayne, was glad to be well and healthy. I was glad to be returning to my family. I realized that I had a lot of love to give to my children and husband and I didn't want to risk dividing it once again, especially in light of the potential health risks for me and for a baby. But, there were more global issues to think about. I had been tested. Why? Had I become too smug, too complacent? I felt certain that while the pregnancy appeared to be unplanned, it really was no accident. Perhaps it was a calling to come out of the closet and become an abortion activist. Perhaps I was chosen because I had the capability to transform the negative aspects of medical care into a positive model for abortion services. Did I want anyone I know and love to have to walk in my shoes? The answer, of course, was "no."

Suddenly, I was abruptly roused from my reverie. "Lynn!" the enthusiastic voice reverberated. "I thought it was you, but I wasn't sure. I haven't seen you in years." I recognized the face from my past. It was an exuberant entrepreneur for whom I had worked as a nurse. His questions continued, never pausing for an answer. I was sure that my surprise at seeing him revealed my deepest, darkest secret. I self-consciously looked around the plane sensing that all eyes were upon us. Had witchcraft emblazoned an "A" on my chest? He and everyone aboard the flight undoubtedly could see through my feigned explanation of returning from a day's visit to New York. Fortunately, he was more interested in talking about himself than sharing conversation. And, in the two hours remaining of the flight he revealed his aspirations to invest a sizable amount of money in a project in Miami. "Perhaps you or your husband know of an interesting proposal?" He gave me his calling card and invited me to submit to him a creative idea needing venture capital. As we parted I couldn't resist the temptation to consider that our meeting was not by chance. After all, how often does a person meet an acquaintance bearing gifts of money?

In a matter of days our life was reasonably back to normal. The physical healing from the abortion was fast. But the mental recovery was slower and more deliberate. Two weeks later when I visited Dr. Greene for an examination he asked if I intended to challenge the Florida statute governing abortion. If I did, he assured me, he would lend his fullest support.

With my husband's assistance, I searched my soul. Choosing abortion was not my proudest moment but it was a decision I emphatically chose. Disclosing the abortion decision could prove hurtful to our family but on the other hand it could provide a model for courage and authenticity. We decided that the ten weeks of anguish imposed upon our lives could be transformed into a meaningful mission. After all, our story spoke for thousands of other women caught in a similar plight. And so, we embarked upon a freedom of choice crusade.

Once we committed our energies to abortion reform a dynamic network emerged. As a state lobbyist I began to engender the support of legislators and health professionals. My husband reread the Florida statutes regulating abortion facilities. In redefining certain specifications he discovered a legal recourse for providing services. Dr. Greene rallied to the cause providing medical expertise and creating a sound medical protocol. The next step was to retrieve the calling card of the angel who in fact financially embraced the "creative proposal" to open the first licensed free-standing abortion facility in the State of Florida.

Within a month I had the seed money to travel to New York and visit a variety of private offices and hospital-based abortion centers. I spoke with medical and counseling personnel as well as patients. I was permitted to observe various counseling techniques and to read existing counseling guidelines. From these observations, a counseling protocol was designed. The course of events seemed to be channeled from a higher source. The medical, nursing, counseling, managerial and financial components magically gravitated to one another like a dream begging to become a reality.

The momentum was contagious. Within six months, the program was complete, including a facility site. The only step remaining was to secure the approval of the Health Planning Board. In our enthusiasm, or perhaps our naivete, we weren't prepared for the onslaught that ensued. For months each Health Planning Board meeting was fraught with conflict about superficial issues that were unrelated to quality health care. Undaunted, we continued to pursue until we were finally given a provisional license from the township.

October, 1972 marked the opening of the first TLC Center for Reproductive Health. It was a newsworthy event that sparked the support of many and the opposition of many more. Hate mail and harassment became a daily occurrence. Our children were harangued and our safety threatened. And, when actual violence was perpetrated, a security guard became our constant companion. In the name of God, the Bible, and the American flag, people sought sanctions to unleash their wrath. We were two factions whose definitions of "blessing" were the antithesis of the other. The establishment of a legal, safe, low-fee abortion service became a double-edged sword.

One day, shortly after our opening, a couple visited the Center requesting a termination of pregnancy. The woman had medical documentation confirming her seven week pregnancy. After counseling with the couple for an hour I had an uneasy feeling about our dialogue. While the man insisted that they both wanted the abortion, the woman expressed comments that indicated ambivalence. I gave them a list of their verbatim responses that I recorded as they enumerated the pros and cons of parenting. I asked that they reflect upon these responses and weigh their options for two days before finalizing their decision. They both strongly objected. I did not relent, and they grudgingly consented to wait.

Two days later they reappeared, anxious to sign the consent form and "get it over with." They adamantly refused to be subjected to another pregnancy test and pelvic exam and chastised me for imposing obstacles to their securing an abortion. It was explained that the reconfirmation of the pregnancy and the physical exam was the mandated policy of the Center and could not be omitted. Under duress they submitted to our requirement. In a matter of minutes it was discovered that the urine tested negative and the internal exam revealed a non-pregnant uterus. They insisted that our findings were incorrect and continued to demand that we perform an abortion. We were puzzled but not intimidated. Their request was rejected. Their money was refunded and they were advised to return to the Center in two weeks if menstruation did not occur. They hesitated to leave. Finally, they revealed a hidden tape recorder and disclosed their identity as two investigative reporters hired to write a story about the exploitive business of abortion. Inadvertently, we had foiled their plans. Certainly the story they transcribed was far less marketable than the story they anticipated recording. How were they now going to present the facts and fulfill the contracted assignment? Rather than displaying anger, we offered our hand in friendship and cooperated in providing insights and research data.

Some months later a five page cover story appeared in the Miami Sunday magazine section. It wasn't pretty; abortion never is. It wasn't flattering, but then the object was not to dignify abortion. It was not balanced or totally accurate but in light of the proposed assignment it was not as ugly as it could have been. It was marketable however. It appeared in more than 100 newspapers throughout the United States. The readers responded with letters of disdain from clergypeople; threats from right-wing activists; embarrassment from conservative family and friends; support from feminists; and curiosity from a wide variety of individuals.

The most poignant letters came from women who had a story to tell. Heroines in search of an opportunity to share their histories. The article, like all the events associated with "the abortion crusade," proved to have a purpose. Rather than diminish our progress, it acted as an oracle. Like a gossamer thread, it bound us with women from coast to coast in a common mission. A retired Army nurse flew to Miami to seek our support in opening a center in upstate Florida. An ex-nun asked that we assist her in fulfilling a dream to open a center in Maine. A health care advocate requested tactical advice for opening a feminist health center in California. A social worker from Arkansas, a counselor from Texas, a reverend from Minnesota, all joined our family of women as the network expanded.

And now, as I am invited to share with you my personal story, I am awed by the confluency of events that have directed my life's path. There was no way of knowing 16 years ago that one unplanned pregnancy could have foretold my mission to initiate 25 women's reproductive health centers throughout the United States. But in looking back, the pattern is clear. Each adversary and obstacle placed in my path was a challenge to be transformed into a positive life force. It is both humbling and inspiring to uncover the neat intermeshing mosaic that has brought meaning and purpose to a single life's crisis. Skeptics may intellectually argue against the concept of inevitability but there is no denying the coincidental or mystical influence that has guided my course. Why did I choose Dr. Greene from the list of pro-choice physicians? Would I have become an activist if my request for an abortion was accepted in Miami? If I had chosen another airline or a different flight schedule would we have secured the financial means to fulfill our project? There is a Yiddish word, *bershert*, which describes the order of the universe: whatever happens, happens because it is supposed to happen.

Does there seem to be a discrepancy between a commitment to Freedom of Choice and a belief in predestination? Does choice really exist? And, if I am merely a vehicle of a master plan, what options do I really have? I believe both philosophies are not only compatible but mutually enhancing. You see, while we may be unable to control our destiny, we can actively participate in the marvelous adventure by being keenly aware of its potential. The way in which we participate in the meeting of choice and chance will determine our purpose and goals. You have the option of myopically viewing life by simply being guided by the light at the end of the tunnel. You have the option of cursing the darkness and resigning yourself to a life of unfulfilled dreams. Or, you can broaden your sights by observing, questioning, and participating in the myriad of opportunities that often are cleverly disguised as disappointments. In essence, choice is a state of mind. It either locks you in a place of inertia or it provides you with options for creative new beginnings.

When Jayne first visited my office for counseling there was little that she could appreciate about her abortion. At 21 years of age Jayne cannot imagine a society without reproductive freedom. Unlike her mother and her grandmother, Jayne's life was not threatened by the illegal, unsanitary, unlicensed abortion options of the past. Jayne was raised in a generation in which abortion rights survived the threats of religious zealots, strident picketers, judiciary debates, political vendettas and even the terrorism of clinic bombing. She, like most of her contemporaries, is inured to the struggle to safeguard a woman's right to choose. She, like most of her contemporaries, views abortion as an inalienable right forever to be protected by the Constitution.

As Jayne takes leave from my office her personal, social and spiritual consciousness has been raised. Of course she's delighted that she's well and healthy, but she never seriously considered how different her options would have been 20 years ago. "Really," she says, "I thought that the back alley and hanger induced abortions were aberrations or tasteless jokes." She assures me that she will be sensitive to the political views of our law makers from now on. In reviewing the abortion experience, Jayne confidently asserts that she feels stronger and more capable of making wiser choices in her own best interest. Jayne observes that in thinking about her life's journey she is beginning to recognize that there really are no mistakes. She relates the genesis of her recovery from anorexia nervosa and declares that the abortion was probably the most poignant expression of her ability to maturely achieve a status of healthy independence. "I certainly don't recommend abortion as a form of therapy," she concludes, "but in my case, I must admit it has really been a blessing."

Sex at Menopause: Each in Her Own Way

Ellen Cole

In 1985 I had the opportunity to spend one day a week, for seven months, at the Yale University Menopause Program. Because the program is directed by a physician who is also a sex therapist, it had a special sensitivity to sexual issues. Although women came to the clinic for a variety of reasons, from routine medical care to consultation for severe distress, an effort was made to provide a comfortable atmosphere in which to discuss sexual concerns if the patient wished to do so. In this article, I present what I heard women say about their sex lives at menopause. I follow with a discussion.[1]

IN HER OWN WORDS

The following statements are excerpted from hour-long, semi-structured intake interviews with 100 women, selected at random from the patient pool. Most of the interviews were conducted by a physician at the clinic, while I (a psychologist and sex therapist) sat quietly in the room and listened. On a few occasions, I alone conducted the interview. It is important to note that these were diagnostic, and therefore problem-centered, interviews. If a woman said "My sex life is fine," that line of inquiry was not pursued. The following statements, then, address problems women encounter, rather than a broader range of responses. However, 85 of the 100

Ellen Cole, PhD, is a licensed psychologist, a certified sex educator and sex therapist, and a professor at Goddard College. She began to study menopause three years ago, when she was a visiting lecturer at Yale University.

This article is based on an earlier draft, first presented at the Advanced Feminist Therapy Institute Conference in May, 1987.

women experienced one or more sexual problems that either began, or were exacerbated, at menopause (for similar findings, see Sarrell & Whitehead, 1985).

Trying to Make Sense of the Changes. Jane, age 45, surgically menopausal, complained of vaginal dryness, loss of desire, loss of clitoral sensation, fewer orgasms, and frequency decrease. "My normal sex urges just aren't there. I don't *want* to not like it anymore. Before the hysterectomy, I was into it, I was so excited. I was ready. I made juices. Now it's harder to arrive at an orgasm. We've both stopped initiating. If I don't respond immediately to my husband, he stops. He's so sensitive. This is all new behavior. Am I withholding from him because of something he's done earlier in the day? Why have I become so petty? I never *used* to take arguments to bed. I love this man; I'd die for this man. It's so important to keep sex going in our marriage, it makes you feel young. We've gone from twice a week to Sunday mornings. I used to like it at 5 o'clock in the afternoon, or before getting up in the morning. Now that it's on a schedule, I don't like it anymore. The fun's gone: the odd times, the odd places, just for the heck of it. My sex drive is zero. A zero minus sex drive for the first time ever."

Loss of Desire. Loss of desire at menopause was described by 66 of the 100 women. Typical comments included the following: "My menopause started at age 45, accompanied by lack of sexual interest. I was just never in the mood. When I stopped having orgasms I went to the family doctor and he told me to fake it." "My sexual desire has been affected in strange ways. I'm still passionate and loving in my head, but my body won't jibe. The feeling of openness doesn't happen any more. It's horrible." "I keep thinking 'if only.' Like if only I had unlimited money in the bank, then sex could be okay. If we were off on a beach, it'd probably be okay sexually. If I could just find the G-spot, then I could get into it. But the truth is, sex doesn't do a thing for me. Right now it's important for *him* to have the experience. I've given up thinking *I* can."

A 52-year-old woman who had a hysterectomy in 1982 says, "My sex drive has left completely. In the final analysis I am now a completely neutered woman. My clitoris has shriveled up and I simply cannot become aroused. It's gone." A 50-year-old woman who hasn't had her period for six months complained of unrelenting hot flashes, night and day. She had this to say about sex: "The vaginal dryness doesn't bother me a bit. I just use Transi-lube, and it's fine. It's the change in desire that really surprises me, because I was always sexually active and interested. It's sad in a way. It worries me. I hope it doesn't diminish totally. We used to make love every other night. Now that same intensity isn't there." And one 47-year-old peri-menopausal (i.e., still ovulating) woman described irregular periods, and hot flashes which were occurring five to ten minutes apart, night and day, for six weeks, and then disappearing for a few weeks before the cycle resumed. She says, "My face feels like a neon sign, and sometimes it is. I feel hot, intense, feverish, clammy. I can't bear the feeling. Afterwards, I'm very cold. The flashes interfere with sleep, and of course with sex. My vagina's been dry for the last six months to a year. There's pain now, with intercourse. I just seem to be so sensitive. My desire's decreased, although a few months ago for four or five weeks I went through a stage of wanting sex all the time. Nothing would satisfy me. It was kind of nice. A high sex drive makes me feel young and alive. But, overall, I feel like I'm losing it sexually. I thought *I'd* never have a problem with menopause. I thought that was a myth. I always thought that menopausal symptoms occurred because of all the other things that were happening, like the empty nest, or a stressful marriage, or problems at work. Boy, was I wrong."

Increased Arousal Time. Here are some typical responses. "Lubrication takes longer to come about, and orgasm longer to get to. Sex is no longer what it should be, and I'm scared." "It sure takes me a long time to get hot." "I have a difficult time getting started." "What turned him on was a lot of secretions, and now I'm afraid he's losing interest in me." One 54-year-old woman says, "Sex response takes a very long time now. It takes me 15 minutes just to build to an intensity that used to take, it seemed, seconds." And another woman, who poignantly speaks for many: "What I feel mostly is confusion. Here I was looking forward to these years, thinking I wouldn't have to worry about birth control, and sex would be more and more pleasurable. Instead I feel like half a woman. I don't respond physically the way I used to respond. It takes forever. The shock of the change is hard for me to accept. It would have been an inconceivable thing five years ago."

Vaginal Imagery. I tried to listen carefully for metaphorical language. Some images that women used to describe their vaginas are: "like the Sahara desert"; "white parchment"; "sand paper"; "fragments of cut glass."

Masturbation. It has become clear that orgasm, whether through partner-sex or self-stimulation, is good for vaginal health. Therefore, masturbation can play a key role in the life of an older woman without a partner, or a coupled woman who enjoys pleasuring herself. The following responses surprised me. "I still do it, but it goes nowhere." "It used to feel good. Now it just tickles." A 73-year-old woman reports that "It hurts when I masturbate." And a 50-year-old single woman, a banking executive, reports, "I notice that I masturbate less than before, from just about daily to maybe twice a week. Sometimes it's not worth the effort."

Touch. I have heard touch described by psychologist Jessie Potter as "the velvet satisfaction of life." Some women at menopause describe it differently. "What happens sexually is still very enjoyable. I can still achieve an orgasm, although it's now a *hill*, not a mountain. My main concern has to do with not having response to touch, not the same reaction I'm used to. Clitorally, there's very *little* reaction. Sex made me alive, happier, it enabled my physical and mental well-being to reach a higher plane. I miss the reaction, the intensity." "My clitoris is de-sensitized." "I don't respond to any kind of touch. Breasts, nipples, vagina. . . . The response is now *gone* with genital touch. When this happened, I was devastated. I think I still am. I could understand it if I were widowed; there'd be no opportunities. And here I am in the same situation." "I draw back from touch now, the roughness of it. It's a fear reaction. I'm afraid of being hurt." "It hurts to be touched. The skin hurts."

Pain. Women described three kinds of pain: painful insertion of the penis with intercourse (related to vaginal dryness); a burning sensation after ejaculation (also related to vaginal dryness – with no or little lubrication to neutralize the alkaline ejaculate); and pain from a vaginal infection (related to the increased susceptibility of women at menopause to vaginitis and cystitis). An active horsewoman complained of vaginal dryness and hot flashes, and was diagnosed as having vaginismus. She says, "I'd like to be more comfortable, and I resent the fact that I am not. The hot flashes, mostly at night, come and go. They're particularly present when I'm under stress. I can't ride when I'm in this state of low energy and fatigue, and I certainly don't have energy for sex. Sex is a very uncomfortable idea. Intercourse is painful; I don't enjoy the whole process, so I attempt to protect myself by avoidance. I don't think I'll ever be able to get used to the mechanics of artificial lubrication. I'm not used to planning this three days in advance. My husband is patient and kind, but I think he's getting bored. Planned obsolescence, that's me."

A peri-menopausal woman says, "I can't use tampons anymore. I'm very sensitive about my body. Even if I'm ready, penetration is painful, and I don't like it. There's discomfort after intercourse. It's just kind of sore. Sometimes there's very serious burning." A cynical 55-year-old woman reports, "My bottom always seems to have an infection or an itch these days. You hear about Herpes and AIDS, and I probably have *them*, too. I *have* no sex life, so maybe I got them at work. I'm a walking bacteria down there. I grow a whole crop. I'd like to take my vagina out and hang it on the clothes line. Between *my* rotten, painful vagina, and *his* heart problems and high blood pressure, we've had no sex life at all for years."

Orgasm. Forty-one of the 100 women reported a change in orgasmic response since menopause. Many of them still orgasm, but with greater difficulty and less regularity. Here are some typical descriptions. "I *had* been orgasmic easily. There's still an orgasm, but it's different now. It takes longer. It's not so intense, not so deeply feeling. It takes a longer time, and lots of stimulation." "Orgasm never *used* to be a problem. After the hysterectomy I stopped having orgasms with intercourse, so I learned to have an orgasm with a vibrator. Now I'm less responsive even with a vibrator." A 55-year-old attorney says, "It's not easy to see your chin get double and your waist get thick and see yourself as not sexually attractive. Things do happen to you that aren't nice. Sexually, you don't feel the same way, there's no question about it. It takes longer to have an orgasm. Whether you want to put a lot of energy into it is the thing. You're tired; it takes longer. But it's not easy to relinquish your sexual self." "I have orgasms only in sleep now." "In the past, just a *little* clitoral touch would produce an orgasm. Now, nothing. Incomplete. Sometimes I prefer not to be touched at all, not to be reminded of my inadequacy."

Frequency. Fifty-one of the 100 women reported a frequency decrease at menopause, and 36 reported periods of abstinence lasting as long as four or five years (2), six or seven years (2), 8 years (1), and 18 years (from a woman whose last menstrual flow was 16 years ago). Some women didn't mind the change, some minded terribly. The following comments come from women with current partners, and no past history of sexual problems. "My husband's had three by-passes; he suffers from hypertension. Sex just doesn't bother me. I wouldn't care if I never had it." "We don't do it much anymore, and I can't say I miss it. Maybe I need STP." A woman who had a hysterectomy one year ago says, "We've had no intercourse in seven months. The happy side of me has been cut off. Even masturbation goes nowhere. I'm just no longer sexual." "There's been no sex in five months. It's not what it should be. *I* wouldn't want to make love to me." "We haven't had intercourse for two months. I'm scared of the bleeding afterwards."

"We used to have intercourse every other day; now it's twice this summer. It's painful. I haven't had an orgasm for two years." "Frequency? From too little to almost none. From once or twice a week to five times a year. I'm so sensitive now to the touch of *any*thing." "Sex used to be anywhere from two or three times a day to two or three times a week. Now it's once a week. It's more *friendly*, not frenzied. I don't like it. I'm less interested now, and it's less interesting." "Our sex has dwindled to once or twice a week since menopause. There's no thrill out of it anymore." "Our sex is reduced now. In the last week and a half we made love once. It was pleasant, but not arousing. And there's the issue of his response. He's under pressure, and he's not always able to have an erection."

Other Issues. Although the above-mentioned issues are those most frequently referred to, and most talked about at length and with depth of feeling, some women spoke, too, of incontinence during sex, sexual problems their male partners had, the effects on sex of sleep disturbance ("I wake up sweating or chilly every hour. Whaddya suppose *that* does to my sex life?"), and interpersonal issues. One articulate woman seemed to speak for herself and others when she said, "Middle-life is like middle-management. You meet everybody's needs and keep on going. There are so many problems with the teenage children, I'm pulled in a million different directions. I don't have time to think about sex."

DISCUSSION

The women quoted here have described sex essentially as an effort. It feels neither as intense nor as intensely satisfying as before menopause. Frequently there is associated physical pain, sometimes even in response to simple touch. Many of the women express their sadness, and worry that their condition will continue to deteriorate. Perhaps, above all, there is a sense of confusion, of utter surprise ("It would have been inconceivable five years ago").

For several reasons, these women cannot be said to be representative of the general population. Each made the decision to visit a menopause clinic; we do not know about the women who stayed at home. Some may have chosen the Yale Menopause Program in particular because its director is a well-known sex therapist, resulting perhaps in an over-representation of sexual problems. As a group, the women were almost entirely white and middle-class, and none identified herself as a lesbian. And yet, despite these limitations, I think the women have some very important things to tell us about the kinds of sexual problems that exist at menopause, what it feels like to experience them, and even about different categories of sexual experience.

I have come to realize that it is crucial not to presume that all menopausal women are the same. Based on the interviews described above, a review of the medical and feminist literature, and informal discussions with friends and colleagues, I have concluded that there are three kinds of women, or three categories of sex at menopause, and that I as a sex therapist must be sensitive to each.

In the first category are women without sexual problems. Several of the 100 Yale women, for instance, report increased sex response, and increased satisfaction. Others notice no changes at all in their sex lives. After a talk I recently gave about menopause, a women who had been in the audience handed me the following note: "During the first 30 years of married sexual life I could arrive at orgasm through stimulation around or above the clitoris, but I could not tolerate direct clitoral touch. Since menopause I can enjoy direct clitoral stimulation, and have found, for the first time ever, that I am multi-orgasmic – a benefit of post-menopausal sex."

In the second category are women who report serious physiological difficulties. It is my opinion that these women require and deserve treatment to relieve their distress, whether that treatment consists of hormone replacement therapy, an "alternative" method such as diet, exercise, vitamins, or biofeedback (see Cobb, 1985; Greenwood, 1988; Morgan, 1986; Taylor, 1986; Trien, 1986; Voda, 1984 for non-medical remedies), or some combination of the two. It is our responsibility as mental health practitioners to know the common sexual complaints, and to let women who experience them know that they are not alone, and that help is available.

In the third category are women who experience mild distress and who are upset by the changes in their sex lives. It is this group that I think is of most interest to the non-medically trained sex therapist or feminist therapist, for it is here that I believe we have the potential to be especially useful.

A 52-year-old friend of mine has said, "Sex is less frequent now and we both prefer it that way. There are great memories, but it's just right for us the way it is now." This is a woman who has gracefully accepted the changes that aging has brought, without fear or resistance. I suspect that at least some of the women in the Yale sample who were in despair about their sex lives might have been holding an image – perhaps a male image, or a youthful image – of how sex is supposed to be.

As feminist therapists we can be particularly useful to these women by providing permission to have a different, more mature kind of sex life than they had at an earlier age, a sex life that is neither better nor worse, but simply different. We can, and should, give women permission to immediately stop any sexual activity that is painful or uncomfortable, and to aim toward a sexual relationship, for those so involved, that is neither demanding nor goal-oriented. Specifically, for women who have focused on intercourse and orgasm for their sexual pleasure, we might discuss the possibilities of an expanded vision of sexuality and sensuality, a vision that might include new kinds of touch, fantasy, play, discovery. We can provide information about the advantages and disadvantages of hormone replacement therapy (see Greenwood, 1988) and non-medical remedies (see references above). We can urge women to discover what works for them, what feels good. We can, and should, convey the message that there is no one "right way" to be sexual. We can offer specific suggestions for improving communication with one's partner about feelings, in general, about sexual pleasure, in particular. When a client's distress is grounded in a sexual dysfunction, whether hers or her partners, we can recommend sex therapy.[2]

When our menopausal clients are experiencing difficulties with their sexual self-esteem, we can point to some of the vigorous and sensual women at mid-life and beyond who are at long-last visible in our culture, women like Robin Morgan, Patricia Schroeder, Tina Turner, Adrienne Rich, Gloria Steinem, Barbara MacDonald. . . . We can encourage women to join menopause support and information groups, and we can start such groups ourselves. With our clients we can think through possibilities for rituals, rites of passage, ways to honor and celebrate the end of one phase of our lives and the beginning of another.

Sex researcher Alfred Kinsey stated 35 years ago that "there is nothing more characteristic of sexual response than the fact that it is not the same in any two individuals." As feminist therapists we need to listen carefully to what our clients at menopause are telling us about their sexual concerns. It is crucial to presume neither that they will sail through menopause nor that they will experience severe distress. Women can take heart from Mary Calderone, an 83-year-old physician. In a recent talk about early childhood sexuality (Calderone, 1986), she reminded her audience that "You are sexual in your own way at 3 and at 23." I know she would want me to add "and at 53, and 83."

NOTES

1. I am grateful to Philip M. Sarrel, MD, the program's creator and director, for the opportunity he so generously provided to do this research. I am also grateful to the women at menopause who allowed me to share a most private piece of their lives.

2. This paragraph follows the outline of Jack Annon's (1976) ever-useful PLISSIT model.

REFERENCES

Annon, J.S. (1976). *Behavioral treatment of sexual problems: Brief therapy*. New York: Harper & Row.

Calderone, M. (1986, October). *Sexuality of the fetus*. Paper presented at the First International Congress on Sexuality Across the Lifespan, Montreal.

Cobb, J. (1985). Alternative remedies. *A Friend Indeed, 2*(6), 1-6.

Greenwood, S. (1988). *Menopause naturally* (rev. ed.). San Francisco: Volcano Press.

Morgan, S. (1986). *Coping with a hysterectomy* (rev. ed.). New York: New American Library.

Sarrel, L.J. & Sarrel, R.M. (1984). Menopause. In *Sexual turning points: The seven stages of adult sexuality* (pp. 249-267). New York: Macmillan.

Sarrell, P.M. & Whitehead, M.I. (1985). Sex and menopause: Defining the issues. *Maturitas*, 7, 217-224.

Taylor, K. (1986). The whole picture: Our health reflects our lives. In M. Adelman (Ed.), *Long time passing: Lives of older lesbians* (pp. 219-235). Boston: Alyson Publications.

Trien, S.F. (1986). *Change of life: The menopause handbook*. New York: Fawcett Columbine.

Voda, A.M. (1984). *Menopause me and you*. Salt Lake City: University of Utah College of Nursing.

Teaching Safe Sex to Women in the Age of AIDS

Deborah Kutzko

AIDS, the Acquired ImmunoDeficiency Syndrome, was first brought to national attention in the spring of 1981. Since then, the covers of many national magazines have shown graphic representations of the horrors of this new disease. Political and public sentiment ranges from a rational concern for people with this disease and those who may contract it in the future, to irrational plans for quarantine of all infected people and increased social pressure to inhibit sexuality. Ads for condoms now speak to disease prevention as frequently as the prevention of pregnancy. Although in the beginning concern about AIDS focused on gay men and Intravenous Drug (IV) users, AIDS is quickly becoming a women's concern.

As the name implies, AIDS is an acquired deficiency or decrease in the immune system, which is that part of the body that fights off diseases. An AIDS syndrome is not one disease, but consists of a syndrome of one or more usually harmless infections, so-called opportunistic infections. These infections are usually harmless in persons with intact immune systems but become serious given the weakened condition of the immune system in people with AIDS.

Studies have concluded that a virus which has been called variously HTLV-III (Human T cell Lymphotrophic Virus Number 3), or LAV (Lymphadenopathy Virus), and now HIV (Human Immunodeficiency Virus) is the cause.

While a majority (66%) of people with AIDS have been men who were exposed to the disease through sexual contact with a man with

---

Deborah Kutzko, FNP, is the AIDS Education Coordinator for the Vermont Department of Health. She is a family nurse practitioner with 10 years of clinical experience in family planning and sexually transmitted diseases.

HIV infection, this was not the only means of transmission. Seventeen percent of the cases were men and women who were exposed through the sharing of IV drug needles and supplies with someone with HIV infection. Other cases included a combination of both homosexual exposure and IV drug exposure among men (8%), men and women who had heterosexual exposure (4%), exposure through transfusions of blood and blood products (including hemophiliacs) (3%), while 3% were lost to follow-up (CDC, May, 1987).

Currently, about 7% of people with AIDS are women. Women with AIDS have been reported in all 50 states, the District of Columbia, and four territories (CDC, May 1987). While the majority of women with AIDS came into contact with HIV through the sharing of IV drugs or needles (50%), sexual contact with a man at risk for HIV infection was the second most common risk group. The proportion of women with AIDS in this group increased from 12% in 1982 to 26% in 1986 (Guinan et al., April, 1987).

Although AIDS is the most talked about and the most serious manifestation of HIV infection, the spectrum is broad. Of the people who show evidence of exposure to HIV, somewhere between 13% and 34% of those studied progressed to AIDS within 6 years of follow-up (Francis, March 13, 1987). Some victims have continued to remain asymptomatic and others will progress to ARC (AIDS Related Complex). People with ARC have symptoms of HIV infection in various degrees (fatigue, lymphadenopathy, night sweats, etc.) without the opportunistic infections that meet the AIDS case definition.

In order to cause illness, viruses must transfer from one host body to another and multiply. HIV has been isolated from various body fluids, blood, semen, tears, saliva, and vaginal secretion. Epidemiologic studies suggest, however, that HIV can only be transmitted through semen, blood, and vaginal secretions. HIV is a retrovirus and, as with all retroviruses, can only multiple in certain human blood cells (lymphocytes and macrophages) and cells of the central nervous system (Francis, March 1987).

With this knowledge in mind, we can address how HIV is transmitted and how to prevent this transmission. Research has taught us that HIV is not spread through casual contact (Friedland et al., Feb., 1986; Sande, Feb., 1986). This virus cannot be spread by sharing drinking glasses, ice cream cones, eating utensils or any other nonsexual activity of daily living. Rather, the three routes of transmission are: (1) sexual – male to male, male to female, female to male, and, although there have not been many documented cases, female to female; (2) blood borne – sharing of IV drug needles, blood transfusions, needle stick and blood spills in health care settings; and (3) perinatal – from infected pregnant women to fetus during the birth process or during breast feeding.

SEXUAL TRANSMISSION

Many people are infected with HIV and, hence, presumed to be infectious, but who show no outward signs of illness. Therefore, women must assess what risks they are willing to take if they contemplate sex with a new partner. It is our job as health care professionals and therapists to help women learn how to make these choices without repressing their sexuality. The answer may at first glance appear to be to insist that all sexual activity take place in the bounds of monogamous relationships. Although this might be the answer for some, it is not realistic to believe that it is suitable for all.

The choices women must now make include how many sexual partners they will have, who these partners will be, and what they will and will not do during sexual activity. The notion of women taking responsibility for these choices is reminiscent of statements regarding contraception, demanding that women take the responsibility for sexual safety. Many women may be angered by once again being asked to consider the sexual health of the couple. Also, some women may have trouble convincing a male partner to use condoms. We must help women deal with these real feelings and help them learn the skills of negotiating sexual acts with prospective partners.

Lesbians and heterosexual women may each face different problems. While studies of women married to men with HIV infection suggest that a woman who has had multiple sexual exposures to HIV infected semen is at high risk for HIV infection (Redfield, March 1985; Schultz, April 1986), there has been little documentation of woman to woman transmission of HIV. Marmor et al. report a case of apparent woman to woman sexual transmission, although "both women had vaginal bleeding as a result of traumatic sexual activities" (Marmor letters, Dec. 1986). Nevertheless, heterosexual women and lesbians need to be aware of how HIV is transmitted.

Since the virus must pass from infected blood, semen, or vaginal secretions of one person to the blood of another, women are at risk whenever there is any tear in the cervix—even small areas of erosion or a tear in the vaginal mucosa—if she has intercourse with a man who has HIV infected semen because the virus will be able to pass from his semen to her blood through the wound. Similarly, if a man with HIV infection has anal intercourse with a woman, the act of intercourse may create small tears in the rectal mucosa and allow the virus to pass through. Conversely, if a man has intercourse with an HIV-infected woman, the virus can pass from her vaginal secretions to his blood through any small openings there might be in his urethra.

Individual women will make individual choices about the amount of risk they are willing to take. To be absolutely safe, a heterosexual woman can be celibate or have sex only with someone with whom she has been in a long term (greater than 10-year) relationship in which both partners have been monogamous and neither partner uses IV drugs or has received a transfusion of blood or blood products. Lesbians who are sexually active only with other women who are not sexually active with men and are not IV drug users nor recipients of transfusions of blood or blood products are also at no risk of contracting this virus. The publicity surrounding this disease has convinced many women that sex is harmful. It is important that we reassure women in no risk or low risk situations.

Lesbians who use IV drugs, who are partners of IV drugs users, or who have a partner known to have HIV infection, and heterosexual women who do not choose celibacy or monogamy, are at greater risk and need to follow safe sex guidelines.

If a woman is having coitus with a man, condoms used consistently and correctly have been shown to reduce the risk of HIV infection during coitus. Women may not have experience with condoms and should be aware of instructions on how to put a condom on, how to take it off, and the use of lubricants with condoms.

Spermicides containing nonoxynol 9 appear to be lethal to HIV in laboratory studies (Conant, April 1986; Peterman, October 1986). These spermicides are available over the counter at most pharmacies. Many women prefer sexual expression that does not include coitus; these women are at less risk for contracting this virus as well as other sexually transmissible diseases. Mutual masturbation, massage, hugging, and kissing all appear not to exchange infected secretions and so appear safe. Oral sex is thought to be risky by some (Mayer et al., 1986). Certainly, cuts or abrasions in the mouth are quite common, often caused by brushing or flossing teeth, thereby producing a portal of entry for infected semen or vaginal secretions into the blood through those openings. Many people are now incorporating the use of condoms when practicing oral sex with a man, and dental dams (a small thin spare of latex used to cover the vulva) when practicing oral sex with a woman. If sex toys are used they should not be shared and should be cleaned after use. Blood to blood contact has been demonstrated to be an effective means of transmission of HIV and so S&M practices that produce bleeding are not considered to be safe.

Dealing with concerns about AIDS is not much different than other concerns, in that fear can be overcome by knowledge. Women who have the facts can assess their own risks and make decisions regarding their sexual lives. When women understand how HIV is transmitted, they will understand that it is not sexual acts per se that cause illness. It is only when those acts allow the exchange of HIV infected semen, vaginal secretions, and blood that they cause an at-risk situation. This information will allow women to take an active rule and make the decisions that will help them protect themselves from HIV infection and AIDS. It is important that when we talk to women about responsible sexuality we allow them to continue to be sexual and not repress their sexuality.

REFERENCES

CDC (1986). Update: Acquired immunodeficiency syndrome. *United States MMWR, 35* (49).

CDC (1987). *AIDS weekly surveillance report*, May 11, 1987.

Conant, M. et al. (1986). Letters – Condoms prevent transmission of AIDS associated retrovirus. *JAMA, 256*, (13), 1703.

Francis, D. et al. (1987). The prevention of acquired immunodeficiency syndrome in the United States: An objective strategy for medicine, public health, business, and the community. *JAMA, 257* (10).

Friedland, G.H. et al. (1986, February). Lack of transmission of HTLV-III/LAV infection to household contacts of patients with AIDS or AIDS-related complex with oral candidiasis. *New England Journal of medicine*, 344-349.

Marmor, M. et al. (1986). Letters—Possible female to female transmission of human immunodeficiency virus. *Annals of Internal Medicine, 105* (6), 969.

Mayer, K. et al. (1986). Association of human T lymphotropic virus type III antibodies with sexual and other behaviors in a cohort of homosexual men from Boston with and without generalized lymphadenopathy. *The American Journal of Medicine, 80*, 357-363.

Peterman, T. A. et al. (1986). Sexual transmission of human immunodeficiency virus. *JAMA, 256*, (16).

Redfield, R. et al. (1985). Frequent transmission of HTLV-III among spouses of patients with AIDS related complex and AIDS. *JAMA, 253* (11), 1571-1573.

Sande, M. (1986). Editorials—Transmission of AIDS, the case against casual contagion. *The New England Journal of Medicine*, 380-382.

Schultz, S. et al. (1986). Letters—Female to male transmission of HTLV-III. *JAMA, 255* (13), 1703.

When the Diagnosis Is Vaginismus: Fighting Misconceptions

Jo Marie Kessler

> I think about sex all the time, not because I have a high sex drive but because it hurts when I have intercourse. As soon as my husband comes home from work, I worry because I'm afraid he'll ask me to make love and I won't want to because of the pain. It isn't that I don't love him. I do. I feel guilty because I am constantly looking for excuses not to have sex with him but I can't help it because it hurts so much. He tries to understand but it's been over a year now and his patience has worn thin. Sometimes he thinks I'm just making it up. I've been to several doctors. When they examine me that say they can't see anything wrong and they tell me to relax. I think they think it's all in my head. Maybe it is, but it still hurts.

This description is representative of the way many heterosexual women with painful intercourse and vaginismus think, day after day. Guilt, shame, fear, and distrust are common emotions for these women. Eventually, those feelings give way to frustration, anger, resentment, and hostility as well as feelings of helplessness, hopelessness, and powerlessness. The women's sexual partners go through the same range of feelings. A vicious cycle is established which often causes the demise of many of these relationships. Sex becomes an arena for conflict instead of a means for experiencing emotional and physical pleasure.

Vaginismus has been defined by a number of experts, in more or less similar ways. Masters and Johnson define it as

---

Jo Marie Kessler, Nurse Practitioner, was an associate at the Crenshaw Clinic in San Diego, CA for seven years and is currently on sabbatical.

> a psychophysiological syndrome affecting woman's freedom of sexual response by severely, if not totally, impeding sexual function. Anatomically, it involves all components of the pelvic musculature investing the perineum and outer third of the vagina. Physiologically, these muscle groups contract spastically as opposed to their rhythmic contractual response in orgasmic experience. This spasm is an involuntary reflex stimulated by imagined, anticipated or real attempts at vaginal penetration. (Masters & Johnson, 1970, p. 113)

Helen Singer Kaplan succinctly points out that in addition to having involuntary muscle spasm of the vaginal orifice, patients with vaginismus are usually phobic of any vaginal penetration which only adds to the frustration and discomfort (Kaplan, 1974, p. 412). There is a high correlation between vaginismus and sexual aversion and dealing with both conditions is necessary for long term success (Crenshaw, 1983, p. 132).

DEFINITIONS

Vaginismus – a condition in females characterized by spastic, reflex contractions of the musculature investing the outer third of the vagina, which produces varying degrees of discomfort ranging from mildly irritating to excruciatingly painful for the woman. Vaginismus can be caused by organic or psychogenic factors. It can prevent intercourse or at best, make it uncomfortable.

Primary vaginismus – a condition which can be congenital or which develops before a female becomes sexually active. The condition is evident from the first sexual intercourse attempt and often produces unconsummated marriages.

Secondary vaginismus – a condition acquired as a result of psychological or organic factors occurring after a woman has become sexually active. Pain-free sexual intercourse was an established pattern prior to the development of this condition.

Dyspareunia – pain experienced during intercourse or as a result of intercourse.

(These are definitions used at the Crenshaw Clinic, San Diego, California.)

Dyspareunia is a more general term and can occur in women without the presence of vaginismus. Dyspareunia may be caused by certain positions for intercourse, vaginal infection, scar tissue or other pelvic pathologies. In dyspareunia there may not be the consistent reflex spastic contraction of the pelvic musculature, characteristic of vaginismus. If immediate attention is given to correcting the cause of dyspareunia then secondary vaginismus can be avoided. However, if intercourse occurs repeatedly under conditions that produce discomfort, in a short time, vaginismus may result. Once vaginismus has developed treatment is required to relieve the problem.

Vaginismus indicates dyspareunia will be present to some degree. The reflex contraction of the vaginal musculature is nature's way of trying to protect the woman. The ultimate body defense is to make the contraction of the muscles so tight and the constriction of the vagina so intense that intromission is impossible.

When a woman has vaginismus, she is dealing with a commonly underdiagnosed problem. The reflex contraction of the vaginal musculature often does not readily give an examiner clear evidence of its presence. If a woman "bears" the discomfort of bimanual and speculum exam during a pelvic and does not volunteer the discomfort she feels, the health care practitioner has no way of knowing it exists, especially in those cases where there is no other pelvic pathology (like a vaginal infection or endometriosis) that would suggest discomfort is present. If the examiner neglects to specifically ask if intercourse, pelvic exams, or tampons are ever uncomfortable and sees no "cause" to suggest discomfort, the conclusion that "everything is okay" seems accurate.

Many women will dismiss the significance of minor discomfort associated with vaginal intromission or containment, not realizing this is the body's way of signalling for help. The woman does not want to appear weak or be labeled as a complainer and besides, "It's not THAT bad," she reasons. This woman obviously doesn't know that vaginal intromission or containment should not be uncomfortable under normal conditions. In other cases, when the pain with intercourse is severe, the woman may minimize it when describing it to the health care practitioner because she's afraid of rejection, ridicule, or judgment. She might be embarrassed, thinking it's too personal to verbalize the specifics of her sex life. She finds it easier to discount the discomfort, hoping it will get better on its own, or she denies the problem altogether.

The woman who is hesitant to describe her condition often hopes the practitioner will "find something" on her/his own that explains the pain. Finding out what is wrong without having to give specific details can be the most appealing approach to that woman. However, when nothing is found and she hears "everything is okay" she is disappointed. For the woman who has tried to explain, hearing "everything is okay" is not only disappointing, it is confusing and frightening. The woman knows she feels pain, but there's no explanation for it or at least an explanation that is readily evident to the practitioner. The woman may begin to doubt herself.

If the woman tries to carefully describe the sensations but the practitioner is unfamiliar with the range of intensity in which vaginismus can present, and particularly if the woman has already born a child or is postmenopausal, then she may sound hypochondriacal or malingering. Some practitioners classify vaginismus as a psychogenic disorder only. With this understanding, a practitioner is less likely to take the woman's complaints seriously, especially if she has the same complaint repeatedly or has been to several other practitioners to no avail. The problem is interpreted to be in her head, rather than her vagina. The woman feels misunderstood or patronized. She feels helpless. How will she explain this to her partner in a way that is understood when she herself does not understand what is happening? How will she make herself understood during sex after the practitioner tells her partner "nothing" is wrong?

In the case of an unconsummated marriage, vaginismus is often suspected and diagnosed because most practitioners have learned to correlate the two. A woman with this intensity of vaginismus usually cannot have a pelvic exam because the muscle constriction is too tight. Pelvic examination under anesthesia might be done in these cases. This does not cure the vaginismus, but it allows for examination of the internal pelvic organs.

Vaginismus that is of lesser intensity, i.e., the type seen in the woman who is sporadically able to participate in intercourse with minimal discomfort, is frequently undiagnosed or dismissed as an attitude problem in the woman. There are no observable tissue changes in the vagina that alert the examiner that something is abnormal. Therefore, when the examiner says, "I don't *see* anything wrong," he or she is technically correct. Frequently, the only sign externally that vaginismus is present is the constriction of the perineum, caused by the reflex contraction of the underlying musculature. If the examiner isn't familiar with vaginismus, that constricting action near the vaginal opening could be interpreted as a manifestation of the woman's self-consciousness at having a genital exam and not a sign of a physical problem that warrants diagnosis and treatment.

During the diagnostic process, after the historical data has been reviewed and if the woman has not volunteered any information about pain or discomfort associated with sex, the following questions must be asked:

1. Is there any discomfort associated with intercourse on entry or deep thrusting?
2. Are pelvic examinations ever uncomfortable?
3. Is there discomfort associated with wearing tampons?
4. Do you have problems with vaginal lubrication?
5. Is there burning or stinging associated with intercourse?

If any of these questions are answered by a yes, vaginismus can be suspected until proven otherwise.

Standard treatment for vaginismus is a combination of short term psychotherapy and vaginal dilations (DeMoor, 1972; Ellison, 1972; Fordney, 1978; Leiblum, 1980; Masters & Johnson, 1970). Masters and Johnson note that the initial and most important step in the treatment of vaginismus is physically demonstrating the existence of involuntary vaginal spasm to both partners (Masters & Johnson, 1970, p. 256).

Vaginal dilations are accomplished by slowly and *painlessly* inserting well lubricated dilators of gradually increasing size into the vagina. This author prefers using Young's plastic vaginal dilators and a water soluble lubricant. The procedure is done diagnostically by the examiner first to determine the presence and intensity of vaginismus. After that the woman is taught to do the dilations. The dilations are done in the exam room under supervision until the woman demonstrates proper technique and confidence in her ability to do the dilations at home. This could take from 4-8 visits. The goal is for the woman to be able to painlessly accommodate a dilator that is equivalent to the girth of the object she and her partner use for vaginal insertion during sex.

Additionally, the treatment must include education, relaxation techniques, systematic desensitization, behavior modification techniques, building of self-esteem and teaching self-responsible behavior. Teaching thought replacement and thought stopping are fundamental aspects of psychological treatment since the woman will have to deal with her anxieties about the recurrence of pain.

Women have been too willing to be "good" patients, often to their own detriment. They have taken pride in being good wives or sexual partners. Socialization processes molded them to be conforming, to please those in positions of authority, to please men. This attitude in combination with the belief that sex will be unpleasant or uncomfortable interferes with some women's ability to act promptly in their own best interest. Women with low self-concepts are very vulnerable to delaying treatment for this dysfunction. For these women, communicating the problem to their partners is only the first step toward resolution. Describing the problem to the health care provider, another authority figure, is the next hurdle.

Part of the psychological focus in the treatment of vaginismus is the process of dispelling misconceptions. For example, the belief that sex is supposed to hurt predisposes a woman to tolerate pain or discomfort during intercourse. If a woman has learned that pain associated with intercourse is what she can expect, then when there is physical discomfort, the woman is unlikely to seek help—at least not at first. If this is normal, she thinks, then there probably isn't anything that can be done about it. So she must grin and bear it. And she does, or she tries to, but a common way to deal with the problem is to avoid sexual contact, which causes conflict with her mate. An essential fact for any woman to know is that intercourse or other vaginal intromission is NOT supposed to hurt and if it does, it is important to discover the cause and have it treated. This is particularly true for the woman with primary vaginismus who has discomfort from the first attempt at intromission and has no other frame of reference.

Other beliefs about women contribute to the confusion experienced by the sexual partner. It is often assumed that women do not like sex and will use any excuse to avoid the activity. Thus, especially if the partner has been told by the practitioner that "nothing" is wrong, when the woman with vaginismus begins avoiding sex (to avoid the pain) the partner interprets her behavior as a manifestation of her dislike of sex, a personal rejection, or both.

Another misconception is the one that says women like to be coaxed to have sex. The male begins asking for sex frequently, often more frequently than even his own appetite dictates. He feels compelled to ask repeatedly because it might take numerous invitations before he can wear down his partner's resistance and get her to agree to have sex with him. He asks excessively and feels angry about having to do so. He feels justified because he observes that once he convinces her to participate, she often is orgasmic and might enjoy the activity. This perpetuates the confusion and the problem.

Whipple and Komisaruk (1984, p. 364) report that vaginal stimulation can increase the threshold to detect and tolerate pain so it is highly feasible that on some occasions for some women the involvement in sexual stimulation diminishes the usual uncomfortable vaginal sensations. It is no wonder that the woman and her partner are confused when the body is inconsistent in its response pattern.

If the woman does not see herself as worthwhile and deserving, she will be reluctant to implement behavior that interrupts or prevents her discomfort during sex. She will not be assertive enough, early enough, to stop intercourse or other vaginal penetration when discomfort occurs. She will be too "other oriented" and put her partner's sexual needs before her own health. If she does not value herself, she will have difficulty acting in her own best interest consistently. Instead she will endure the discomfort, hoping that it will soon be over. She will only take care of herself if it does not inconvenience her partner. With this attitude, vaginismus will persist or recur.

The woman who has experienced vaginismus and the accompanying discomfort must learn how to neutralize the negative spectatoring associated with intercourse. (Spectatoring refers to anxiously observing one's self or one's partner.) The woman who has felt pain will be on the lookout for it as the moment of penetration approaches. Reflexively her body will become guarded and tense. To overcome this action during sex, instruct the woman to take charge of inserting the penis into the vagina during intercourse. By being in control of penile insertion, she can be assured of a process that will not proceed faster than she can handle and if the process needs to be stopped at a second's notice, it can be done. By assuming control of intromission, the spectatoring will be reduced. It is necessary to have the woman's partner be supportive, cooperative, and reassuring so the spectatoring will diminish.

Enlisting the woman's partner in the therapy process is essential (Masters & Johnson, 1970). Encourage him to attend all the office visits. It will enhance the desensitization process; he will learn and provide emotional support for his partner. As the dilations progress and the woman is developing confidence and comfort, instruct her in teaching her partner to insert the dilators at home. This promotes intimacy and trust. When intercourse is reintegrated into the couple's sexual activity, tell them the purpose and benefits of the woman doing the inserting of the penis. For the woman, it reduces the fear of intromission and containment. The male can keep focusing on the erotic thoughts and sensations and not have his concentration interrupted trying to avoid hurting the woman. Assure the man that it is not a problem if his penis is not 100% erect during the times when the couple is experimenting with and exploring containment anew. A slightly softer penis may even be an advantage because it might be less threatening and feel more comfortable to the woman during the first few insertions. On the other hand if the penis is fully erect, that is all right because the woman can be reassured that she has the ability to accommodate an object of that girth because of her experience with the dilators. The couple can be assured that the penis is more malleable (even fully erect) than the plastic dilators and therefore more easily inserted.

An antagonistic partner can rapidly impede, or totally sabotage, therapy. For example, if the man does not understand the rationale for the ban on intercourse during the dilation phase, he may coax, threaten, or manipulate his partner into disregarding the therapist's recommendations. He could also react in a manner that would make it more difficult for the woman to stop intercourse in the event it became uncomfortable.

> Carmen and Gil's marriage was in jeopardy. Carmen had painful intercourse following surgery for a malignancy that had been removed from the posterior aspect of the vaginal orifice and consequently, she avoided intercourse. After thorough evaluation by her gynecologist who confirmed there was no other organic basis for the discomfort except scar tissue, Carmen was assessed for the presence of vaginismus and the diagnosis was confirmed. Carmen made weekly appointments even though she was advised to schedule visits closer together. The marital discord was reaching crisis proportions and her partner was threatening to leave. Being sexually functional was imperative to Carmen although her actions contradicted her words. Supervised serial dilations began in the office; Gil attended most of the sessions, but seemed to be annoyed and impatient. At the fourth session Carmen could barely accommodate the #5 dilator. However, she revealed that during sex the night before she had had intercourse with Gil even though it had been uncomfortable. Gil laughingly said they had been drinking and he "couldn't stop" when he got aroused. He made it clear other sexual behaviors were not of much interest to him—he preferred intercourse. Carmen indicated she was reluctant to say no especially because he "insisted."

The emotions a man experiences when his partner has vaginismus are multiple and conflicting. On the one hand, he feels guilty; he has been causing her physical distress and has not known how to alleviate it. On the other hand, he feels deprived, rejected, and cheated. He wonders if she knew this before they got married or moved in together and just didn't tell him. He is vulnerable to the widely held belief that women don't like sex and will find any excuse to avoid it. Even though he doesn't think this applies to his partner, how does he know for sure? The practitioner even said she couldn't find anything wrong! A guilt/resentment cycle develops for the male and he is at risk for developing sexual aversion or erectile problems. Extramarital affairs may become appealing.

Helping the male develop acceptance and tolerance is a goal of therapy. The reward will be a woman who more easily overcomes the vaginismus. The man will be asked to cope with interrupted sexual experiences, spurned sexual overtures, a hesitantly passionate woman, tears, frustrations and many unknowns until the problem is completely solved. Explain to the male that when his partner stops the sexual encounter because she is uncomfortable, he is not to interpret the message as "I'm doing something wrong." The message is simply "Ouch!", a cue that change is necessary before continuing. Often, just a few seconds break in the activity or position adjustment or slight downward pressure on the penis is all that is necessary. It is important to learn how to be flexible and participate in other mutually acceptable sexual behaviors to achieve satisfaction during the time intercourse is off limits. With an expanded sexual repertoire, boredom can be avoided regardless of the longevity of the relationship.

What is the psychotherapist's responsibility? First, believe what you hear. Take the woman's complaints and descriptions seriously. If you are unable to do the actual physical assessment yourself, refer her to a competent colleague who understands vaginismus and will be sympathetic and helpful. Emphasize the need for psychotherapy in addition to the physical treatment. During the psychotherapy sessions, ask about the progress of the dilations. Find out about her concerns. Address any and all questions. Get input from both the woman and her partner. As with other sexual dysfunctions, this problem affects both people.

To act in her own best interest, the woman must describe her symptoms and sensations and volunteer the information instead of waiting for the practitioner to ask the right questions. In health care, it is necessary to be an informed consumer. It is necessary to be assertive. It may be necessary to do comparative shopping, i.e., find a practitioner who is familiar with the problem and cooperates with her in finding a solution instead of leaving her with feelings of inadequacy and confusion. This does not mean that women who have a positive self-image and who can be assertive are immune to the problems associated with vaginismus. Even when the assertive woman articulates clearly what she is experiencing, an examiner uninformed about the scope of vaginismus may leave the self-assured female feeling defeated. Fortunately, the assertive female is not easily thwarted and will risk dealing with another examiner and another until she ultimately finds someone who can help her.

Working with the woman with vaginismus requires understanding and patience as well as a willingness to be supportive and resourceful. Giving detailed explanations and reassurance repeatedly will facilitate the treatment process and compliance. Help the woman take actions that are beneficial to her both long-term and short-term, taking into account the effects her actions have on those for whom she cares. With a combination of short-term psychotherapy and painless vaginal dilation the condition can be successfully treated.

REFERENCES

American Psychiatric Association (1980). *Diagnostic and statistical manual of mental disorders, third edition*. Washington, DC.

Barbach, L.G. (1984). *For each other*. New York: New American Library.

Crenshaw. T. (1983). *Bedside manners*. New York: McGraw Hill.

Crenshaw, T. & Kessler, J.M. (1985). Vaginismus. *Medical Aspects of Human Sexuality, 27* (32), 21-22.

Crenshaw, T. (1985). The sexual aversion syndrome. *Journal of Sex and Marital Therapy, 4*, 285-292.

De Moor, W. (1972). Vaginismus: Etiology and treatment. *American Journal of Psychotherapy*, April, 207-214.

Ellison, C. (1972). Vaginismus. *Medical Aspects of Human Sexuality*, August, 34-54.

Fertel, N. (1977). Vaginismus: A review. *Journal of Sex and Marital Therapy, 3*, 113-121.

Fordney, D. (1978). Dyspareunia and vaginismus. *Clinical Obstetrics and Gynecology, 21*, 205-221.

Kaplan, H.S. (1987). *Sexual aversion, sexual phobias, and panic disorders*. New York: Brunner/Mazel.

Kaplan, H.S. (1983). *The evaluation of sexual disorders*. New York: Brunner/Mazel.

Kaplan, H.S. (1974). *The new sex therapy*. New York: Brunner/Mazel.

Kessler, J.M. (1987, May). Sexual aversion and vaginismus. Paper presented 20th annual conference of American Association of Sex Educators, Counselors, and Therapists, New York, NY.

Ladas, A., Whipple, B. & Perry, J. (1982). *The G spot*. New York: Dell.

Leiblum, S. et al. (1980). Treatment of vaginismus: Success and failure. In Leiblum, S. and Pervin, L., eds., *Principles and practices of sex therapy*. New York: Guilford Press.

Masters, W. & Johnson, V. (1970). *Human sexual inadequacy*. Boston: Little, Brown.

Whipple, B. & Komisaruk, B. (1985). Elevation of pain threshold by vaginal stimulation in women. *Pain, 21*, 357-367.

SECTION IV: CLINICAL IMPLICATIONS FOR PARTICULAR POPULATIONS

Issues in Sex Therapy with Ethnic and Racial Minority Women

Carole Pigler Christensen

Helping professionals have long recognized that the well-being of the individual and satisfaction in relationships are closely related to sexuality. Similarly, helpers of all disciplines are cognizant of the importance of rapport between therapist and client, and of the conditions that facilitate effective relationships. The near simultaneous occurrence of the legitimization of sex therapy as a distinct form of treatment, and the culmination of the feminist movement during the 1970s, resulted in attention being focused on women's sexual functioning. Moreover, helping professionals and medical

---

Carole Pigler Christensen, MSW, DEd, is Associate Professor at McGill University, School of Social Work, in Montreal, Canada, where she has initiated and developed courses in human sexuality and in cross-cultural counseling over the last decade. She has extensive clinical, supervisory, and consultation experience in these areas, and regularly conducts training workshops for helping professionals at home and abroad. Her research interests include the evaluation of therapists' knowledge base for practice with minority women.

researchers began to consider women's sexual concerns from a female perspective. Sex therapists and, increasingly, social workers, psychologists, counselors, and psychiatrists began to provide sexuality counseling to individual women, women's groups, and women in heterosexual and lesbian relationships.

Despite the growth in awareness regarding women's sexuality, the particular concerns of ethnic and racial minority women have continued to be largely ignored. Apparently, few minority women seek the specific services of sex therapists, but many are involved in various forms of counseling relating to sexuality. This article examines some of the issues relating to minority women and sexuality counseling and sex therapy, and suggests a framework for further investigation of areas in critical need of attention.

The arguments set forth are based on the following assumptions:

1. All people have a right to enjoy satisfying and responsible sexual expression in accordance with their needs;
2. At present, some groups are more likely than others to have their right to satisfying and responsible sexual expression sanctioned, promoted, and validated;
3. As products of a society in which racism, ethnic stereotypes, and cultural myths abound, therapists' preconceptions about various ethnic and racial groups often interface with the helping process; and,
4. Barriers to effective sex therapy with ethnic and racial minorities can, and must, be overcome.

An underlying premise of this paper is that most racial and ethnic minority groups are among the sexually oppressed populations in North American societies. Sexually oppressed populations are generally defined as those whose sexual needs are ignored, distorted, or suppressed (Gochros, 1972). For the present purposes, minority groups are defined as being singled out for different and unequal treatment by those representing the dominant groups(s), based on assumed genetic, cultural, or behavioral characteristics. In the North American context (i.e., the United States and Canada), racial minorities tend to be identified first by skin color, or as "non-White." Ethnic minorities are generally defined by the degree to which they are perceived to differ from the Anglo-European norm in terms of social customs, mores, and life-style. Since the vast majority of those working in the area of sex counseling and therapy are White, and have developed theories based on working with White middle-class populations (Wyatt, Strayer, & Lobitz, 1978), this paper addresses issues likely to arise when the helper represents the dominant group, but the client is from a different background.

HISTORICAL FACTORS

In order to fully comprehend the complexities of current issues relating to minority women and sexuality counseling and sex therapy, the historical roots of these issues, and their development over time, must be understood.

North American societies are products of a colonial past, where the dominant group consists of people of European origin (in particular Great Britain, France, and Northern Europe) described as having "conquered," "colonized," or "settled" lands originally inhabited by people of a different race (i.e., the Aboriginal peoples of North America). The dominant group hold the bulk of the power, privilege, and prestige in society, and determines the position other groups will occupy (Kallen, 1982). European settlers soon brought African slaves to North America to work under conditions that changed their traditional folkways, including those affecting sexual behaviors, roles, and mores (Rodgers-Rose, 1980). It was never intended that the slaves, or their descendants, should be other than a separate and unequal source of labor. Settlers from Eastern and Southern Europe, as well as non-European groups, were later added to the population, resulting in the pluralistic mix that comprises North American societies today (Christensen, 1986).

Each new group was, naturally, viewed from an ethnocentric standpoint point by the dominant group. Behavior relating to sexuality, like all other forms of behavior, was evaluated and ranked in terms of Anglo-Saxon values and standards. The greater the differences perceived between the dominant group and the minority population, the lower the evaluation and ranking (Hughes & Kallen, 1974).

The earliest European immigrants had family life-styles and religious beliefs governing sexual behavior, whether Catholic, Protestant, or Jewish, which closely resembled those of the American colonists (e.g., patriarchal families, taboos about behaviors such as masturbation, and the expectation of chastity for unmarried women). More importantly, in societies that considered race a more determining factor than either class or religion, people of European ancestry, whatever their values and beliefs, were eventually absorbed into the mainstream culture. Although stereotypes developed around sexual attributes of some European groups (e.g., Latin Lovers), none were as insidious and harmful as those which came to be associated with identifiable racial groups (e.g., Black male studs). Beginning with the phenomenon of slavery, racism and sexual oppression have been inexorably linked together in North America in a manner still evident today.

Social Darwinist beliefs supporting the physical, mental, and temperamental superiority of the White race had spread throughout Europe, and were eventually transported to the colonies in the form of antimiscegenation laws (Davis, 1978). These laws, which forbade racial mixing on the grounds that it would lower the biological quality of the White race, affected all interactions between White and non-White races, both sexual and non-sexual. Consequently, women who happened to be members of racial minorities have since been subjected to oppression based on both gender and race.

ETHNOSEXUAL AND RACIAL OPPRESSION

The control of the sexual freedom of ethnic minority peoples has been referred to as ethnosexual oppression, manifested by a set of beliefs about ethnic minorities to justify individual and institutional sexual discrimination against them (Mokuau, 1986). Rationalization for acts of socioeconomic, political, and sexual oppression directed toward some ethnic groups is provided by beliefs, myths, and stereotypes. In addition, "ethnic" categorizations create arbitrary classifications (often of culturally dissimilar groups), based on visible racial features, including skin color (e.g., Blacks), and other identifiable characteristics such as mother tongue (e.g., Hispanics), and assumed geographic origin (e.g., Asians). Although North Americans differentiate between White ethnic groups based on national origin, they tend to use race and ethnicity interchangeably when referring to non-White groups. Class differences are often ignored, creating a false picture of homogeneity that helping professionals also fall prey to.

Minority Women and Sexual Oppression

Although beliefs, myths, and stereotypes about ethnic and racial groups have adversely affected the sexual expression of men and women, some of the most deleterious effects have been directed toward minority women. Furthermore, women representing the dominant cultural group are as prone as men to beliefs and behaviors contributing to the oppression of minority women. A brief consideration of some major historical factors still affecting the sexual expression and satisfaction of Black, Hispanic, and Asian women follow. Although helpers may be familiar with some of the occurrences below, the effects of the resulting oppression on the self-concept and sexuality of women belonging to these groups remains undocumented (Mokuau, 1986); similarly, there is still much to be learned about the effects of ethnicity and race on the therapeutic process (Christensen, 1984).

Black women. No other woman has suffered physical and mental abuse, degradation, and exploitation on North American shores comparable to that experienced by the Black female. During slavery, legal in Canada and in the United States for more than 150 years, masters exercised near total control over the sexuality of their slaves. The racist ideology on which this treatment was based included many contradictory beliefs, apparent to this day. Like Black males, females were said to be hypersexual, sensuous, and immoral, as opposed to the "virtuous" White woman. This stereotype was used to suggest her desire for White males, and their right to abuse her sexually, for pleasure and to augment the slave population. Black women were denied the right to enjoy their role as mothers, since their children, whether from a union with a Black or a White male, were also slaves, sold for the slave owner's profit whenever he desired. Black women formed stable unions with Black men and, when allowed, were legally married (Rodgers-Rose, 1980). Although laws soon forbade intermarriage between

Black men and White women, Black men were unable to protect their wives, sisters, and daughters from sexual exploitation by White males. Paradoxically, the only women to ever suffer socially sanctioned and induced sexual abuse were branded "loose and immoral."

The legacy of slavery is ever present in the United States, where Black women are more often unemployed and underpaid than any other group (Rodgers-Rose, 1980). Economic and social pressures, fueled by racism, have resulted in growing numbers of female-headed households and teenage pregnancies. Decision-makers associating welfare mothers with single Black women continue to devise punitive policies based on the belief in their immorality, lack of intelligent child-care, and laziness. In Canada, Black women who clean the homes and care for the children of White women are often labeled neglectful housekeepers and mothers by social workers (Christensen, 1986). At the same time, there is the contradictory myth of the Black matriarch, a tower of strength holding the Black family together, despite limits to the advancement of Black males by the wider society. The consequences to women of the depletion of available Black males as many succumb to drugs, are imprisoned, or were killed on the front lines in combat are seldom recognized.

White women, as well as men, have defined Black women's roles and abilities in terms of inferiority to her White counterpart. Damaging stereotypes are perpetuated in the media and the social science literature. When the perfect woman was supposedly disinterested in sex, Black women were said to be sexually liberated; when White women gained sexual liberation, studies began to suggest that Black women are "frigid," restrained partners (Wyatt, Strayer, and Lobitz, 1976). Black women recognize the distortions and contradictions outlined above and struggle to establish positive sexual identities and relationships, despite pressure to fit them arbitrarily into a mold. Too often, sexuality counseling is but one of many encounters of this kind, leading Black female to seldom seek such services voluntarily. Rather, the extended family and close friends are relied upon for advice and emotional support in matters concerning sexuality.

Hispanic women. The history of Hispanic peoples in North

America predates more recent influxes of migrants, immigrants, and refugees from Mexico, the Caribbean, and Latin America. Long before the Mexican-American war of 1846, the descendants of Spanish colonists, Aboriginal Indians, and African slaves had made their presence known (Valdez & Gallegos, 1982). In areas now parts of Texas, California, and the southwestern states, Mexicans have continued to cross borders into the United States; Puerto Ricans have come since the 1920s; and Cuban Americans have been present since the 1960s (Mokuau, 1986). More recently, Spanish speaking refugees from South America have come north seeking a higher standard of living and freedom from political unrest. Although there are cultural differences between Hispanic groups based on their history and traditions, common threads exist, resulting from the shared experience of Spanish colonial rule. From the very beginning, there were tensions about racial, religious, language, and cultural differences. Hispanic groups faced poverty through exclusion, based mainly on racist beliefs assuming their inferiority and lack of initiative to better their lot (Mokuau, 1986). Racism has also resulted in differential encounters with discrimination for these racially mixed groups, since family members vary in color. Fair-skinned women may dye their hair and apply cosmetics, hoping to emulate white beauty standards.

Most of the literature on sex roles refers to the machismo-marinismo stereotype of the virile and powerful male, complemented by a submissive, morally superior female. Such oversimplications are used by many, including helping professionals, to explain "deviance" in Hispanic families, viewed as too patriarchal, too large and, therefore, too poor. Not unlike Black women, many Hispanic women have been punitively sterilized, without their consent (Valdez & Gallegos, 1982). Therapists often view family structures in which the duties of motherhood are above the role of wife as pathological. There have been waves of migration of Hispanic peoples, of various cultural backgrounds, and under varied circumstances. The therapist must strive to understand the meaning of family roles for a particular woman. Degrees of acculturation differ, and affect attitudes about a woman's proper role. Catholicism has also shaped values and attitudes regarding sexuality (e.g., chastity, abortion, and motherhood), marriage, and divorce. The post-

Civil Rights era has brought an upsurge in ethnic identity on the part of Hispanic peoples, now the fastest growing community in the United States (Valdez & Gallegos, 1982). Demands for more equal treatment, from women as well as men, are increasingly being directed toward the helping professions.

Asian women. Asian immigrants have been coming to North American since the mid-1800s, when Chinese and Japanese laborers were recruited to work in the mines and on railway construction (Li and Bolaria, 1983). Unlike patterns for Europeans, Asian immigration can best be understood by examining restrictive immigration policies, such as head taxes and enactments of exclusion. The attitudes of governments in Canada and the United States closely followed the generally negative popular opinion concerning Asian populations, especially on the west coast. Sexual oppression played a major role from the very beginning. The first generation of Asians were mostly young men, recruited as cheap labor. Considered an unassimilable race, laws against intermarriage were passed. White society feared "lascivious Oriental men" who might ravish "pure" White women (Mokuau, 1986). At the same time, however, White men frequented Chinese and Japanese prostitutes found on the west coast since the days of the gold rush (Daniels & Kitano, 1970). Chinese "married bachelors," forbidden by law from sending for wives, could only hope to earn enough to visit wives and children left in their homelands. When restrictions were finally lifted, many Chinese women joined old husbands whom they hardly knew (Ishisaka & Takagi, 1982). Widespread hostility led early Asian immigrants to develop their own service associations, many of which still serve communities known to underuse mainstream agencies (Christensen, 1986). There are now several generations of Chinese and Japanese North Americans, having various degrees of acculturation. Since the lifting of racially restrictive legislation in the 1960s, newer immigrants of Filipino and East Indian origin have settled in Canada and the United States. Recent refugees of Southeast Asian descent are struggling to adjust to a new and racist culture. Unmarried women may find themselves ostracized by White males, or sought after as curiously exotic. Many are torn between the values and beauty standards of their group and those of the dominant culture.

Most Asian women share a strong emphasis on family roles as daughters, sisters, wives, and daughters-in-law. Loyalties cross several generations, and are to the extended, rather than nuclear, family. There is usually a clear double standard, with males more highly valued than females (Shon & Ja, 1982). Sex is not openly discussed, and a women's role as mother is more highly valued than her role as wife or sexual partner. Traditionally, the oldest son cares for his elderly mother in his home, particularly if she is widowed, allowing her considerable power over the household. Helping professionals often hold contradictory views of Asian women, viewed as both a "model minority," whose strong families make outside help unnecessary, and as difficult to understand, since many appear content in a subordinate role. Research suggests that the expectation that their culture will not be understood, often compounded by language difficulties, leads many Asian women to avoid encounters with helpers from the dominant culture (Christensen, 1986).

Summary. Sexual oppression is deeply rooted in past and present forms of racism. Should sexual oppression disappear, racial oppression, which overrides sexism, would remain (Leggon, 1980). Lack of power prevents the concerns of minority women from receiving equal and effective representation. As the mothers, wives, sisters, and daughters of White decision-makers, dominant group womens' needs receive public attention and response (e.g., witness the recent upsurge in interest in funding day-care, now that over 50% of White women work). White men may behave in a manner harmful to minority women and their families, in order to protect the perceived interests of White women (e.g., denying Black children equal access to education, and job opportunities to their parents).

HELPING PROFESSIONALS AS THE SEXUAL ELITE

It is widely recognized that professional helpers are overwhelmingly drawn from the White middle-class (Atkinson, Morten, & Sue, 1983). Some authors have noted that, like most people in positions of influence and control (e.g., law-makers, professors, elected officials, physicians), the majority are also male, middle-aged, and well-educated (Gochros, Gochros, & Fischer, 1986). Most belong to the "sexual elite" population, whose sexual behaviors are sanctioned by significant social institutions such as the church, the law, and the helping professions, because their attributes and sexual behaviors approximate those necessary to create a socially approved pregnancy (Gochros & Gochros, 1977). Helping professionals are generally socialized in environments which lead them to adopt the values, standards, belief systems, and behaviors of the dominant culture, and of the more privileged in our society. Unfortunately, the training of most professional helpers does not provide opportunities to become aware of the effects of their class and ethnic backgrounds, stereotypes, and racist beliefs, on their ability to help minority clients with sexual concerns (Christensen, 1983). Nonetheless, as representatives of the sexual elite, professional helpers are among the agents of social control that determine which sexual behaviors will be sanctioned, and how. Many shape the very policies that have a determining effect on the sexual well-being of minority women and their children. It has been suggested that in an age when the influence of religion and the law has decreased, the helping professions have become the new arbiters of sex, and now exert more control over sexuality than any other social institution (Gochros, Gochros, & Fischer, 1986, p. 7).

Many professional helpers work in institutions such as social welfare agencies, hospitals, and community mental health clinics, where sexual behaviors are regulated, directly and indirectly, and where the majority of the clients or patients are women from less privileged, or sexually oppressed groups, "who cannot produce socially approved additions to their number as determined by those with more social influence than they" (Gochros, Gochros, & Fischer, 1986). Socioeconomic and political oppression is closely related to sexual oppression, and disproportionate numbers of ethnic and racial minority women with children are poor. Most earn less than equally qualified White women and men of both races, limiting their opportunities to acquire the material wealth necessary to increase their standard of living (Smith, Burlew, Mosley, & Whitney, 1978). Many single mothers receive welfare payments only because they have given up hope of rising above the poverty level through gainful employment at wages that would not allow them to afford day-care services. Moreover, most non-White women apparently feel that the feminist movement has neglected their concerns, at best, and has been openly hostile, at worst, toward sharing their new-found economic and political strength with the sisters from minority backgrounds (Hemmons, 1980).

Sex therapists and others, of both genders, who assist minority women with sexual concerns must not underestimate the importance of the factors discussed above. Despite the obstacles to establishing trusting relationships between therapists representing the dominant culture and minority clients, recognition of critical issues relating to assessment and intervention, which are outlined below, should help professionals to avoid some major pitfalls. A detailed consideration of issues peculiar to specific groups is beyond the scope of this paper, but helpers working with particular groups have an ethical obligation to learn as much as possible about issues affecting their sexuality.

SEX COUNSELING AND THERAPY WITH MINORITY WOMEN

Assessment Issues

Although important differences in ethnic and racial backgrounds must never be overlooked, certain issues are generally common to minority women seeking help with sexual concerns. These issues involve: the underuse of sexuality counseling and sex therapy services by minority women; the therapists' lack of sensitivity to the cultural backgrounds, world views, and systemically induced problems of minority women; the therapists' inability to recognize and assess factors relating to racism, intertwined with sexual problems.

Surely, the most important factor affecting the diagnosis and assessment of minority women with sexual problems is that they are likely to go unattended. For a variety of reasons, rooted in the cultures of the women themselves, as well as in the culture of the helping professions, women from certain ethnic and racial backgrounds seldom present themselves to sex therapists asking for help. More often than not, the sexual problems of minority women are discovered when they seek help with concerns around contraception or birth, gynecological or other medical problems, or for reasons apparently unrelated to sexuality. Nonetheless (Mokuau,

1986; Wyatt, Strayer, & Lobitz, 1978), there is reason to believe that minority women suffer the entire range of sexual problems and dysfunctions experienced by women from the dominant group.

Factors Relating to Ethnic and Racial Minority Cultures

Among the most common reasons for the underuse of sex therapists by minority women are the following:

1. The seeking of help from strangers, rather than from relatives or close friends, is an anathema to many cultures represented by ethnic and racial minority women.
2. If help is sought, it is usually in times of crisis, and when the presenting problem is of a practical or concrete nature (e.g., relating to physical health, finances, housing, translation, immigration status), rather than due to a relationship or mental health problem.
3. Discussion of most matters relating to sexuality, and particularly to sexual intercourse, are taboo in any event, and would be considered too intimate, embarrassing, or shameful to talk about with anyone but a long-trusted confidant.
4. Many minority women come from cultural and social class backgrounds where they lacked information about the kinds of services offered by social services agencies and marriage and family counselors; and they know even less about what to expect from sex therapists.
5. Some minority women may make it difficult, even for the sensitive therapist, to accurately diagnose the problem—either because of negative feelings about self-disclosure, or because of having internalized the views of the dominant culture regarding their minority group and its problems.
6. Most non-White minority women will have encountered racism and prejudice from the dominant group that the helper and/or the agency represent. For this reason, it is most unlikely that an open, trusting relationship, including the sharing of honest feelings, will be forthcoming in an initial assessment interview.
7. To the surprise and disbelief of many White helpers, minority

persons who have lived for generations in a hostile environment seem to have developed a "sixth sense," which often helps them to recognize and survive efforts to put them into harmful situations. Those perceiving "therapeutic" situations as potentially harmful do not return after an initial, or assessment, interview.

Factors Relating to the Culture of the Helping Professions

The assessment procedures used by professional helpers are shrouded in mystery, full of jargon, filled with intrusive and often irrelevant questions, and imply an attitude of judgment, as perceived by many minority women. Moreover, in the course of their middle-class upbringing, most professional helpers have incorporated belief systems rife with misconceptions and myths about the sexuality of minority women, which tend to be reinforced by professional education, and the socialization processes of mainstream institutions (Christensen, 1983, p. 59). Furthermore, many minority women have had negative encounters with helping professionals and social service agencies, and view them with suspicion, hostility, or the expectation that their perception of the problem will not be understood. The following may result when the therapist's culture interferes with assessment:

1. The root causes of the minority women's problem may be misunderstood and misdiagnosed, due to the helper's lack of knowledge or biased perceptions. Based on the author's clinical experience, it is suggested that an additional category called *systemically induced dysfunction* must be considered when dealing with certain problems experienced by minority (and other) single mothers on welfare. For example, anxiety leading to low sexual desire and secondary anorgasmia may be induced when a stable relationship with a male threatens to result in loss of welfare payments.
2. The culturally encapsulated helper may be certain that s/he knows and understands the motives, feelings, and attitudes of some client groups, without realizing that what is actually at

play are learned expectations and myths about the client's racial or ethnic group.

3. Stereotypes about the sexuality of some minority women may lead helpers to ignore, deemphasize, or exaggerate aspects of their sexuality. Consequently, those who are victims may be perceived as having invited the problem, or as not having been traumatized by certain experiences (e.g., rape).
4. Oblivious to the racist overtones of their assessment, helpers working with poverty-stricken clients (a disproportionate number of whom are representatives of non-White groups), may find themselves more interested in controlling aspects of their clients' sexuality or fertility than in helping them to make personally satisfying choices (e.g., whether to abort a fetus, keep the baby, or give it up for adoption).
5. Helping professionals may be unaware of the extent to which minority women are bicultural, and assume that their cultural attitudes are defined by their race or ethnic origin. In fact, although the helper may be unfamiliar with the client's values, it is most unlikely that a woman who has lived and worked in North America would not be aware of prevailing norms, and have acculturated to some degree.
6. Assessment formats may not leave room for an evaluation of the role of spiritual or folk healers, herbal cures, or practices that allow for transcending one's problems, all of which may play a role in the lives of minority women. Similarly, informal networks may offer an unrecognized source of support.
7. The combination of lack of knowledge, bias, and the expectation that minority women *should* be like White women in sex role behaviors, values, life-styles, and perceptions of the desirable often lead to the diagnosis of pathology and deviance where none exists.
8. A number of studies indicate that, when helpers are uncomfortable dealing with minority clients, they tend to offer them only "one shot" crisis intervention, or "bandaid" therapy, rather than a thorough assessment leading to an offer of treatment for a longer term. Since discussions of sexuality and racism are likely to arouse anxiety, especially in combination,

helpers tend to deny aspects of one or both problems when presented by a non-White woman.

Interventive Issues

Although knowledge and understanding of the minority woman's life experience and world view are important, they are insufficient unless accompanied by the ability to implement appropriate interventions (Christensen, 1985). Perhaps the greatest dilemma facing therapists helping minority women with sexual problems is whether to treat them "just like everyone else," and fit them into neat categories applicable to women from the dominant group. This is especially tempting, because there is, as yet, no approach to sexuality counseling that fully incorporates the sexuality of minority women. A review of the literature on major sex therapy approaches indicates that both the clinical and research evidence upon which they are based stem from samples and case studies of White, middle-class women. From the time of Freud (1938), through the research of Kinsey (1953), and, finally, Masters and Johnson (1970), there have been innumerable studies of women who represent the sexual elite, but few of ethnic and racial minority women, except as they deviate from the White female "norm." The fact that there are so few well-documented and unbiased studies of minority and poor women is, in itself, a form of oppression – exclusion by omission. A brief consideration of the theories underlying major approaches to sex therapy suggests the following shortcoming, when applied to minority women. It should be noted, however, that all commonly used approaches and the policies of the institutions in which they are practiced share cultural attributes such as use of time (50 minute hour at proscribed time), space (office and desk or couch), orientation (intrapsychic), and role expectations (nonegalitarian) which may alienate some ethnic and racial groups.

Psychodynamic approaches. Interventions based on psychodynamic theories are limited by a monocultural and gender bias (Leiblum & Pervin, 1982). Those relying on the use of symbols, such as represented in penis envy or dreams and their classic psychoanalytic interpretations, will be locked into a cognitive framework that was appropriate for Western European women of a particular era, ethnic background, and social class. Moreover, reliance on verbal skills and abstract concepts creates difficulties for minority women whose first language is not English, and those for whom manipulation of abstractions is perhaps not an acquired, or desired skill. When transference and countertransference are examined, there is no model for the systematic examination of racial factors. Furthermore, therapists basing their analysis and treatment of minorities on psychodynamic perspectives alone tend to highlight the dysfunctional, or deficit, aspects of individuals and their families, since neither the role of systemically induced stress, nor the strengths of minorities who survive them, are considered. More importantly, no interventive procedures are suggested for changing policies or institutions that affect the sexuality of some minority women adversely. These shortcomings often lead to misguided treatment emphases and poor outcomes in sexuality counseling and sex therapy.

Behavioral approaches. Behavioral approaches are emphasized in the work of Masters and Johnson (1970), and many who have adopted a modified direct treatment approach. Although aspects of the treatment procedures are derived from other therapeutic models (e.g., cognitive), anxiety reduction and learning or reeducation techniques, common to behavior therapy, are paramount. This emphasis means that the approach could be used to help minority women to investigate the causes of anxiety in sexual relationships, and to design a program of information and education to alleviate distress. However, the role played by the imposition of, or identification with, stereotyped expectations and sexual exploitation, rooted in racial and ethnic myths, are seldom explored. Therapists using this model usually search for the etiology of anxiety and faulty learning in the individual, couple relationships, or early learning experiences in the family; in fact, deleterious effects of racially motivated stereotypes, originating from the wider society, will seldom have escaped minority women. Fear of racial slurs, sexual harassment, suggestions of unattractiveness (by White beauty standards), ostracism or over-attentiveness in mixed gender situations, lack of suitable partners of the same ethnic or racial background, and many other factors relating to the realities of minority status are seldom considered in treatment planning for sexually oppressed women. In addition, given the common acceptance of racist myths concerning the sexual desires and behaviors of minority women, and the fact that unconscious feelings of the client (e.g., anger, sadness, powerlessness) and the therapist (e.g., envy, curiosity, seductiveness) are not explored is no guarantee that they may not be exacerbated as the therapist directs, proscribes, and prescribes sexual activity for the minority woman or couple.

CONCLUSION

Research evidence is lacking to allow definite conclusions about the effectiveness of sex therapy, and fewer still are the studies documenting success rates with ethnic and racial minorities. This fact, coupled with the inconclusive evidence about the effects of ethnic and racial variables on the counseling process, underscores the critical need for research examining issues relating to minority women, sexuality counseling, and sex therapy. If the sexual oppression of minority women is to end, professional helpers, who are part of the sexual elite, must actively seek opportunities to intervene, not only in the personal lives of minority women, but on an institutional level, to dispel harmful stereotypes, myths, agency policies, and societal conditions that continue to oppress them.

REFERENCES

Atkinson, D. R., Morten, G. & Sue, D. W. (1983). *Counseling American minorities: A cross cultural perspective* (2nd Ed.). Dubuque, Iowa: Wm. C. Brown Company.

Christensen, C.P. (1983). The influence of culture in undergraduate sexuality education: A course experience. *Intervention, 65-66*, 58-63.

Christensen, C. P. (1984). Effects of cross-cultural training on counselor response. *Counselor Education and Supervision, 23*, 311-320.

Christensen, C. P. (1985). A perceptual approach to cross-cultural counselling. *Canadian Counsellor, 19*, 63-81.

Christensen, C. P. (1986). Chinese resident's perceptions and expectations of mainstream social services; Keys to service underuse? *Intervention, 74*, 6-15.

Daniels, F., & Kitano, H. L. (1970). *American racism: Exploration of the nature of prejudice*. Englewood Cliffs, New Jersey: Prentice Hall.

Davis, J. F. (1978). *Minority-dominant relations*. Chicago: AHM Publishing Corporation.

Freud, S. (1938). Three contributions to the theory of sex. A.A. Brill (Ed.), *The basic writings of Sigmund Freud*. New York: Modern Library.

Gochros, H. L. (Ed.) (1972). *Human sexuality and social work*. New York: Association Press.

Gochros, H. L., & Gochros, J. S., (Eds.) (1977). *The sexually oppressed*. New York: Association Press.

Gochros, H. L., Gochros, J. S., & Fischer, J. (1986). *Helping the sexually oppressed*. Englewood Cliffs, New Jersey: Prentice-Hall, Inc.

Hemmons, W. M. (1980). The women's liberation movement: Understanding Black women's attitudes. In L. Rodgers-Rose, (Ed.), *The Black woman* (pp. 274-284). Beverly Hills, California: Sage Publications.

Hughes, D. & Kallen, E. (1974). *The anatomy of racism, Canadian dimensions*. Montreal: Harvest House.

Ishisaki, H. A., & Takagi, C. Y. (1982). Social work with Asian- and Pacific-Americans. In J. E. Green (Ed.), *Cultural awareness in the human services* (pp. 122-123). Englewood Cliffs, New Jersey: Prentice-Hall.

Kallen, E. (1982). *Ethnicity and human rights in Canada*. Toronto: Gage, Ltd.

Kinsey, A. C., et al. (1948). *Sexual behavior in the human female*. Philadelphia: Saunders.

Leggon, C. B. (1980). Black female professionals: Dilemmas and contradictions of status. In L. Rodgers-Rose, (Ed.), *The Black woman* (pp. 189-202). Beverly Hills, California: Sage Publications.

Leiblum, S. R., & Pervin, L. A. (1982). Introduction: The development of sex therapy from a sociocultural perspective. In S. R. Leiblum & L. A. Pervin (Eds.), *Principles and practice of sex therapy* (pp. 1-24). New York: The Guilford Press.

Li, P. S. & Bolaria, B. S. (1983). *Racial minorities in multicultural Canada*. Toronto: Garamond Press.

Makuau, N. Chapter 11, Ethnic minorities (1986). In H. L. Gochros, J. S. Gochros, & J. Fischer (Eds.), *Helping the sexually oppressed* (pp. 141-161). Englewood Cliffs, New Jersey: Prentice-Hall, Inc.

Masters, W. H., & Johnson, V. E. (1970). *Human sexual inadequacy*. Boston: Little, Brown.

Rodgers-Rose, L. (1980). Some demographic characteristics of the Black woman: 1940 to 1975. In L. Rodgers-Rose, (Ed.), *The Black woman* (pp. 29-41). Beverly Hills, California: Sage Publications, Inc.

Shon, S. P., & Ja. D. Y. Asian families (1982). In M. McGoldrick, J. K. Pearce, & J. Giordano, (Eds.), *Ethnicity and family therapy* (pp. 208-228). New York: The Gilford Press.

Smith, W. D., Burlew, A. K., Mosley, M. H., & Whitney, W. M. (1978). *Minority issues in mental health*. Reading, Massachusetts: Addison-Wesley Publishing Co.

Valdez, T. A., & Gallegos, J. (1982). The Chicano familia in social work. In

J. W. Green (Ed.), *Cultural awareness in the human services* (pp. 186-203). Englewood Cliffs, New Jersey: Prentice-Hall.

Wyatt, G. E., Strayer, R. G., & Lobitz, W. C. (1978). Issues in the treatment of sexually dysfunctioning couples of Afro-American descent. In J. LoPiccolo & L. LoPiccolo (Eds.), *Handbook of sex therapy* (pp. 441-451). New York: Plenum Press.

Lesbian Sexuality in the Framework of Psychotherapy: A Practical Model for the Lesbian Therapist

Susan Hamadock

This article is based on the premise that sexual health is fundamental to overall mental health. As women and as lesbians, we have been systematically traumatized and shamed with regard to our sexuality. The result is disease and ill health. It is incumbent upon the lesbian therapist to incorporate sexuality into work with lesbian clients. In the following pages, I will present a practice model to the lesbian therapist who is interested in exploring her clients' sexuality more fully. After briefly discussing characteristics of the subject matter and common problems our clients encounter, I will provide an operational definition of lesbian sexuality which lays the foundation for the utilization of the practice model. My intention is not to provide specific information about sexuality, but to describe the model and demonstrate ways in which it might be useful. The reader is encouraged to adapt the model to meet her own needs.

The lack of sex education and therapy services available to lesbians is a reflection of the pervasive heterosexual bias that continues to dominate the field of sexology. The predominance of this bias suggests that sex educators and therapists continue to define and view female sexuality primarily in its relationship to male sexuality.

Susan Hamadock is a feminist therapist, teacher, and advocate who works with lesbians, children, and people with developmental disabilities. She and her partner, Carol, share their family life with Carrie, Allen, Brian, Cleo, Shaun, and Margaret.

A review of the literature reveals a paucity of information and research specific to the sexual functioning of women independent of that of men. I am speaking, of course, about lesbians. This lack of information and subsequent lack of training available to lesbian therapists in the area of sexuality creates a void in the delivery of psychotherapeutic services within the lesbian community. Although many lesbian therapists attempt to address sexuality with their clients, it is usually on a limited basis. Too often, lesbians who are experiencing problems with their sexuality feel that there is no place to turn for help. This leads to feelings of isolation, a sense of helplessness, and a resignation to existing problems. Often embarrassment and fears of being judged inhibit lesbians who are in therapy from initiating discussions about sex with their therapists.

Concomitantly, lesbian therapists are likely to feel somewhat helpless and without direction or support in treating sexual problems or in engaging a client in an in-depth exploration of her sexuality. Our own discomfort with the subject matter or confusion about some aspect of our sexuality can limit our willingness to work with our clients in this area. For some, unresolved conflict between our radical feminist politics and particular forms of sexual expression such as S&M contribute to our reluctance to bring sexuality into our work as therapists. Many of us feel insecure about our lack of training and the availability of resources. Additionally, we are often influenced by the socially accepted norm that only "specialists" should deal with sexuality and sexual problems.

Historically, we have approached sexuality from a reactive position, addressing the subject if and when our clients identify a problem. The client has borne the primary responsibility for articulating problems and initiating discussions. Due to the sensitive nature of the subject of sexuality for many clients, this is too difficult. As a result, problems related to sexuality, have, for the most part, gone unaddressed. Unwittingly, therapists who have operated from this reactive position regarding sexuality have perpetuated the age-old taboo that surrounds this subject.

Based on a belief that there is a need to "normalize" sexuality in the delivery of mental health services, this article advocates a proactive approach to sexuality and sexual problems. I suggest that lesbian therapists should assume responsibility for sex education and counseling in work with all of our clients. The rationale set forth by Masters and Johnson (1970) advocating dual-sex therapy teams in work with heterosexual couples affirms my belief that lesbian therapists are the best candidates for work with lesbian clients. Their research findings indicated that a male therapist cannot ever fully understand the sexual responses of a woman nor can a female therapist ever fully understand the sexual functioning of a man. Similarly, a heterosexual therapist cannot fully understand a lesbian's sexual functioning because she has never had the experience of an ongoing sexual relationship with another woman. She can only imagine this experience. What she learns about lesbian sexuality she learns indirectly through observation, exposure, or report. Regardless of her objectivity, she cannot be completely secure in her concepts because she has not experienced sexual intimacy with another woman. While it is true that certain problems cannot be effectively treated by a non-specialist, it is possible for a lesbian therapist with little or no special training to provide significant help to her clients and often accomplish much of what the sex therapist does.

The necessity of adopting a pro-active approach to sexuality within the context of psychotherapy is further supported by the following definition. Lesbian sexuality in its fullest and most meaningful sense refers to an integral component of a woman's total identity. It is a lifelong phenomenon that begins at birth and continues throughout the entire life cycle. Role and gender identity, crucial in how we define ourselves, are central aspects of our sexuality. No individual's self-concept can be separated from her feelings about herself as a sexual being (Kempton & Forman, 1976). Self-esteem and body image are part of every woman's sexuality. Our ability to love and to be loved are intrinsic elements of sexuality as is our capacity for intimacy and tenderness, our ability to bond, and our feelings about our relationships.

If we accept this definition of sexuality as a primary component of one's total identity, then it follows that sexuality should be included as an integral aspect of therapy. Weaving sexuality into the fabric of psychotherapy requires that the therapist actively engage the client in exploring all aspects of her sexuality throughout the entire therapy process. The shift from a reactive to a pro-active position necessitates a commitment on the part of the therapist to establish a climate of safety and acceptance that encourages sexual exploration and growth. In attempting to establish this atmosphere, the therapist must be aware of some troublesome characteristics regarding the subject matter itself and common problems clients encounter when beginning to explore their own sexuality. It is also important for the therapist to be "approachable" in the eyes of her clients. Objectivity and comfort with her own sexuality are two essential ingredients.

The most outstanding feature of sexuality is that it is an emotionally charged, value-laden, and taboo subject that in most women elicits considerable anxiety and guilt. All of us, at one time in our lives, have been made to feel ashamed of some aspect of our sexuality. Many of us have been traumatized by incest, assault, and rape. From this perspective, it can be said that to varying degrees we are all sexually handicapped. Most of us have not had the benefit of meaningful sexuality education. As a result, we are sexually illiterate. We arrive in adulthood harboring bad feelings and misinformation about sex and continue to be plagued by negative childhood experiences. Characteristically, lesbian life is either hidden from public view or portrayed in a negative manner. Lesbians lack positive role models and images. Regardless of when in life we address our lesbianism for the first time, our guilt, anxiety, and confusion about sexuality are compounded by myths about lesbian sexuality. To varying degrees, we feel ashamed and troubled in our struggle for our identities. As lesbians and as therapists, this is the sexual legacy we have inherited and we are often as uncomfortable with this subject as are clients.

Most clients share common problems as they begin to explore their sexuality within the context of therapy. Many experience a high degree of anxiety, guilt, and shame. Many women have never been given permission to discuss sex without fear of being punished or judged. Some women are uncomfortable with sexual language, feeling that medical terms are too sterile and other words too crude or misogynistic. Laboring under myths and self-doubt, many women feel overwhelmed by guilt, shame, embarrassment, and fear. For some, discussing sexuality is initially impossible.

In order to maximize the potential for ongoing dialogue, there are desirable qualities which help us to become "approachable" in the eyes of our clients. Desirable qualities helpful to clients include warmth, interest, objectivity, and acceptance. Using natural talents such as humor and creativity is effective in reinforcing our common bond regarding sexuality.

Comfort with our own sexuality is the key. Unfortunately, we do not instantly become comfortable with our sexuality simply because we think it's a good idea. For this reason, I recommend participation in a brief but invaluable training process known as a Sexual Attitudes Reassessment (SAR). An SAR is an explicit multi-media presentation depicting all aspects of human sexual behavior. Experiential in nature, it is designed to help participants get in touch with and become more comfortable with their own sexuality. A mini-SAR can be as brief as one day, while a full SAR can require one week.

Possessing an awareness of troublesome characteristics of the subject matter and some of the problems clients face enables the therapist to prepare herself for working more intensively with her client's sexuality. An SAR increases her comfort with her own sexuality. Demonstrating empathic and interested behaviors help her set the tone for continued dialogue. The following model is intended to assist the therapist in helping her clients grow as sexual beings.

In order to explore sexual attitudes and feelings and help clients move toward a greater degree of sexual health, certain aspects of Annon's PLISSIT (Permission, Limited Information, Specific Suggestion and Intensive Therapy) model (1974) can be employed. PLISSIT describes four ways of approaching sexual problems. I have framed the basic concepts of PLISSIT within the context of psychotherapy, placing a slightly greater emphasis on exploration and growth than on problem-solving. The goal of the model that follows is to help the client become more comfortable with her own sexuality, thus more accepting of herself. It is designed to assist the therapist who chooses to include sexuality in her work by presenting an organized system for gathering data, setting goals, selecting areas requiring further education, and encouraging change. It is intended as a guide, not a recipe, and can be adapted to meet the needs of the particular client-therapist unit. The model identifies three progressive stages of therapy:

Level I	– establish sexuality as an integral component of therapy – learn the client's sex language – gather data regarding sexual history
Level II	– set learning goals – give permission – give reassurance – provide selected education – provide resource information
Level III	– promote and encourage change in attitude, affect, or behavior – limited problem-solving

The intent of Level I is to establish an atmosphere of safety and to communicate the message that sexuality is a significant part of every woman's life and as such will be included in her therapy. During the early sessions, the therapist needs to communicate empathy and warmth, explaining that for many women sex is a difficult and anxiety-producing subject. Discussing why we are so anxious about sex is often helpful in disarming the anxiety and fear. It is important to provide the client with a broad definition of sexuality and to reassure her that her sexual health is as important as her physical, emotional, and spiritual health. This integrative approach helps the client begin to re-frame her thinking about sexuality. It is essential that the therapist convey her own comfort with the subject and her acceptance of all aspects of her client's sexuality. These qualities help to establish a safe climate which encourages exploration.

The primary objective of Level I is to gather data. Including a sexual history as part of the initial assessment process reinforces the importance of sexuality in overall health. A comprehensive sexual history (Masters & Johnson, 1970) need not be taken. However, the following types of questions can be interspersed throughout the diagnostic assessment:

- –Where did you first learn about sex?
- –What is your earliest memory related to sex?
- –How did your family deal with nudity; with affection?
- –When did you first become aware that girls and boys are different?
- –When did you begin to masturbate?
- –Can you remember childhood sexual experimentation with friends, brothers and sisters, or with family pets?
- –Where you ever caught in any type of sexual experimentation or play?
- –Were you prepared for your period?
- –What happened when you first started your period?

It is particularly helpful to discuss the client's feelings about these experiences. Additional questions about her adolescence and early adult sexual experiences help the therapist get a sense of how the client presently feels about her sexuality. Exploring her adolescent experimentation, successes or failures in early love relationships, and how she first became aware of her lesbian sexuality are also useful in this process. Investigating the specifics of her current sexual relationships provides relevant information about her feelings about herself as a sexual being. During Level I, it is important to reassure clients that there are no authorities when it comes to understanding lesbian sexuality, that we all experience some degree of discomfort around sexuality, and that change will come gradually.

As the therapist gathers a sexual history, she is also able to observe and assess the client's level of discomfort with the subject matter, the degree of guilt and shame she experiences, the impact of any sexual trauma she might have experienced, and whether her sexual value system is syntonic or dystonic. This information is vital in planning her learning goals and in helping her identify her need or desire to become more comfortable with her own sexuality.

There are further considerations at this level. For some clients sexuality is too threatening a subject to address so early in the therapeutic relationship. For others, the presenting problem requires immediate and exclusive attention. In such cases, sound therapeutic judgement dictates that sexuality not be included until the client is stable and ready to approach the subject. The second consideration has to do with language. Whenever possible, it is desirable to learn and utilize our clients' language when discussing sex. This helps establish safety, communicates a nonjudgemental attitude, and builds rapport. Finally, it is imperative that we give clients who have been sexually victimized the power to set the pace and depth of discussions about sexuality (Maltz & Holman, 1987).

As she gathers important data, the therapist uses herself in such a way as to establish safety and to foster continued discussion about sexuality. The Level II stage unfolds in a natural progression. At this level the therapist concerns herself with giving the client permission or reassurance. In this fashion, potential problems can be minimized or eliminated. Many lesbians have never received explicit permission to be sexual beings or to actively engage in and enjoy expression of their sexuality. Experiencing the "go ahead" can be liberating and can produce instantaneous growth. Lesbians need to hear reassurance that we are okay sexually and that all thoughts, feelings, and fantasies are normal.

Based on the information gathered during Level I, as well as her own insights regarding the client's level of comfort, the therapist selects learning goals and shares those goals with her client. The primary objective of Level II centers around education. For example, if the client harbors a belief that oral sex is dirty, information regarding anatomy and hygiene will be of use to her. Similarly, if she believes that manual penetration is nothing more than an imitation of intercourse and therefore repulsive to her because that is what men do to women, it may be useful for her to read about the way other lesbians feel about penetration (Godiva, 1975).

If during the initial assessment it has become clear that she is ashamed of her genitals because she believes them to be unclean or unlovely, it might be helpful to her to review photographs of female genitalia (Blank & Cottrell, 1978) and to discuss her responses. Concern about the presence of men in sexual fantasies is common among some lesbians. Others are very uncomfortable about the presence of rape fantasies or those which include children or animals. Clients need to be reassured that these fantasies are common (Califia, 1980), that there is a difference between fantasy and reality, and that a sexual fantasy does not represent a wish to act out a particular behavior.

It is important for the therapist to keep in mind that clients employ the same defense mechanisms to ward off unwanted thoughts and feelings regarding sexuality as they do for other aspects of their lives. Some women will find it impossible to purchase a book about sexuality. This degree of discomfort needs to be interpreted as an indication of how she feels about herself and her sexuality. Gradually, as the encouraging therapist models comfort with her own sexuality and an unconditional acceptance of the client, she will be able to make changes.

General reading materials are effective tools for eliciting discussions about feelings related to various aspects of sexuality. For example, Dodson (1974) provides a focus for discussing the positive and affirming qualities of masturbation. Similarly, Califia (1980) suggests ways to improve sexual communication. This reading material and the client's responses provide additional material for exploration in therapy.

Frequently, lesbians express concern about orgasm. Loulan (1984) provides valuable information regarding this subject with suggestions for change. I find it particularly useful to frame orgasmic problems in a social context before exploring the psychological or physiological underpinnings. As a society, we tend to define sexuality from a male dominated heterosexual bias and, therefore, too often accept the male viewpoint regarding orgasm. We typically equate ejaculation with male orgasm and since an adequately functioning man orgasms (ejaculates) nearly every time he has sex, we erroneously conclude that an adequately functioning woman should also orgasm every time she has sex. Even our lesbian literature is full of suggestions of how to improve one's orgasms. I believe this over-emphasis perpetuates a certain amount of performance anxiety. My clinical experience suggests that for many lesbians, the journey of mutual pleasuring and the spiritual and emotional interchange holds as much or more significance than what society considers to be the journey's end—orgasm. However, we continue to be plagued by the commonly-held belief that we are somehow diminished or dysfunctional if we do not produce orgasms. Often reframing these beliefs, using the theory of male bias, helps eliminate some of the negative feelings and lifts the pressure to perform and produce orgasms. Exploring internalized homophobia as it impacts on a client's sexual expression is another problem for which it is helpful to explore the social context.

Throughout Level II, the therapist focuses on selecting areas that require re-learning or re-evaluation based on her continued insights and therapeutic judgment. At this level, education and the accompanying re-assessment are curative factors which can help the client toward greater self-awareness, acceptance, and sexual health. Due to the heavy emphasis on growth through education in Level II, it is important for the therapist to have immediate access to readings and resource materials.

Much of the content of Level III is based on the strength of the therapeutic alliance, the client's level of comfort, and the specific content of the previous sessions. The primary objective of Level III is to promote new experiences and sexual growth. The message is that sexual growth, like emotional, intellectual, and spiritual growth, is not only possible but desirable. At this level, the installation of hope can be a curative factor.

Tenacious and persistent troublesome aspects of her sexuality which have not responded to the earlier interventions of permission, reassurance, or re-education become the focus for work of Level III. De-sensitization is a primary tool at this level. Repeated exposure to, and supportive discussion about, specific aspects of her sexuality can help the client overcome the repulsion, fear, and guilt that continue to limit her growth or enjoyment of her own sexuality.

The specific therapeutic content of Level III is so individualized that it is difficult to describe without detailed case study examples. The length of this article prohibits such an undertaking. However, I have included a few brief examples to illustrate the basic process of Level III. Drawing on her own experiences and reading materials, the therapist works closely with the client, suggesting practice exercises and encouraging creativity. Loulan (1984) offers many specific suggestions for effectively dealing with a wide variety of sexual issues. These suggestions can guide the therapist until she is confident in her own ideas and can create practice activities which will help her client. Each time the client has a new sexual experience or practices an assignment, she will benefit from discussing her physical and emotional responses.

If a client believes her genitals to be unclean and odorous, progressive de-sensitization exercises might be instrumental. For instance, encourage her to bathe, taking care to wash her genitals. Suggest that after bathing she stimulate her genitals with her hands. Exploring the color, temperature, and texture of her vaginal fluid by rubbing it between her fingers, smelling and tasting it might be a useful step in de-sensitizing her to her negative feelings about her genitals. In this, as in most cases, practice exercises at this level require much repetition, and discussion of her reactions is essential during each therapy session.

Similarly, if a client has problems telling her partner what she wants because she is repulsed or uncomfortable with sexual language, a language de-sensitization activity might be useful. In the therapy session, ask her to select one word she can tolerate for either a body part or a sexual activity. Suggest that she repeated the words in a soft and then a loud voice for one minute every day. Add new words, one at a time, to her list until she has developed a sexual vocabulary with which she is comfortable.

In assigning practice exercises, it is important for the therapist to always be specific and explicit, taking care not to leave anything up to the client's imagination unless the goal is for her to create her own experience. The therapist always pre-determines a brief time limit, increasing the length and flexibility of time as the client becomes more familiar with the exercises and more comfortable with a particular aspect of her sexuality.

In describing the process of Level III, I have attempted to illustrate the common sense approach to sexual change. There are no authorities with regard to lesbian sexuality. The therapist already possesses expertise in this subject by virtue of the fact that she is a lesbian. Helping clients grow sexually can be accomplished by the lesbian therapist who is committed to the process and who is comfortable with her own sexuality.

Using a systematic approach of gathering data, providing reassurance, permission, education, and experimentation with change enables the therapist and client to dramatically improve sexual health. This intervention model, which defines a pro-active approach to sexual problems, is equally applicable when working with lesbian couples or families. Bandler (1985) provides practical suggestions for helping couples enjoy greater sexual intimacy and resolve sexual conflict. The same techniques used to help clients solve problems, resolve conflict, develop more effective communication skills, and raise self-esteem apply when working with issues of sexuality.

Of course, there may be problems that the general practitioner cannot treat. A referral to a sex therapist may be indicated. However, neither the therapist nor the client need perceive this as a failure. To the contrary, the work done thus far will have laid the groundwork for sex therapy. In most cases, the continuation of the therapeutic relationship is recommended using sex therapy in a short-term, adjunctive manner.

Since sexuality is an integral component of identity development and the capacity to give and receive love, including it within the course of psychotherapy is critical. In order to become more comfortable with the subject matter itself, the therapist may need to explore her own sexuality through a SAR process. Beyond this, however, she needs no special training or expertise. Comfort with her own sexuality and genuine interest in her client's sexuality are the key ingredients to successful integration. The creative energy that evolves as lesbian therapist and client commit themselves to exploration, learning, and growth enables the client to move toward sexual health, viewing sexuality as a positive and integral part of her identity.

REFERENCES

Anon, J. S. (1974). *The behavioral treatment of sexual problems*. Honolulu: Enabling Systems, Inc.

Bandler, L. C. (1985). *Solutions practical and effective antidotes for sexual and relationship problems*. San Raphael, CA: Future Pace, Inc.

Blank, J. & Cottrell, H. J. (1978). *I am my lover*. Burlingame, CA: Down There Press.

Califia, P. (1980). *Saphistry: The book of lesbian sexuality*. Tallahassee: Niad Press, Inc.

Dodson, B. (1974). *Liberating masturbation: A meditation of self love*. New York: Dodson.

Godiva (1975). *What lesbians do*. CA: Godiva.

Kempton, W. & Forman, R. (1976). *Guidelines for training in sexuality and the mentally handicapped*. Philadelphia: Planned Parenthood of Southeastern Pennsylvania.

Loulan, J. (1984). *Lesbian sex*. San Francisco: Spinster's Ink.

Maltz, W. & Holman, B. (1987). *Incest and sexuality: A guide to understanding and healing*. Lexington, MA: Lexington Books.

Masters, W. H. & Johnson, V. E. (1970). *Human sexual inadequacy*. New York: Bantam Books.

Research on the Sex Practices of 1566 Lesbians and the Clinical Applications

JoAnn Loulan

When working with lesbians, I believe that one must consider and analyze the sociology of the majority culture. Lesbians live in a homophobic, misogynist world. Therefore, when working with lesbians on the most intimate part of their behavior, that of their sexual encounters, one must be willing to take into account the impact the culture has on their sense of self and their self-worth. In addition, because the culture identifies lesbians by whom they have genital contact with, sexual activity becomes more than behavior, it becomes an entire identity.

I believe that this does not happen in other sexual orientations. Even gay men have at least been raised in a culture that teaches men that they can be sexual. The fact that lesbians are raised in a culture that teaches women that they cannot be sexual, and that teaches lesbians their identity is determined by their sexual partner, becomes a double bind. This creates a great deal of anxiety, ambivalence, and pressure on the sex lives of lesbians.

Little needs to be said about the homophobia of a culture that has a Supreme Court that condemns oral and anal sex between members of the same gender. This court states it cannot make similar judgments about the activities of two people who are differently gendered. Homophobia is rife in a culture in which families of origin will abandon their lesbian daughters simply because they are lesbi-

---

JoAnn Loulan is the author of *Lesbian Sex, Lesbian Passion: Loving Ourselves and Each Other*. She has worked with lesbians for twelve years on issues of self-esteem and sexuality.

ans; a culture in which lesbians can lose their children, jobs, and housing because of their sexual orientation.

It is significant that lesbians do not consciously think they are being affected by the AIDS crisis unless one of their gay male friends or relatives dies. I find in working with lesbians throughout the United States that our internalized homophobia is profoundly affected by AIDS. A lesbian cannot pick up a newspaper, listen to the radio, or watch the television without hearing that homosexual sex kills you. The fact that lesbians are homosexuals and that hatred and anger is being directed at the homosexual community at this time means that these women are deeply affected. The problem in the lesbian community is that we are once again invisible as society focuses its reaction to AIDS on the gay male population, and we are blind to the impact of the crisis on our own sense of sexuality.

Lesbians are often torn between being "good girls" and having an identity within the lesbian community. There is a dilemma about whether to be sexual or not. Can we have sex with women and still fit into the mainstream culture? If we do not have sex with women regularly, does that mean we are not lesbians and thus do not fit into the lesbian community?

There are many aspects of being a lesbian: cultural, emotional spiritual, sexual, intellectual, and artistic, to name a few. Most people in the world are sexual a small percentage of their lives and that applies to lesbians as well. To be plagued by sexual activity as an identification makes sex overemphasized.

I have done a research project on sex practices of 1566 lesbians. This, along with my experience in working with the sexual issues of lesbians for 10 years, is the basis of this article. The techniques established by Masters and Johnson, Lonnie Barbach, Helen Singer Kaplan, Marny Hall, along with educational models such as those developed by Jack Annon, Joani Blank, and Jack Morin are all basics of my therapeutic model. In addition, I rely heavily on the family therapy model of dynamics in a couple to explore the impact on the sexual relationship.

The results of my survey will be woven through this paper. The data were gathered through a questionnaire that I distributed at lectures, workshops, and other speaking engagements given in different locations. Some questionnaires were taken by attendees to their home towns. Some women's bookstores distributed the questionnaire. Others were distributed through ads in women's and gay newspapers in the United States. Obviously, this was not a random sample. It is impossible to create such a scientifically "pure" sample due to the homophobia in this culture. The sample group came from over 150 cities and towns throughout the United States and Canada.

The demographics of the respondents covered a wide range. It is important to establish who the majority of the respondents were to make sure we do not generalize the information to all lesbians. Their ages ranged from under 25 to over 60. There was representation from all socioeconomic classes, most racial groups, and each of the major religions. However, the majority of the sample described themselves as follows: 70% were 25-39 years old; 40% were middle class; 92% were Caucasian; 37% were raised Protestant; 89% were able-bodied; 69% were college graduates or held advanced degrees. The women identified themselves as being lesbians for varying lengths of time: 25%, less than five years; 32%, five to 10 years; 31%, 10 to 20 years; and 12%, over 20 years. For the most part, these women were at a lecture, workshop, or speaking engagement on lesbian sexuality, and therefore would probably not be afraid of being seen at a predominantly lesbian event.

With this in mind, I intend to show in this paper how some of the questionnaire results can and should impact lesbian sex therapy, and how I use them in my work. For a fuller discussion of these findings, see my new book, *Lesbian Passion: Loving Ourselves and Each Other* (Loulan, 1987).

Perhaps the statistic that most shows vividly my premise that homophobia and misogyny put lesbians in a unique position as a group is that regarding hand holding. When asked if they held hands, 80% said they did. When asked if they held hands in public, only 27% said yes. This is a shocking reality for most lesbians: holding hands in public is off limits. The fact that this benign expression of sexual bonding is impossible for most lesbians to share in public creates more pressure for their private sex lives. How do you have sex in private when you have been denying sexual feelings all day?

Internalized homophobia probably needs to be the most crucial concern for lesbian sex therapy. To work effectively with the lesbian woman, therapists need to help her work consciously toward accepting her sexual self as positive, good, and exciting. The bounds of the culture notwithstanding, lesbians can indeed have fun with sex.

It is important in sex therapy to establish the kinds of sex activity that clients participate in so that precise, realistic goals for therapy can be established. This includes specifics about masturbation, partner sex, and what other practices they use with their own or another's body, including frequency of sex with themselves and others. Those who have not had partner sex within the preceding year will need different work from those who have had sex once a week but are not satisfied with the quality. The information will also establish what kinds of sex education clients need.

Clients should write down their goals to eliminate vagueness. How often do they want to have sex in a month? What kind of enhancement do they want to bring to their union? What level of satisfaction are they hoping to achieve? How will they measure their success?

Sex histories are also a crucial part of the therapy. It is important to find out specifics about if and when certain stages of sexual development occurred and the circumstances surrounding each stage. I gather information on: history of sexual abuse, onset of menses, first masturbation, first sex with same gender, first sex with opposite gender, adult sexual abuse or rape, and sexual histories of past and present relationships.

Thirty-eight percent of my sample group reported sexual abuse before the age of 18. This corresponds directly with the statistics of Diana Russell (1986). She studied a random sample of 930 females and found that 38% of them had suffered childhood sexual abuse. My study revealed that the ages at which this trauma occurred in the group that was abused were as follows: under five, 32%; five to 10, 55%; 11-15, 55%; 16-18, 23%. This would of course make a profound impact on these women and their intimacy with future sex partners. The resulting issues for these women must be discussed openly in the therapeutic sessions.

The perpetrators of the sexual violence were overwhelmingly men, but there were also female abusers. A partial list of the categories is: father, 35%; older male relative, 20%; male stranger, 20%; sibling, 20%; mother, 8%; male lover/partner of mother, 7%; female stranger, 2%; older female relative, 2%; same-age female relative, 1%; female lover/partner of mother, 1%.

In considering the actual current sexual activity of the respondents, there was no difference between those who were survivors of sexual abuse and those who were not. Comparing the amount of masturbation and partner sex in a month and satisfaction with sex, the two groups were not statistically different. This is helpful information for survivors and their partners. Many times when beginning a process of recovery from childhood sexual abuse, survivors feel unwilling to have sex. They and their partners wonder if sex will ever be part of their lives again.

Lesbians must often make a conscious effort to have sex. In my survey, I asked the women to identify themselves as single (27%), casually sexually involved with another woman (12%), or partnered (61%). In all three groups, sexual satisfaction decreased the longer they were in that situation. In addition, they masturbated and had partner sex fewer times in a month the longer they were single, casually involved, or partnered.

My conclusion from this and from the women I have worked with in therapy over 10 years is that lesbians must make an effort in order to have sex on a regular basis. The fact that all three groups have decreasing sex means several things to me. Women have been taught not to be sexual and when the newness of a partnership, single life, or a casual sexual involvement wears off, sex must become more intentional. No longer overwhelmed by our new status, we are thus less able to cross boundaries as we did in the new flush of partnership or single life. When our conscious self takes over, we become bored and often scared, exacerbating common non-recognition of sexual desire. We were never taught to initiate sex, which makes intentional sex even more difficult. There is no definitive data on why this is so, but there is most certainly a sociocultural component: i.e. "Women are not supposed to be sexual."

In therapy, when a woman's sex life is diminishing, I work with her on my "Willingness Model" (Loulan, 1984). This model has been effective for the women with whom I have worked. It is based on the sexual response cycle first described by Masters and Johnson (excitement, plateau, orgasm, and resolution) and then modified by Helen Singer Kaplan (desire, excitement, orgasm). I believe that for women sex is more complicated than it is for men. Most women begin their sexual response from willingness, which is where my model begins. Women skip some or all of the remaining stages, or skip around between them. Any of the stages can lead to pleasure or a feeling of being shut down. Sexual response is varied and unique to each woman; therefore, the stages of the sexual response cycle I use in my therapy are: willingness, desire, excitement, engorgement, orgasm; yet, this does not imply that there is necessarily a linear development.

Willingness is often the beginning for women. This does not mean they just give in and let someone have sex with them. Rather, women can choose to have sex without waiting for desire or excitement. This concept is paramount, and can be a source of great power for some. Sex does not have to be erased from her life; in fact, she can have regular sex at her conscious choosing. This is an especially powerful concept for a woman whose partner is always ready to have sex when she herself never seems to want sex. The woman in the position of usually saying no has an opportunity in this model to actually choose sex, rather than waiting for her partner or her desire to lead her into it.

Desire is a stage of the sexual response cycle with which most women are familiar, but do not consciously experience with regularity. There are sociocultural and perhaps hormonal reasons why women do not recognize sexual desire. There is certainly a cultural imperative that states that only "bad" women recognize their sexual feelings. During the course of therapy, it can be valuable for a woman to keep a notebook—secretly, if necessary—of when she has sexual thoughts or feelings, or desires to have sex.

Many women are afraid of their desire. For some women, it triggers painful feelings about sexual abuse. Others have a rekindling of feelings for an unrequited love. Still others fear that if they have these feelings they must act on them. Many believe that if they tell their partners about such feelings, their partners will insist on having sex. These problems can be helped through educating that we have feelings, feelings do not have us. It is helpful to educate women about boundaries and how to establish them. For others, the separation of desire for a peer and the memories of sexual abuse are crucial.

Excitement is a stage of the sex response cycle that is also frightening for some women. For them, the idea of allowing emotional excitement to build once sex has begun is alien. Some may feel it is vulgar to be excited about sex. Still others may believe that excitement is overwhelming to those around them as it had been, abusively so, in their childhood. If this is the case, encourage the client to allow excitement into her life on all levels. I often suggest she allow herself to get excited about little things, and build toward bigger things. I also suggest that she start and stop the excitement to allow her to see that, indeed, she has control over it.

Engorgement of the genital tissues with fluid occurs with genital stimulation. This increases pressure on the nerves and is essentially physiological excitement. Many women have access to this kind of physical excitement, but never achieve desire or emotional excitement. Differentiating between emotional excitement and physical excitement is critical for educating clients about their sexual response cycle and actual levels of eagerness.

Many women stop having sex because they do not have desire or emotional excitement. Most women report that once stimulation of their bodies is sufficient, they begin to have physical excitement and then enjoy the sexual experience. In my work with such women, I encourage them to make sex dates with themselves or their partners to create regular times during which there is opportunity for physical excitement. This validates their individual experience of sexual response and satisfaction.

We often forget what is pleasurable and remember only the negative, so there can be a resistance to these dates. I suggest techniques to minimize unconscious sabotage. Mark the dates on a calendar. Cancellations must be made 24 hours in advance and another date rescheduled for within two days.

Many women complain that this is not spontaneous and romantic. This calls for a great deal of education about the cultural mandates that say sex is only worthwhile if it looks like the movies. I remind my clients that movie stars are paid enormous sums of money to make their sexual encounters on the screen look spontaneous and romantic. Hollywood certainly offers few visions of lesbian sex, and we should not be caught by the male heterosexual standards that are presented by the entertainment industry. Besides, even heterosexuals are not having the kind of sex that is portrayed in movies, and the advantages of reintroducing pleasurable, affirming sex in the relationship through formal agreements outweighs the discomfort caused by this structure.

The orgasm stage is the last stage of this sex response cycle. This stage is frequently skipped in sexual encounters. As I mentioned earlier, any of the stages can result in either pleasure or a feeling of being shut down. This stage often intensifies that differentiation. When educating on the sexual response of women, I state my belief that we live in a culture in which there is a tyranny of orgasm. This is often difficult for lesbians to embrace. They commonly use orgasm as the sign that sex is over, or the sign that sex has been fulfilling for one or both partners. If orgasm is not regularly a part of one or both partners' sexual response, it is usually a point of anxiety and friction. Single women often do not want to date if they cannot be assured of an orgasmic response during sex.

In my survey, 14% occasionally or never have orgasms with masturbation. Nineteen percent occasionally or never orgasm with a partner. This is a significant number of the respondents. This information is reassuring for many women who believe they are the only ones who do not orgasm.

I work with orgasmic response with great caution and only after much education and various assignments that do not include having an orgasm. The difficulty in trying to help clients create orgasms in their lives is that the real goal of being sexual gets lost in the overwhelming struggle for orgasm. My work concentrates on the totality of the pleasuring experience rather than on the importance of orgasms.

I spend time in therapy making sure that clients continue to understand sexual realities for them, not what they wish were true. If one does not orgasm, the emphasis needs to be taken away from that goal. If they orgasm only with the kind of increased stimulation given by a vibrator, I suggest that it may be the vibrator or no orgasm and perhaps they should consciously choose one or the other. If one wants to have orgasm as part of the sex response cycle, then one must accept what brings on this muscle spasm.

When discussing the possibility of orgasmic response in the women who do not experience this as they would like, I refer them to Lonnie Barbach's work (1975). This book desensitizes women to masturbation, teaches them about their orgasmic response, and suggests ways to translate that into partner sex. In my survey, 90% masturbate. When asked how often they masturbate in a month, they reported as follows: less than once, 9%; once, 6%; two to five, 37%; six to 10, 26%; 10-20, 14%; over 20, 8%.

Since most of my clients do masturbate, it makes the desensitization process easier. Through the use of Barbach's techniques, clients can usually learn to figure out their orgasmic response. I also commonly recommend a vibrator as an answer to orgasmic problems.

After working with the sexual response cycle in various ways, I also educate on information about lesbian sexual realities. This information is difficult to find since we do not talk to each other about the specifics of sex, and thus have little information from which to draw. This is when the information from my survey is helpful.

Most of the women in the research – 78% – have been celibate for varying periods of time. The majority had been celibate for under one year, but 35% had not had sex with a partner for one to five years and 8% had abstained for over six years.

Four percent of the respondents were currently celibate and in a relationship. This is a small number in light of what I observe occurs in the couples I work with. This discrepancy between my observations and the survey results may have occurred because I believe most women do not want to admit they are celibate, especially in a relationship. In addition, this was a self-report, and the respondents conceivably have different notions about what celibacy means. These are important data in view of the fact that the culture identifies lesbians by their sexual activity. This shows clients that, indeed, many lesbians have periods of no sexual contact with a partner.

When asked how often they had partner sex in a month, the women answered as follows: never, 12%; less than once, 11%; once, 7.5%; two to five times, 35%; six to 10, 20%; 10-20, 11%; over 20, 3%. This was correlated with how long they had been either single, casually sexually involved with another woman, or coupled. Of those who had sex 10 or more times per month, 94% had been in their situation less than three years. In fact, 68% who had sex more than 10 times in a month had been single, casually involved, or partnered for less than one year.

When using the survey to analyze the sex practices of couples, it was found that satisfaction with sex was at its height in the first year of the relationship. The incidence of sexual activity decreased significantly as the relationships got longer, but satisfaction with sex stays essentially the same after the first year.

Clients may be relieved to know that having sex often is not an essential ingredient of satisfaction for many lesbians. I feel as though many women respond to the pressures of a culture that identifies sexual activity by the white male standard. We would find many interesting aspects of sex activity with further study of lesbians who are not directly responding to the pressures or expectations of men for sexual activity.

The question of adult sexual abuse is also an important factor in working with lesbian clients in sex therapy. In this survey, 26% had been physically harassed; 9% had been beaten; and 16% had been raped as adults. Those who were abused as adults were abused by the following: male stranger, 53%; male lover/friend, 21%; female lover/friend, 13%; male relative, 9%; male husband/mate, 9%; female mate, 3%; female stranger, 2%; other, 10%. Clearly, the women who were abused were frequently abused by more than one person.

Many women were abused by other women, which challenges the myth that women are hurt only by men. In this survey, 16% of the women were abused in lesbian relationships specifically. Lesbians who were abused by lesbian lovers in the past have a particularly difficult time in sex therapy. Violence in the former relationship was an assertion of power. In working with women in battering relationships, I have found that many times, violence was related to sex, sometimes preceding or following sex. Discussions about sex also triggered violence in some relationships.

Certainly, issues of power are present in sex and often cause difficulty for a woman who was battered by men or women, or a woman who battered. Often when having sex, the gender of the person does not matter: it is the re-experiencing of feelings of vulnerability that brings up fear. Dealing with this fear often becomes the focus of sex therapy.

If there is violence in the current relationship, the therapist needs to deal with this directly. Sex therapy is contraindicated, as the clients usually have such a volatile union that sex is too overwhelming an experience. This will make the therapy frustrating and will often trigger more violence. It is difficult to address this issue since lesbian battering is such a deep secret that couples will often not admit to the reality.

There was a significant correlation in the survey between being sexually abused as a child and being abused as an adult. Those who were sexually abused as children had a 27% incidence of adult rape; those who were not abused as children had an 8% incidence. Russell's (1986) findings were similar. This should not be misconstrued to imply that those who are abused as children bring adult abuse on themselves. Remember, there is no excuse for rape. No one ever has the right to rape someone else.

It may be true that childhood sexual abuse survivors have few skills to protect themselves in potentially dangerous situations. Some women may feel so full of self-hatred that they do not remove themselves from situations that may result in adult abuse. This statistic is not to be used against women, but rather used to help them understand the impact of early trauma.

Working with women who have been sexually abused as children and adults brings up needs for clear and basic education. These women often need to learn that using their bodies with a safe peer can be loving and positive. Survivors of childhood abuse may need to be taught how to set boundaries even in peer relationships. For many women, giving suggestions for activities to counteract negative experiences is helpful in working through the trauma of sexual violence.

It is my belief that in any work with lesbians, one must investigate substance abuse. In my survey, 29% of the women described themselves as in recovery from substance abuse. Another 2% said they were currently addicted; 3% were heavy users; 51% were casual users; 15% never used chemical substances. I believe there is such severe denial about substance abuse that most women who abuse drugs would not admit that they do. I feel this is why so few stated they were currently addicted or heavy users. Eric Rolfes (1983) writes that 30% of the gay community is alcoholic. I concur that this accurately describes the population, based on my practice over the last decade. In fact, a recent Gallup Poll states that one-third of the people in the United States are alcoholic.

The import of investigating addiction during sex therapy is that for many women in the addictive cycle, sex often becomes a dramatic battle ground. In my opinion, sex is used as a red herring to distract attention from something more serious putting stress on the system. Besides, no amount of therapy is going to work for a woman who is currently addicted to chemical substances unless the focus of the therapy is the addiction.

Sex therapy for women who are currently in recovery from substance abuse needs to take into consideration the recovery process. It often takes one to three years for women in recovery to regain a sense of their bodies. In my survey, 9% of those who had been celibate listed recovery from substance abuse as the reason.

Once the clients in recovery are ready to have sex, or more fulfilling sex, the therapeutic process may need to proceed slowly. They may believe that the sex they had while under the influence of drugs will translate to the sober experience. Often this is not possible because the chemical so altered their sense of reality that they may have done or felt things they would not ordinarily. In addition, their memories of these encounters may well be distorted. Some women in recovery have to start at the beginning, learning how to have sex again. The therapist needs to be aware of this and encourage the client to proceed at her own pace.

Being therapists puts many of us in the position of believing that all people have problems and difficulties like our clients'; however, we see only a sample of the lesbian population that is having problems with sex. Overall in my survey, one can see that lesbians are being sexual with themselves and others, and having some degree of satisfaction with their sex lives. According to my statistics, 89% of these women are masturbating and 88% are having partner sex.

When asked how satisfied they were with their sex lives, the women replied: not at all, 15%; somewhat, 24%; passibly, 8%; fairly well, 39%; and completely, 14%.

There was no significant difference in sex activity and satisfaction between the following groups: disabled and able-bodied; those sexually abused in childhood and those not sexually abused in childhood; different ages, although the women over 60 masturbated more and had somewhat less partner sex than the women in the other age groups.

CONCLUSION

The results of this survey of 1566 lesbians can be used by all those working with lesbian women. The statistics are significant, at least for the demographics of the respondents. It is important to remember that the homophobia of the client and that of the therapist can significantly influence the course of therapy. One must glean the specific sexual activities of clients and, with this knowledge, establish goals for the therapeutic process. Taking the sex history of the clients, including current and past relationships, is helpful. Sex abuse is so prevalent in the childhoods of women that establishing if this is the case with particular clients is important.

Working with the Willingness Model of sex response can be useful. The therapist can establish both what stages the client experiences, and use the model to explain female sexual function.

Commonalities showed frequently with this research. Most women had been celibate, masturbated, had partner sex, and were at least somewhat satisfied with their sex lives. Some women suffered adult sexual abuse and it correlated significantly with abuse in childhood. Substance abuse figured significantly in the lives of some of the women in this survey.

In sexual activity and satisfaction with sex there was no difference between disabled and able-bodied women; those abused in childhood and those not abused in childhood; and older and younger women.

REFERENCES

Barbach, L. (1975). *For yourself: Fulfillment of female sexuality*. New York: Doubleday.

Loulan, J. (1987). *Lesbian passion: Loving ourselves and each other*. San Francisco: Spinsters/Aunt Lute.

Loulan, J. (1984). *Lesbian sex*. San Francisco: Spinsters/Aunt Lute.

Rolfes, E. (1983). *I thought people like that killed themselves*. San Francisco: Fox Press.

Russell, D. (1986). *The secret trauma: Incest in the lives of girls and women*. New York: Basic Books.

Bisexuality in Women: Myths, Realities, and Implications for Therapy

Margaret Nichols

INTRODUCTION

As Fritz Klein and Timothy Wolf point out in their introduction to *Bisexualities: Theory and Research* (1985, p. xv): "The history of research into bisexuality until now could almost be characterized as nonexistent." In recent decades, bisexuality has been variously described as counterfeit, illusory, or pathological. Although some notable figures in psychology, including Sigmund Freud and John Money, have believed that all humans have a bisexual potential, and despite the evidence from Alfred Kinsey showing that significantly higher percentages of people exhibit bisexual behavior than exclusively homosexual behavior, it is still widely believed that any individual with sexual experience with both sexes is either "really" heterosexual, or more recently, "really" gay.

Gary Zinik describes this belief as the "conflict model" of bisexuality:

> Underlying the conflict model of bisexuality is the notion that sexual orientation is a dichotomy: One is either heterosexual or homosexual. This dichotomous notion derives from the following logic. Since men and women are viewed as opposite

---

Margaret Nichols is a licensed psychologist and certified sex therapist. She is the Executive Director of the Institute for Personal Growth, a counseling center in New Brunswick, NJ, with a large gay, lesbian, and bisexual clientele. She is also the founder of the Hyacinth Foundation AIDS Project, a psychosocial support program for those affected by the AIDS epidemic.

> sexes, it appears contradictory that anyone could eroticize two opposite things at the same time. Attraction to one sex would logically rule out attraction to the other, or else lead to psychological dissonance and conflict. It follows that people claiming to be bisexual are: (1) experiencing identity conflict or confusion; (2) living in an inherently temporary or transitional stage which masks the person's true underlying sexual orientation (presumably homosexual); and (3) employing the label as a method of either consciously denying or unconsciously defending against one's true homosexual preference. (1985, p. 9)

While hundreds of research studies have investigated homosexuality, little interest has been taken in bisexuality. The investigation of bisexuality holds rich promise for our understanding of some of the basic structures of human sexuality; but to look clearly at bisexuality requires discarding some cherished conceptions. Most basically, one must move from a dualistic notion of sexual orientation to a more expansive vision of sexuality. At the very least, one must acknowledge the existence of what Hanson and Evans (1985) call the "Excluded Middle": that is, those people whose sexual orientation lies between the endpoints of the Kinsey Scale. Just as recent research on psychological androgyny has emphasized the mutual compatibility of "masculine" and "feminine" attributes, in contrast to dualistic notions that once viewed these traits as mutually exclusive, concepts of sexual orientation must include the reality that attractions to men and women can exist side by side in the same person. Exploring bisexuality in depth leads to an even more radical revising of our views on sexuality. Klein, Sepekoff, and Wolf (1985) have a model of sexual orientation that differentiates seven variables, including sexual attraction, behavior, fantasies, emotional preference, social preference, self-identification, and hetero/gay lifestyle. Some feminist theorists have gone further and challenge the idea of the primacy of gender of object choice as a dimension of sexual orientation. Califia (1983), for example, reveals that many men and women who practice S&M care more about whether a potential partner is dominant or submissive than they do about the gender of that partner. And in fact, several reports corroborate that some bisexuals maintain that gender is an irrelevant dimension of their attractions to people (Coons, 1972; Zinik, 1983). To understand bisexuality in women, then, and to do therapy with women who may be bisexual, requires nothing less than completely discarding some of the concepts of sexuality with which we have been raised, which have been considered scientific axioms and psychotherapeutic truths.

BISEXUALITY IN WOMEN: THE EVIDENCE FROM RESEARCH

It is difficult to ascertain the rates of bisexuality in women, and one can do so only inferentially. Part of the problem lines in how one defines bisexuality. Most researchers have found that individuals who report exactly equal attractions to both men and women (the most narrow definition of bisexuality) are quire rare. Beyond this narrow definition, estimates of bisexuality vary according to whether one uses the criterion of *attraction or fantasy* only, *actual behavior*, or *self-identification/self-label*. As one would expect, estimates based only on fantasy or attraction are quite high. Masters and Johnson (1978), for example, found that what they term "cross-preference encounters" were the third most frequent category of sexual fantasy for both homosexual males and homosexual females, the fourth most frequent fantasy for heterosexual males and the fifth most frequent fantasy for heterosexual females. Bell and Weinberg (1978) report that only about half of gay men and half of gay women rate their *feelings* as exclusively gay. Hyde (1982), in interpreting data from both the Kinsey surveys of the 1940s and the Hunt survey of the 1970s, estimates that *behaviorally*, about 75% of men and 85% of women are exclusively heterosexual, 2% of men and less than 1% of women are exclusively homosexual, and nearly 25% of men and 15% of women are behaviorally bisexual. Bell and Weinberg (1978) report that nearly all of their samples of gay men and women have had behavioral heterosexual experience, and estimate that one-third of men and an even higher percentage of lesbians exhibit what they call a "partial bisexual style": i.e., attractions and behavior that are somewhat heterosexual. Moreover, even among their "heterosexual" control group, only three-quarters of the males and 90% of the women were exclusively behaviorally heterosexual! The "Playboy Sex Survey" (*Playboy*, 1983) found that 3% of males and 1% of females *identified* themselves as bisexual, and Klein (1980), in a *Forum* magazine survey, found that 56% of his respondents identified themselves as bisexual, with more men than women reporting this bisexual orientation.

Clearly, bisexual self-identification is much lower than bisexual behavior, which is in turn lower than bisexual fantasy or attraction. Bisexual behavior, and perhaps bisexual attractions, are higher among self-identified gays than among self-identified heterosexuals. This data is not surprising in a society which, first, stigmatizes homosexuality and, second, teaches us to polarize sexual orientation. In such a society, one would expect the incidence of bisexual behavior to lag far behind incidence of bisexual fantasy or attraction. Furthermore, one would expect individuals to "choose up sides": i.e., to self-identify as either gay or straight, with far fewer people identifying as homosexual. One would also expect, in such a culture, that the label "gay" might become something of a "residual category," a label that might more precisely mean "not exclusively heterosexual." Nichols (1985), found that measures of various dimensions of sexual orientation (fantasy, romantic attraction, past and current sexual behavior, etc.) were more discrepant for those who self-label as gay than for those who self-label as heterosexual. This data, together with the studies reporting high degrees of bisexual feelings and behavior among homosexuals, corroborate the notion that "gay" is a residual category in this culture. In general, we can assume that self-label gives us less than a total picture of sexual orientation. In the same study, Nichols found that self-label correlated highly only with "behavior in the last year."

Interestingly, there is little or no data to confirm the popular view that women are more bisexual than men. It is true, however, that lesbians are more likely to have been married than gay men (Bell & Weinberg, 1978; Jay & Young, 1979; Masters & Johnson, 1979); but gay men tend to *stay* married longer than lesbian women and report more marital satisfaction (Bell & Weinberg, 1978). Thus, it appears that women are "less likely to behave sexually in accordance to their true interests" (Bell & Weinberg, 1978, p. 60), perhaps explaining findings of less bisexual and homosexual behavior in women and further complicating the clinical picture of sexual orientation for women.

What characterizes bisexuality in women, beyond data on incidence? How do bisexual men and women compare with one another? Most of what we know comes from research on *self-identified* bisexuals; this research is summarized well by Zinik (1985). He reports that:

1. Most bisexuals, whether male or female, first eroticize the opposite sex and identify as heterosexual, recognizing their homosexual interests in adulthood. However, some "life-long homosexuals" spontaneously develop heterosexual interests and become bisexual in mid-life. The incidence of this later phenomenon may be rising (Nichols & Paul, 1986).
2. Bisexual males and bisexual females both report similar levels of erotic excitement with male and female partners. However, both males and females report more emotional satisfaction with female partners.
3. Both male and female bisexuals report falling in love with women more often than with men, although many report falling in love with both genders. These data are interesting because they echo observations of many gay men, who say they are more *sexually* attracted to men but more emotionally attracted to women (and thus define their orientation on the basis of their *sexual* preference). And some lesbians, who say they are sexually attracted to men and women are emotionally satisfied by women (thus defining themselves by *emotional* preference).
4. Bisexual men report that their relationships with men are of shorter duration than their relationships with women. Bisexual women tend to have fewer but more lasting relationships with both women and men.
5. Many bisexuals report that they are attracted to qualities of particular people rather than to aspects of gender per se; they transcend gender. Blumstein and Schwartz (1977), however, state that their female subjects, in contrast to male subjects,

> more often report that they get different things from relationships with men and women.

A second source of information on bisexuality in women comes from studies of bisexual women in marriages. Both Coleman (1985) and Dixon (1985) found fewer than half of these women were aware of homosexual feelings prior to marriage. Many appeared to make dramatic swings in Kinsey ratings of both behavior and fantasy over the course of the marriage. These findings cast doubt upon the widely held belief in the inflexibility of sexual orientation and attraction over a lifetime. For some women, at least, not only behavior but attraction and fantasy can be quite fluid and changeable with time. The Dixon data are particularly interesting. In her sample of women in "swinging" marriages, few subjects reported homoerotic fantasies or attractions before engaging in lesbian activities during "swinging" scenes, but most reported such fantasies and attractions *after* pleasurable lesbian sex. It seems then, for some women, fantasy can follow pleasurable behavior rather than be an antecedent to it.

What begins to emerge from studies of bisexuality in women is that there are a number of very different *patterns* of bisexuality. Some of these patterns are as follows:

1. Most bisexual women move from a heterosexual to a bisexual orientation. However, given the fact that women seem less likely than men to actualize their sexual inclinations, it is not always easy to determine the meaning of this transition. For some women who married for reasons purely of social conformity, the bisexual self-identification may be a "shield" for a truer identification as an exclusive lesbian. For other women, it may be an acknowledgement of bisexual feelings that have existed all along but have previously been unacknowledged. Some of this latter group may prefer eventually to identify as lesbian, or to only act upon their lesbian attractions, for reasons related to the quality of their *emotional* relationships with women, despite a substantial or even greater erotic attraction to men. These women can be considered to have genuinely "chosen" a lesbian lifestyle. Some of them frame their choice in feminist political terms, and have sometimes been called "political lesbians":

> Women who come to lesbianism through radical feminism reject the notion that lesbianism is a sexual identity. This is not to say that sexual expression is usually absent in the new gay woman's lives; rather, sexual activity is for them generally only one aspect and perhaps a relatively unimportant aspect of their commitment to a lesbian lifestyle. Lesbianism in this context, or, more precisely, lesbian-feminism, is defined as a political choice more than a sexual preference. (Faderman, 1986, p. 86)

2. Still other women who move from a heterosexual to a bisexual orientation genuinely become aware of the homosexual component to their bisexuality only in adulthood, after marriage, perhaps only after a homosexual erotic experience. These women seem to be fairly fluid in their sexual attractions and fantasies.

3. A smaller number of women identify as bisexual after a lesbian identification. Some of these women, like the women described in (2) above, seem to have developed heterosexual attractions only after a lifetime of primarily homosexual attractions. Many more of them are probably women who always experienced bisexual erotic attractions but self-identified as lesbian for emotional/relationship reasons, for political motives, and/or because of the perceived absence of a bisexual "category" and community.

4. Many women continue to self-identify as heterosexual or lesbian despite conscious awareness of bisexual feelings, for reasons of social pressure. These women may never choose to act upon the aspect of their erotic attractions that does not conform to their self-label or, if they do, will act upon these feelings only in secrecy and possibly with much internal conflict, guilt, and shame.

5. Some women express their bisexuality in the form of serial monogamy with alternating gender of partner, a pattern that has occasionally been observed (Nichols & Paul, 1986). The explanation for this is unclear. It may reflect a true transcendence of gender. Alternately, for bisexual women who view their relationships with women as substantially different in nature from their relationships with men, it may reflect different personal needs at different stages of the life cycle. For example, it has been observed that female-female pairings seem to be more intensely intimate than fe-

male-male or male-male pairings. Thus, varying gender choice may reflect different needs for intimacy versus autonomy; or it may represent varying desires for similarity versus difference in a partner.

6. Some women may express their bisexuality by only having sex with one gender and full relationships with the other. For example, some women enter into couple relationships with men but have sexual "flings" with women. While some self-identified lesbians may have sex with men but only with to enter relationships with women.

7. Some women assume that their bisexuality automatically involves non-monogamy. These women are perhaps more likely to be women who view their relationships with men and women as substantially different in nature, and feel a need for both in order to be "fulfilled." Other women see the issues of monogamy and bisexuality as unrelated.

THE MEANING OF THE DATA

It should be clear by now that the term "bisexuality" covers a very diverse and only partially understood group of phenomena. It must also be clear that it is impossible to divorce the various aspects of bisexual attraction—especially of bisexual behavior and identity—from their social and political underpinnings, just as it is impossible to divorce lesbianism or, for that matter, heterosexuality in women from the social fabric from which these roles, behaviors, and identities emerge (Nichols & Leiblum, 1986).

On the most obvious level, the absence of social supports for a bisexual identity certainly impeded self-identification as bisexual, probably inhibits behavioral expression of bisexual attractions, and possibly serves to block conscious awareness of bisexual feelings. The heterosexist bias and strong homophobic messages of our culture act to prevent many people from actualizing any homosexual component of their sexuality. The Gay and Lesbian Liberation Movement, so crucial in combatting heterosexism has, in the process, done a disservice to bisexuals. When gay and lesbian activists claim bisexuality to be fraudulent or as no more than denied homosexuality, when they denounce self-identified bisexuals as traitors to the community, or when they rush to claim every woman who has experienced same-sex feelings or a same-sex affair as "really" a lesbian (e.g., Joan Baez, Margaret Mead, Eleanor Roosevelt), they perpetrate upon women the exact mirror of the oppression women experience from the heterosexual mainstream. Under these circumstances, it is not surprising that many women suppress their bisexuality, cloak it in secrecy, or experience personal conflict. To claim an identity as bisexual in our current culture is to isolate oneself in a grey area where little sense of community or support exists. It is not surprising that, despite data that consistently suggest that bisexuality is more prevalent than exclusive homosexuality, there are far fewer self-labeled bisexuals than homosexuals or heterosexuals. One would predict that, if cultural sanction for bisexuality increases, the numbers of identified bisexuals will also increase, with a substantial proportion of these individuals coming from within the gay and lesbian communities.

An examination of the complex forms of bisexuality also yields a more subtle understanding of the interactions of social factors and sexual orientation. Many of these social factors relate to sexism and the ways in which men and women are differently conditioned. For example, the interesting finding that both male and female bisexuals report better relationships with women and relationships of longer duration may well be related to women's socialization towards intimacy and valuing intimate relationships. When bisexuals report viewing their relationships with men and women as different in nature, these differences are probably social in origin. Women who are bisexual in erotic attraction but actively choose to engage in lesbian relationships are doing so for reasons that are, at their root, political. It is not only true that socio-political conditions determine who will express their bisexuality and how those bisexual attractions will be experienced, interpreted, and manifested; it is also the case that the study of bisexuality can teach us a great deal about the social construction of gender.

> This are of investigation—looking at how homosexuals, heterosexuals and bisexuals experience same-sex and other-sex relationships—seems rich in the possibilities for elucidating the role of gender socialization in human relationships. Bisexuals who have experienced male and female sexual relations and intimacy may hold a key to our understanding of differ-

ences in male-male, male-female, and female-female pairings. (Nichols & Paul, 1986, p. 6)

CLINICAL ISSUES: WORKING WITH BISEXUAL WOMEN

The multiplicity of ways in which bisexuality is expressed implies that therapeutic interventions must be greatly tailored to the individual case. Let us consider here not only women who self-label as bisexual but also those who exhibit bisexual feelings, fantasies, attractions, and/or behaviors while self-labeling as heterosexual, homosexual, or "confused."

Therapists who are experienced in working with individuals who are gay or lesbian and engaged in the "coming out" process will recognize many of the clinical issues described here as parallels to the processes of identity conflict and identity integration that lesbian women undergo.

Successful therapy with bisexual women must begin, as with lesbian women, with examination of whether the bisexuality is a clinical issue. Just as there has often been a tendency for heterosexually biased therapists to assume that homosexuality is a therapeutic issue for all gay and lesbian clients, many therapists may assume that bisexuality is a clinical concern for all bisexuals. Some bisexuals enter treatment with no conflict about their orientation; the first order of business for a therapist working with a woman who displays a bisexual identity, behavior, or attraction is to determine whether the client herself considers her sexual orientation in any way worthy of discussion.

For those women who report a need to work on issues of sexual identity, a detailed sexual/relationship history is essential. Such a psycho-sexual inventory would include answers to the following questions:

1. What is the client's history of the emergence and expression of both heterosexual and homoerotic fantasy, attractions, and behavior, including masturbation fantasies and limerant experiences?
2. What is the relative *power* of homo- verses hetero-erotic at-

tractions? Does one seem more primary than the other? Have attractions and behavior remained consistent over time, or have they varied over the life history of the client? Most importantly, what are the recent experiences of the client, and is some future direction suggested?

3. How have homo- and hetero-attractions and experiences differed from each other qualitatively? Is one more sexual and another more limerant or emotional in nature? Is one type of experience more personally satisfying than another? Have her major relationships been heterosexual, homosexual, or both, and what has been her experience of these relationships?
4. What meaning does the client attach to these experiences? Is one orientation more ego-dystonic or ego-syntonic than another?
5. What social supports does the client have for a bisexual identity? Has she revealed her bisexuality to others? If she has not, what sexual orientation does she claim socially? Such self-labeling may reveal internalized homophobia or heterophobia. For example, a woman may claim only a heterosexual or homosexual identity, or she may differentially label herself with different people, e.g., claiming to be lesbian with lesbians and straight or bisexual with heterosexuals.
6. If she has not fully integrated a bisexual identity, what would it mean to her life if she did? Is she prepared to deal with the issues she would face if she changed her behavior or self-label? Is this a goal of treatment?

Clinicians not experienced in dealing with gay and lesbian clients might consult the writings of gay and lesbian therapists and theorists on gay and lesbian identity formation. Cass (1979), for example, has formulated a stage model of homosexual identity which is a classic and quite translatable to bisexual terms. In Cass's model, the client's personal journey of identity integration begins when she perceives that her behavior/feelings are discrepant from her self-perception; Cass assumes that, in this culture, all people start from a base of a heterosexual self-identification (though that self-identification may begin to be disrupted in childhood). For example, a child or adolescent may begin to recognize homosexual attractions, which are almost inevitably at first ego-dystonic. The journey to self-integration includes information-seeking behavioral exploration, the need for social supports, and self-revelation, and invariably includes periods of defensive strategies that seek to deny, compartmentalize, or repress certain aspects of self.

Transposing this model to bisexual identity, one sees that many variations are possible. Some women may move from a heterosexual to a bisexual identity and comfortably remain there. Other women will move from a heterosexual, to a bisexual and eventually a lesbian identity; still others will perceive themselves as heterosexual, then lesbian, then bisexual. When dealing with women undergoing a second major transformation of sexual identity, it is clinically helpful to point this out to the client. A woman who has self-identified as lesbian, for example, and is currently struggling to understand attractions to men, can be reminded of the process she went through when "coming out" as lesbian. As she notices the similarities in process, she can access past experiences and past skills to help her with her current situation. One conflict often experienced by some women who undergo a second sexual identity reorganization is the feeling of an almost schizophrenic-like sense of personal discontinuity. Such clients can be helped by pointing out aspects of their life that represent ongoing continuity rather than cataclysmic change.

Perhaps the single most important thing a therapist can do for bisexual women clients is to validate the concept of bisexuality and give information. This can be important even for women whose bisexual component seems rather insignificant. For example, many primarily heterosexual or primarily homosexual women have bisexual fantasies; i.e., lesbian or heterosexual erotic fantasies, respectively. For women still in the grip of dualistic notions of sexual orientation, it can be reassuring for the therapist to explain bisexuality in terms of the Kinsey Scale continuum. In this situation, while it is of course important to point out that fantasy or attraction does not inevitably lead to behavior change, it is equally important not to minimize the potential significance of such attractions. Given the fluidity of some women's sexual orientation, one cannot assume that a fantasy will always remain a fantasy. The "heterosexual" woman of today may choose to actualize her lesbian fantasies tomorrow.

For the women whose bisexuality is more than incidental or takes a form greater than mere fantasy, validation and information from the therapist is even more important. The therapist may be the only person in the client's social system who corroborates even the existence of bisexuality as a sexual identity, so he/she must be able to provide unwavering support as well as information that may include reading material and access to support groups, bisexual organizations, and bisexual newsletters (two of which are produced by the Boston Bisexual Women's Collective and the Chicago Bisexual Women's Network).

Some therapeutic issues that may need to be addressed, in addition to those mentioned above, are enumerated in Lourea's article on counseling bisexuals (1985). The special edition of the *Journal of Homosexuality* in which this article and others mentioned herein can be found also contains a bibliography on bisexuality (Stein, 1985). Some of the problems bisexuals may encounter are, for example, dealing with potential partners who may be homophobic, heterophobic, or "biphobic," grappling with the role that monogamy versus non-monogamy plays in their bisexuality, deciding when and how to "come out" about their bisexuality to friends, family, and associates, and, for some, considering the implications of their bisexuality for current marriages or love relationships. Women who have previously identified as heterosexual need to deal with many of the same issues that lesbians face, as they confront the "gay side" of their personalities. Women who have previously identified as lesbian often experience guilt and a sense of having betrayed their community. In addition, many women who have lived an open lesbian lifestyle, especially those with a feminist background, experience a profound "culture shock" when they find themselves relating to men again and having to deal with sexism, inequality in relationships, and traditional role expectations. Although they may find sex with men exciting and fulfilling, and although they may enjoy the greater sense of differentness and autonomy they experience with men, they can feel frustrated or even hopeless about finding a man with whom they can have a truly equal relationship.

SIX CASE VIGNETTES

In order to illustrate some of the clinical issues faced when counseling bisexual women, six case vignettes are offered below.

Susan is a forty-two-year-old owner of her own business, married for sixteen years at the time she entered therapy. While she immediately identified herself as bisexual to her therapist, she also indicated that her bisexuality was not a source of personal concern. She had sought out a clinician she believed to be lesbian precisely because she did *not* want her bisexual activity to become a focus of treatment. This activity took the form of occasional "three way" sexual encounters between herself, her husband, and various other women. These liaisons usually lasted for a few months, with no lesbian activity taking place outside the context of the *menage*, after which Susan reported that the relationships between her and the third woman usually evolved into friendships. Susan maintained that she had never fallen in love with a woman and that she had no inclination to pursue her "lesbian side" further. At her request, her bisexuality was not discussed as a clinical issue, despite some suggestion that she manifested a certain degree of internalized homophobia (for example, she told no one of her bisexual encounters and somewhat irrationally believed that her business would be destroyed should word ever "leak out"). At the time of this writing, Susan was grappling with marital conflict partially complicated by her affair with another man. Her bisexuality did not appear to be a factor in her marital discord. It is not inconceivable that should Susan separate from her husband she might choose to explore lesbian relationships a bit further, although there is no indication of this at the present time.

Alice was a thirty-five-year-old suburban housewife with three children at the time she entered treatment for what she reported as sexual identity confusion. Although her behavior was bisexual, a sexual history revealed little or no heteroerotic component despite her marriage, and a recognition of lesbian attractions and furtive affairs since adolescence. She was blocked in fully expressing her lesbianism by considerable internalized homophobia, a lifetime of trying to be a "good girl," and realistic fears of losing custody of her children. In addition, she quite liked her "Princess" lifestyle and had very substantial fears of independence and of having to take care of herself without the financial support of a man. Eventually, however, she decided to give up the Gilded Cage and now identified exclusively as a lesbian.

Helen was a forty-year-old self-identified lesbian at the time she entered therapy for reasons unrelated to her sexual identity. Until her mid-thirties, her attractions, fantasy, and behavior were all entirely heterosexual. At the age of thirty-six, after fifteen years of a dismal marriage and four children, she joined a local feminist organization and quite spontaneously fell in love with another woman who was a member of the group. Within a year, she left her marriage and began to live with this woman. At the time of treatment, she reported a mixture of hetero- and homo erotic attractions and fantasies. However, she considered herself a lesbian for emotional and political reasons and quite adamantly maintained that she would never again act upon her heterosexual impulses; she says she's "had it" with men. Some time in therapy was spent in helping her integrate her heterosexual attractions with her lesbian identity. She currently maintains an exclusively lesbian lifestyle and self-label.

Lisa is a thirty-three-year-old self-identified lesbian. Her sexual history reveals a mixture of hetero- and homo erotic attractions, behavior, and fantasies, however, she only falls in love with women, and all her relationships have been with women. Within the last year she separated from a female lover of nine years. She currently has sex with both men and women. However, she explicitly seeks out men because, she says, she can have sex with men without becoming emotionally involved. During this time of healing her wounds from her broken relationship, she feels she sometimes needs what she sees as the "safe" sexual outlets of men. Although her therapist sometimes uses the term "bisexual" to describe her behavior, Lisa rejects this label as a self-identification. She defines her identity on the basis of her limerant attractions, rather than sexual impulses or behavior.

Diane is a thirty-year-old self-labeled bisexual. Married to the same man since the age of eighteen, with a three-year-old child, Diane first became aware of attractions to women in her early twenties. From the time she recognized these feelings, she was open with her husband and, with his knowledge, had several affairs with women. She is also quite open about her bisexuality with others and is active in a local bisexual organization. Her current attractions and fantasies are quite mixed. She is confused, however, about how to "manage" her bisexuality. She experiences her relationships with women as different from her relationships with men. While she has had a number of lesbian relationships, her husband was her first and remains her only male partner, so she is unclear about whether her experience of "differentness" in relationships is related to gender or simply to the quality of her marriage (she describes the difference as feeling closer and more intimate with women than with her spouse). The "open marriage," which has included three-way affairs, has created problems for her and her husband. She is inclined to monogamy at the moment, yet yearns for a relationship with a woman. She is not sure whether her dissatisfaction with her marriage is a by-product of unfulfilled bisexuality or is simply a function of the perceived lack of intimacy with her spouse. She is very much in flux regarding her future lifestyle, but has a clear sense of personal identity. Diane feels she will always remain bisexual whether she is monogamous or non-monogamous and regardless of the gender of her partner of the moment.

Amy is a twenty-seven-year-old who now considers herself bisexual. During high school she experienced heterosexual attractions and had the usual round of boyfriends and heterosexual dates, including some heterosexual sexual experience. Early in her college career, she met lesbians through her feminist activities and became aware of attractions to women. She fell in love with and lived with a woman, identified herself as lesbian, and became open and active in the lesbian-feminist community. She always maintained both hetero- and homoerotic attractions and defined herself as a "political lesbian" who had chosen lesbianism consciously. In law school, she fell in love with a male fellow student while still living with her female lover; she had been experiencing problems in her lesbian relationship for quite some time. She entered treatment at this time in considerable conflict. Amy deliberately chose an open lesbian therapist. In addition to experiencing guilt over what she considered her betrayal of her female lover, she felt a profound sense that she had "abandoned" and "betrayed" the lesbian community. In fact, she experienced substantial rejection from her lesbian friends, and felt very isolated, yet she was appalled at the idea of joining the heterosexual mainstream. It was very important to her that her lesbian therapist accepted her bisexuality; this was a major validation of Amy's identity. A turning point in treatment came when Amy realized that some of her guilt stemmed from the fact that she had never "come out" as lesbian to her parents. Since she had introduced her current boyfriend to her parents, they assumed she was straight. Much of her conflict was reduced when she "came out" as bisexual to her family. She left her female lover and married the boyfriend, but became active in forming the first women's bisexual support group in the area. Her marriage is monogamous but, like Diane, she considers her bisexual identity to be independent of the gender of her partner. She and her husband have just had their first child.

CONCLUSION

We have seen here that bisexuality is a complex, multifaceted phenomenon, and that many types of bisexuality exist in women. In many ways, the best preparation a clinician can have for working with bisexual women is prior experience working with lesbians. Therapists, however, must have themselves gone beyond a dualistic view of sexual orientation and have gained more sophisticated appreciation of the variability of sexuality from woman to woman and, indeed, within one woman over the course of a lifetime. In a culture that, at worst, allows women only a heterosexual option and, at best, acknowledges two options – heterosexual or lesbian – the most important function a clinician can fill is that of validating the existence of bisexuality.

REFERENCES

Bell, A.P., & Weinberg, M.S. (1978). *Homosexualities: A study of diversity among men and women*. New York: Simon & Schuster.

Blumstein, P.W., & Schwartz, P. (1977). Bisexuality: Some social psychological issues. *Journal of Social Issues, 33*(2), 30-45.

Califia, P. (1983). A secret side of lesbian sexuality. *S and M: Studies in sado-*

masochism. Ed. by Weinberg, T. & Levi Kamel, G.W., Buffalo, N.Y.: Prometheus Books.

Cass, V. (1979). Homosexual identity formation: A theoretical model. *Journal of Homosexuality, 4*, 219-233.

Coleman, E. (1985). Bisexual women in marriages. *Journal of Homosexuality, 11*(1/2), 87-99.

Coons, F.W. (1972). Ambisexuality as an alternative adaptation. *Journal of the American College Health Association, 21*, 142-144.

Dixon, J.K. (1985). Sexuality and relationship changes in married females following the commencement of bisexual activity. *Journal of Homosexuality, 11*(1/2), 115-133.

Faderman, L. (1981). *Surpassing the love of men: Romantic friendships and love between women from the Renaissance to the present.* New York: William Morrow.

Hanson, C.E., & Evans, A. (1985). Bisexuality reconsidered: An idea in pursuit of a definition. *Journal of Homosexuality, 11*(1/2), 1-6.

Hunt, M. (1974). *Sexual behavior in the 1970s*. Chicago: Playboy Press.

Hyde, J.S. (1982). *Understanding human sexuality*. New York: McGraw Hill.

Jay, K., & Young, A. (1979). *The gay report*. New York: Summit.

Klein, F. (1980). Are you sure you're heterosexual? Or homosexual? Or even bisexual? *Forum Magazine*, 41-45.

Klein, F., Sepekoff, B., & Wolf, T.J. (1985). Sexual orientation: A multi-variable dynamic process. *Journal of Homosexuality, 11*(1/2), 35-50.

Klein, F., & Wolf, T.J. (1985). Bisexualities: Theory and research. *Journal of Homosexuality, 11*(1/2).

Lourea, D.N. (1985). Psycho-social issues related to counseling bisexuals. *Journal of Homosexuality, 11*(1/2), 51-62.

Masters, W.H., & Johnson, V.E. (1979). *Homosexuality in perspective*. Boston: Little, Brown & Co.

Nichols, M. (1985). *Relationships between sexual behavior, erotic arousal, romantic attraction, and self-labeled sexual orientation*. Presented at SSSS conference, San Diego, September, 1985.

Nichols, M., & Leiblum, S. (1986). Lesbianism as personal identity and social role: A model affilia. *Journal of Women and Social Work, 1*(1), 48-60.

Nichols, M., & Paul, J. (1986). *Patterns of bisexuality: Separating fact from biphobic fiction.* Unpublished paper.

Stein, A. (1985). A bibliography on bisexuality. *Journal of Homosexuality, 11*(1/2), 235-248.

Zinik, G. (1983). *The relationship between sexual orientation and eroticism, cognitive flexibility, and negative affect*. Unpublished doctoral dissertation, University of California, Santa Barbara, Ca.

Zinik, G. (1985). Identity conflict or adaptive flexibility? Bisexuality reconsidered. *Journal of Homosexuality, 11*(1/2), 7-20.

Issues in Sex Therapy with Survivors of Intrafamily Sexual Abuse

Linda J. Weiner

Clinicians working with women who are survivors of childhood sexual abuse have described a variety of disturbing long-term effects, including depression, "self-destructive tendencies," anxiety disorders, eating disorders, disassociation, feelings of isolation and stigmatization, negative self-concept, inability to trust which results in difficulty forming and maintaining healthy intimate relationships, chemical abuse, and increased likelihood of revictimization through vulnerability to later assault, all too often at the hands of physically and/or sexually violent husbands or lovers. (Note: many clinicians believe that the diagnosis of post-traumatic stress disorder is an appropriate diagnosis to describe the constellation of "symptoms" observed in these survivors.) Perhaps one of the most widely reported negative effects is the potential impact of early sexual abuse on adult sexuality, with numerous nonclinical studies noting a tendency toward later sexual problems among child sexual abuse survivors (Briere & Runtz, 1985; Finkelhor, 1979; Russell, 1986).

CHARACTERISTICS OF SEXUAL ASSAULT AND SEXUAL DYSFUNCTION

It appears that intrafamily sexual abuse survivors, especially when the perpetrator is a father or father figure, may be at greater risk for subsequent sexual difficulties than survivors of other forms of sexual assault. A recent study comparing the incidence and types

---

Linda J. Weiner, MSW, is Director of the Child Sexual Abuse Treatment Program and a sex therapist and researcher at the Masters and Johnson Institute in St. Louis, MO.

of sexual dysfunctions in survivors of rape and intrafamily sexual abuse ("incest") by Becker, Skinner, Abel, Axelrod, and Cichon (1984) seems to confirm the results of other studies, indicating that women whose assault history included incest were more likely to experience assault-related sexual problems than were survivors with no history of incest. While incest in the Becker study was defined as sexual abuse by a family member, other studies (Russell, 1986; Finkelhor, 1979; Briere and Runtz, 1985) have found that sexual abuse by a father or stepfather was significantly more traumatic than abuse occurring either inside or outside the family. Thus, we can expect that adult survivors of sexual abuse by a father or stepfather would be at greater risk of developing sexual difficulties. The greater risk is postulated to result from the more chronic nature of the abuse, the internalization of guilt and shame, the betrayal engendered by sexual abuse by a trusted caretaker, and the lack of support and protection from other family members.

ANALYSIS OF SEXUAL DIFFICULTIES

A review of the literature reflects the following sexual problems as experienced by adult survivors: fear of sex, including phobic response to perceived sexual situations (sexual aversion); inhibited sexual desire; inability to experience sexual arousal; lack of subjective pleasure or satisfaction from sexual response (including orgasm); avoidance of being touched; disgust or revulsion about their own bodies as well as those of their partner's; low sexual self-esteem; primary and secondary anorgasmia; inability to tolerate genital touching with preference for and responsivity to intercourse; compulsive desire for sex; and potential for resolution of feelings of powerlessness by becoming, themselves, sexual abusers of children. It is not unusual for an individual survivor to experience multiple sexual difficulties.

A study by Becker, Skinner, Abel and Treacy (1982), comparing the incidence and types of sexual dysfunction in rape and intrafamily sexual abuse ("incest") survivors indicated the following: Of the nine types of sexual problems identified, incest survivors ranked as suffering from: (1) fear of sex – 75%; (2) arousal dysfunction – 41.7%; (3) desire dysfunction – 33.3%; (4) secondary non-anorgasmia–33.3%; (5) primary non-anorgasmia–8.3%; and, other sexual problems–8.3%. One need only examine the percentages of sexual problems in each category to note the extraordinary disruption in the first stages of the sexual response cycle. Inhibition of receptivity to sexual opportunity, and/or inability to take in sexual stimulation with positive attribution results in desire phase disorders which may or may not interfere with the survivor's physiological responses (orgasmic component). Arousal difficulties may result when a survivor perceives sexual stimuli as anxiety-provoking and subsequently relabels her sexual feelings as reduced or absent altogether. This conditioned fear which reduces perception of sexual feelings may result in significant disruptions in a survivor's sexual functioning.

THE GROWTH OF TREATMENT SERVICES

Treatment services for adult survivors has greatly expanded in the past five years in response to the large number of women coming forward as the taboo against "sharing the secret" has diminished. Numerous rape and sexual assault treatment centers have modified their approach for the treatment of adults molested as children, including the expansion of group treatment services, a modality which provides support, reduces the sense of isolation and shame, and empowers women by actively engaging them in the resolution of their struggle for emotional well-being. However, subsequent to treatment, many women find that their sexual dysfunctions and difficulties remain, and additional treatment by a professional skilled in the techniques of sex therapy appear warranted.

It is my impression that the most effective treatment for sexual difficulties is contingent upon the survivor having worked through the more cogent issues associated with the sexual abuse by family members, including recognition of her feelings of anger and betrayal, and acknowledging, if not internalizing, that she was not to blame. In addition, the other two requirements for effective intervention in resolution of sexual difficulties appear to be the absence of severely limiting difficulties (major depression, psychosis, etc.), and involvement in a noncoercive relationship. Assuming these three conditions have been met, the following relates to some special issues for consideration in treatment of sexual difficulties.

SPECIAL ISSUES

Motivation for Treatment

All too often the survivor's motivation for treatment is based upon her guilt about denying her partner a fully satisfying sexual relationship, fears of divorce and/or emotional abandonment. Obviously, these rationales for treatment are reminiscent of the coercive elements in her victimization and confirm the frequently internalized message that sex is to be exchanged for love, security and acceptance, or that access to her body is something a woman provides for the benefit of a man. Obviously, with the help of the therapist, the survivor must explore what there might be of benefit to her in resolution of the sexual difficulties. The concept of entitlement to sexual pleasure and satisfaction for the woman is often a totally alien concept.

Partner Response

One of the most important factors in the effective treatment of sexually dysfunctional survivors of intrafamily sexual abuse is the cooperative participation of a supportive sexual partner who neither over protects nor pressures his partner (relevant for both gender; however, my discussion will focus on male partners due to significantly more experience with heterosexual couples). Whether or not a male partner has previously been informed of the abusive history, induction into therapy may trigger or rekindle similar responses. Often partners feel anger in response to their powerlessness to have intervened (to have protected the survivor from abuse); they may become consumed with thoughts of retribution; they may express resentment of their partner's seeming calm and may become angry with her for her perceived "lack of outrage . . . "; all of which only serves to destabilize their partners emotionally. Sometimes partners are angry not only at the perpetrator for the anguish caused the partner, but also because, as a result of the abuse, they themselves feel robbed of a full sexual relationship. Feelings of guilt are often engendered by their perception of their own selfishness. Another frequently encountered response is the partner's questioning of the survivor's complicity in the sexual activity and either implicit or direct blame of the partner for her "failure" to avoid and/or stop the abuse. Some men, without a great deal of insight into the emotional dynamics of abuse, may simply admonish their partner to stop making so much of this, expecting her to "move on" in recognition that the "past is gone." Some partners are hurt and angry that the survivor does not seem to be able to differentiate between him and the abuser in the context of the sexual encounter. In some situations the male partner may be traumatized by his partner's residual behavior patterns and sexual difficulties such that inhibited sexual desire or impotence may develop to complicate the picture.

The involvement of the partner in therapy aimed at providing individual support while facilitating his understanding of the dynamics of the survivor's trauma is critical.

Trust and Vulnerability

One of the most traumatic repercussions of early sexual abuse by family members is that the child's trust and vulnerability has been manipulated by those who were supposed to provide care and protection. For therapy to be effective, the issue of trust between client and therapist, between the woman and her partner, as well as her trust in her own feelings and perceptions, must be consistently explored and encouraged throughout the course of treatment. Allowing oneself to be sexual with another person always involves a high degree of vulnerability. Such a level of vulnerability may produce severe levels of anxiety for an individual who has experienced sexual abuse at the hands of trusted family members.

Powerlessness and Control

One of the major issues for women whose body territory has been repeatedly invaded in a situation in which she felt unable to protect herself is the development of a sense of powerlessness in subsequent sexual situations. Previous attempts to cope with a situation in which she felt no control often involved disassociating from what was occurring ("I couldn't stop him from using my body but my mind was somewhere else") or later, by avoiding sexual thought, feelings, or situations altogether. The anxiety which may be experienced at the initiation of sex therapy comes, in part, from the woman's sense of powerlessness and fear, especially as she understands the need to give up her previous coping mechanisms of avoidance and disassociation.

Thus, at the onset of therapy, the woman must be given full control of the initiation, timing, pace, and cessation of each sensual encounter and must also have the privilege of deciding when she is ready to move on to the next suggestion in what amounts to a systematic desensitization experience through the medium of sensate focus (a structured hierarchy of sensual opportunities). The survivor is the expert on how much anxiety or discomfort she can tolerate before termination of the sensate opportunity. At the same time, she must be prepared to experience some anxiety at each therapeutic stage. This is particularly true as issues associated with the sexual abuse are often buried or forgotten until a particular touch, interaction or feeling facilitates a resurfacing of the issue which must then be dynamically addressed.

The survivor is taught to master barriers both inside and outside the bedroom through expression of feelings, use of relaxation techniques, visualization, cognitive reframing, and learning to refocus on sensation, as well as through other techniques employed in sex therapy. A delicate therapeutic balance must be struck between coddling and permitting the woman to move at her own pace. She must be supported and encouraged, and she must come to recognize that courage is not the absence of fear, but the mastery of it. At each stage, as the woman masters her anxiety, moves ahead and experiences either a neutral or positive outcome, she is empowered, her self-esteem increases, and her natural responsivity is reconstituted. Eventually the woman is encouraged to experiment with turning over initiation of sexual activity to her partner with the understanding that she is always in control, and that being in control does not necessarily mean controlling.

Repression of Memory/Guilt

For some women sexual abuse conditions a fear response paired to sexual activity. For others who were sexually abused without the experience of pain or fear (and often the abuse occurred prior to recognition of the meaning of the experience), extreme guilt associated with their pleasure or responsivity may result in repression of the experience. Many women presenting for sex therapy are consciously unaware of their abusive experiences, having repressed the memory for other reasons which are often more available to conscious awareness when "breakthrough" occurs in the course of sensate focus opportunities. For women who have experienced sexual pleasure, extreme feelings of horror and guilt may be engendered. The resolution of this guilt is subsequently effected by disallowing the experience of pleasure in the sexual interaction, or by allowing themselves to experience pleasure up to the point of orgasm. At this juncture, at high levels of arousal, the woman will experience a high degree of anxiety and/or will "shut down" through distraction or disassociation. Experiencing sexual pleasure or allowing themselves to respond to orgasm is threatening because it may engender recall of their past pleasure which results in the resurfacing of guilt. In order to assist in therapy, it is critical that the woman be made acutely aware of the link between her current reactions and past experience, thus affording the opportunity to restructure her attitudes, beliefs and experiences.

CASE EXAMPLE

The following case example is presented in order to illustrate many of the dynamics of work with adult survivors of intrafamily sexual abuse. While there were also some significant marital and developmental issues addressed in the therapy, for purposes of clarity and brevity, these issues will not be fully discussed. A complicating factor in this case which should be noted, as well, is that at the time of therapy, Barbara was consciously unaware of early sexual molestation by her father.

Capsule Summary

Barbara and David, both in their early twenties, presented to the Institute for two-week, intensive sex therapy with the complaint of rapid ejaculation and primary anorgasmia. They had been childhood sweethearts who married several years before when Barbara became pregnant. The unplanned pregnancy appears to have been a very traumatic event for Barbara, in that she had been planning to complete high school and attend college. Her decision to marry rather than proceed with her career left her feeling angry and emotionally alienated toward her husband, who was unaware of the conflict she experienced about the decision.

During the initial interview Barbara described a generalized history of sexual inhibition, including discomfort with nudity, with her own genitals, and with the thought of masturbation. She also suffered from an extreme sense of propriety, feeling discomfort, for example, with public displays of affection.

Barbara characterized the sexual relationship prior to marriage as highly sexually stimulating although she was unable to be orgasmic, ostensively because her husband ejaculated rapidly and also because the type of stimulation she found most arousing would result in her bleeding rather profusely. (The stimulation she described involved her husband moving her uterus violently back and forth with his fingers.) Subsequent to the marriage, when issues such as lack of privacy and fear of being caught by parents were not paramount, no improvement was noted in their sexual relationship. Indeed, the unplanned pregnancy and subsequent move to another city as a result of her husband's employment left Barbara with a loss of environmental supports and a sense of hopelessness which turned to depression, further removing her from interest in, and response to, sexual stimulation. The couple's sexual interaction was reduced to approximately one to two times a month during which time Barbara "felt nothing" and engaged in the sexual activity merely to "fulfill her role and obligation as a wife."

Subsequent to the birth of their daughter, the sexual relationship continued to decline with Barbara moving from infrequent sexual contact in the service of her husband to total sexual withdrawal. At the point Barbara began to experience sexual thoughts and feelings toward another man, she began to question whether or not she loved her husband and withdrew from the marriage, although contact was maintained. Happening upon Masters and Johnson's *Human Sexual Inadequacy*, the couple felt there might be some hope to rectify the marriage if David's rapid ejaculation could be brought under control.

It was only upon questioning about possible inappropriate sexual contact in the family during history taking that Barbara offhandedly recalled that her father had fondled several of her girlfriends during a sleepover party when she was approximately eight-years-old and that she never again invited friends for the night. Delving deeper, Barbara was able to recall a vague memory of shouting "no" at her father but did not recall what prompted this response from her. She also recalled the time, subsequent to the birth of her daughter, that she experienced a panic attack upon leaving her young daughter in her father's care and rushed back to retrieve her. Despite these recollections, Barbara steadfastly asserted that she, herself, was never sexually abused by her father.

During the course of the first week of daily therapy, Barbara and David's relationship issues were uncovered and addressed and they were offered a number of tools to improve their verbal communication, negotiation and problem-solving skills. The couple was also involved in a series of structured sensate focus exercises, and individual assignments were given Barbara to explore her own sensuality and develop comfort and appreciation for her body. During the course of the first week of therapy, Barbara was able to resolve a great number of her sexual inhibitions and issues. These included concerns about nudity, taking sexual initiative, allowing herself to enjoy her husband stimulating himself to ejaculation without feeling the need to "service" him, learning about her own body through self-exploration, overcoming revulsion with her genitalia, learning to insert a diaphragm, allowing her husband to examine and become familiar with her genitals, learning to provide information about what she enjoyed sexually, and attempting a variety of sexual activities. During this time she also developed comfort and facility in employing the coronal squeeze technique to assist in reconditioning her husband's rapid ejaculatory pattern.

By the eighth session Barbara was able to experience sexual arousal which continued with regularity until she became quite close to orgasmic release on a couple of occasions via partner's manual stimulation at the vaginal outlet. However, Barbara reported that she was beginning to feel extremely tense throughout the touching opportunities, and at the juncture of being orgasmic, would simply stop her husband from continuing the stimulation that could possibly have resulted in her being orgasmic for the first time in memory. Barbara could offer no explanation as to why she was stopping the stimulation. Initially she felt it was because the stimulation was so intense that it was verging on pain. However, as we examined the issue more closely, it became increasingly apparent that her unidentified and unresolved issues around sexual abuse by her father were preventing her from allowing herself to be orgasmic.

A variety of suggestions were offered to assist Barbara in going beyond her tendency to stop herself from being orgasmic. Among the suggestions were for Barbara to focus in on the pleasurable feelings, to relabel the intense stimulation as pleasurable rather than as pain, to attempt to become more in control of the situation by "handriding" or alternating self-stimulation with partner stimulation, to maintain a more playful and neutral approach to the touching, to utilize sexual fantasies, etc. However, these suggestions proved ineffective in facilitating her responsivity and ultimately Barbara began experiencing a number of sexual dreams with the theme of victimization, loss of control, and powerlessness. At this juncture, Barbara began to accept the probability that molestation had occurred, representing the key to her sexual difficulties. She asked for our support in sharing her insights with her husband, who responded initially in an over-protective, but ultimately supportive way.

Over the course of the next several days, both Barbara and David were offered both individual and joint therapy sessions to assist them in grappling with the issues raised. During these days, Barbara required massive support from both her husband and the therapists as memories unfolded and anxiety, depression, and hurt feelings surfaced. Barbara struggled with the recognition that she *had* experienced genital fondling, resulting in orgasmic release with her father. Recognizing that this was socially unsanctioned behavior, she had "resolved" the emotional conflict by blocking memory of the abuse, as well as by disallowing herself from being orgasmic, fearing that this might trigger her recollection.

Again, during the next several sessions, therapy was focused on assisting Barbara to acknowledge the abuse, supporting expression of a range of emotions, and providing encouragement to deal with some of the primary issues such as sharing the secret with her mother and her absolute right to refuse to see her father until such time as she felt ready to do so.

At the termination of the two week intensive phase of therapy, the couple, who had continued to address their sexual issues at a pace and in a manner comfortable with Barbara's reactions and responses, reported that they had been able to have insertion for a fifteen minute period of time without David ejaculating. Both were delighted with the amount of ejaculatory control acquired. At this juncture, Barbara was encouraged to take care of her own needs and was given information on adjunct therapy options, including group therapy for adults molested as children. She was also given some suggested reading materials on incest, and encouraged to have regular follow-up telephone contact with us.

Over the course of the next several months, as Barbara participated in a therapy group for adults molested as children, she was able to work simultaneously on being able to confront her father, gain the support and understanding of her mother, learn to relate to her husband as a resource, and move ahead to acknowledge and fully experience her own sexuality. During this time, Barbara was able to learn to respond sexually to her husband and to be orgasmic with oral and manual stimulation.

CONCLUDING REMARKS

It is hoped that this review of the sexual and emotional difficulties and issues, frequently encountered in sex therapy with adult survivors of intrafamily sexual abuse, will prove helpful to those readers committed to assisting survivors in reaffirming their personhood through enjoyment rather than estrangement from their own bodies. While we must continue to resist the notion that sexual abuse of children of either sex is "expectable" and focus our energies on prevention, we must also commit our energies to assisting in repairing the damage done.

REFERENCES

Becker, J.V., Skinner, L.J., Abel, G.G., Axelrod & Cichon, J. (Winter, 1984). Sexual problems of sexual assault survivors. *Women & Health, 9*(4), 5-20.

Becker, J.V., Skinner, L.J., Abel, G.G., & Treacy, E.C. (Spring, 1982). Incidence and types of sexual dysfunctions in rape and incest victims. *Journal of Sex & Marital Therapy, 8*(1), 65-74.

Finkelhor, D. *A sourcebook on child sexual abuse*. Beverly Hills, CA: Sage Publications.

Gilbert, B. & Cunningham, J. (October, 1986). Women's postrape sexual functioning: Review and implications for counseling. *Journal of Counseling and Development, 65*, 71-73.

Masters, W.H. & Johnson, V.E. (1970). *Human sexual inadequacy*. Boston: Little, Brown and Company.

McGuire, L.S. & Wagner, N.N. (Spring, 1978). Sexual dysfunction in women who were molested as children: One response pattern and suggestions for treatment. *Journal of Sex and Marital Therapy, 4*(1), 11-15.

Divorced Women's Sexual and Contraceptive Issues

Norma J. Leslie

INTRODUCTION

> I can't believe it. My dreams are shattered. He wants a divorce but maybe I want one too. What will I do?—What will I become? I don't want to be in the dating scene again. Where do I begin to start over? Alone—my thoughts center momentarily on that word, a small word, yet so meaningful. A word that I have to define—to attach a meaning that makes sense to me. It is still in the embryo state—maybe it will become clearer to me as time passes. I just want someone to love me and tell me I'm o.k.
>
> Journal entry of a divorced woman, 1980

The United States has the highest divorce rate in the world at 5.1 per 1000 population (U.S. Bureau of the Census, 1983). Demographers say the increased number of divorces over the past twenty years is one of the most significant social changes in the United States. Although unanticipated and undesired in American lives, marital separation has become almost commonplace (Weiss, 1975). The National Center for Health Statistics projects that about half (49.6%) of all new marriages will end in divorce. It is estimated that over 49% of couples who married ten years ago will eventually divorce.

The number of U.S. households also rose by 58% between 1960

Norma J. Leslie, RNC, PhD, is on the faculty of the University of Oklahoma College of Medicine, Department of Obstetrics and Gynecology. She is the director of the Women's Health Education and Counseling Center and has a private practice, specializing in sex therapy, marital, and individual counseling.

and 1983 with non-traditional household types accounting for most of the increase. One-parent households increased by 175%; one-person households by 173%, and households composed of unmarried couples by 33%. Married couples account for only six in ten U.S. households. Adults living alone accounted for the second most common household type. Single parent households represent nearly one in ten households. Ten percent of single parent households are women who are separated or divorced. One-fourth of these have never been married, and fewer than one in ten of them are widows (Glick, 1984).

Divorce is the action that dissolves the legal relationship of marriage. Divorce affects every phase of life; altering sexual mores, the rearing of children, laws, economics, and the concept of marriage itself. Major adjustments have to be made; attitudes and behaviors will likely change. One of the most important changes is one's identity from "wife" to "single," and divorced. Bogue (1949) states:

> Few events in the life cycle require more extensive changes in activities, responsibilities, and living habits (or cause greater alterations in attitudes, re-ranking of values, and alteration of outlook on life) than does a change from one marital status to another. (p. 212)

Divorce supposedly creates an identity crisis, which results in separation distress, depression, loneliness, denial, and use of maladaptive coping mechanisms (Weiss, 1975). Vital to the task of developing an identity is knowledge of one's self as a sexual person. One of the difficulties facing the divorced single woman is reentry into the single world, sexual and contraceptive decisions and development of relationships. Could it be that through divorce a sense of alienation occurs which causes one to feel vulnerable and detached; making sexual decision-making and planning difficult?

SEXUAL AND CONTRACEPTIVE PATTERNS IN DIVORCED WOMEN

The previously married single woman has been in a marital relationship in which sex was available as needed. Society sanctions the marital relationship and expects her to plan her family. As her marital status changes, so do her sexual relationships. She is faced with many of the same conflicts as the young unmarried woman – guilt, planning for contraceptive use, and coming to terms with her sexual behavior.

Historically, little attention has been given to contraceptive use by the unmarried. Research reflected the widespread assumption that women generally did not have intercourse before marriage and, until recently, the subject was investigated only in connection with illegitimate pregnancy. As recently as 1969, Pohlman's authoritative review of the literature on birth planning contained no reference to unmarried users and cited the meager data on premarital contraceptive use. Gebhard (1958) states:

> Despite the fact that the proportion of women who have been separated or divorced has risen greatly in the twentieth century, virtually nothing has been known of their reproductive behavior during the time following the end of marriage and before marriage. Much of this lack of knowledge is due to a reluctance to face what many would consider an insolvable moral problem. One can find hundreds of articles in newspapers and magazines, and hundreds of chapters in marriage manuals directed at the woman who has yet to marry, but one has to search diligently to find discussions of sexual problems of the previously married woman. (p. 143)

Gebhard made the above observations 27 years ago, yet they are still true today. Most of the research is directed toward the unmarried adolescent and little toward women of older ages. Although books on "how to be single" have been written for the popular market, very little research has explored the divorced woman's sexual adjustment, contraceptive behavior, and dating patterns.

Clinical Observations

As a women's health care nurse practitioner and sex therapist, I observed a number of pregnant divorced women. In an obstetrical department at a large teaching hospital, I also completed a chart audit and found on a specific day there were 459 prenatal patients. Of that number, 28% were divorced. I then randomly interviewed several of these women regarding their pregnancy. The following statements were typical: "I don't know why I got pregnant, I just did," "I guess I thought I needed something to love," "I know I'm old enough to know better, I just didn't think I would get pregnant." Another said, "I just couldn't go to my gynecologist for birth control, he knows I'm not married." One said, "My gynecologist asked me why I needed birth control."

I began to realize that this is a group of women who have special needs, yet the health care profession is ignoring their problems. It also occurred to me that their sexual and contraceptive behaviors may be similar to that of adolescents.

These clinical observations, along with a lack of literature that describes sexual and contraceptive behaviors of single, divorced women led me to complete a research study that attempts to answer these questions.

Research Study

The purpose of this study was to search for answers to the problem of unplanned pregnancies, and to describe the needs of the divorced single woman as they relate to the psycho-social phenomena of sexual behavior and contraceptive practices. An additional purpose of this study was to increase the available knowledge related to divorced single women's characteristics, lifestyles, and adjustment to loss of spouse.

The study sample consisted of 101 sexually active, legally divorced, single women between the ages of 18 and 44 and physiologically capable of becoming pregnant. Within the overall sample, 53 had experienced a pregnancy after divorce and 48 had not.

Each woman was interviewed, given a questionnaire and Rosenberg's (1965) Self-Acceptance Scale, Snyder's (1974) Self-Monitoring Scale and Beckham's (1984) Coping Strategies Scale. This paper will describe the results as it relates to the respondent's dating, sexual, and contraceptive patterns.

Dating Patterns. The majority of both study groups (65%) had begun to date within six months of their divorce. A still higher proportion (80%) of both groups preferred to be monogamous in their dating and sexual relationships. Those who were not in a "significant relationship" at the time of interview reported the reason as not being able to "find a decent man" (80% of both groups). One said, "There are at least five sharp, stable women to every one sharp, stable man." This fact alone seems to cause much concern in both groups of women. All of the study women appeared to want a warm, comfortable relationship, but not necessarily marriage. Sixty percent of both groups expressed the need to sense their new freedom; to "run and play." Some likened it to being an adolescent again. Their responses were: "I feel free again to run with my friends." "I really didn't date that much in high school." "I thought about different boyfriends and I wanted to go back and do those things." "I have done things I did when I was a teenager." "I never did some of the things I'm doing now when I was a teenager, such as date, because I married young." Another said, "Not really, I never roamed like this in adolescence before. I was looking for someone to take his place."

The need to feel free and be involved lasted at least a year for most of the study respondents. During this time, they ran with friends, socialized, drank, danced, and developed relationships.

Contraceptive Use and Sexual Relationships. All but two of the study women were sexually involved on the average of one to three times per week. It is obviously a myth that divorced women are not sexually active. Many said sex during marriage was boring, and they did not know how good a sexual relationship could be until they divorced. One said, "I feel I was sort of being awakened to what sex is all about." One of the prevailing themes among respondents in both groups was that they had a tendency to discontinue contraceptives when a relationship was terminated, be it marriage or boyfriends. All of them admitted that termination of a relationship leaves them lonely, with a need for closeness, and more vulnerable to an unprotected sexual encounter. But as one said, "Well, if I'm not on contraceptives, I will stay out of his bed," though she admitted to several unprotected encounters. Another said, "It isn't OK to plan for sex, mine just happened, I don't really believe in non-marital sex." Those who have had a pregnancy after divorce tended to not use contraceptives regardless of marital status. They also seemed to intellectualize that they were not going to be sexually involved. However they recognized, somewhat reluctantly, that when involvement did occur, no contraceptives were used.

These findings are similar to those in previous studies. Luker (1975), for example, theorized that contraception, like sex, carries many social taboos. Contraception means acknowledging and planning intercourse, and possibly being sexually available. Planning for sex suggests that the woman may be actively anticipating intercourse. For some women their values prohibit planning for sex. Thus, no contraceptives are used. Walsok (1975) also found that contraceptive use is positively related to the anticipation, planning, and acceptance of sexual encounters. He asked his study respondents "on last intercourse when you or your partner had not used contraceptive devices or practice, was it because of. . . ." The single most frequent answer to this question was, "Intercourse should be spontaneous." Another frequent response was, "Did not expect intercourse to occur." Similarly, Maxwell (1977), Scanzoni (1975), and Foriet and Foriet (1978) report that the frequency and use of reliable methods increased in relation to an increased level of emotional involvement in the relationship. The pregnancy group was also more likely to see themselves as non-compliant with their contraceptives and to not know when ovulation occurs in relation to the menstrual cycle.

Another interesting finding in the present study is the importance of age at first sexual intercourse. The pregnant group started sex at an earlier age than the not pregnant group. These findings coincide with research (Zelnik & Katner, 1977; Maxwell, 1977) which indicates that those who were older at first intercourse were more likely to be better contraceptive users throughout the childbearing years.

In a more recent study, Cook (1981) studied a group of young women in England and reported similar findings. She found age at first intercourse ranged from thirteen to twenty-eight, with a mean of eighteen years. The numbers peaked at age seventeen. Sixty percent of her group had used contraception at the time of first intercourse. When respondents were grouped by age at first intercourse, the most careful contraceptive users were those who became sexually active over the age of twenty-one.

Pregnancy Occurrence. Rationale for pregnancy and non-monitoring of sexual behavior were varied. Refusing to foresee another sexual encounter appears to be an important reason for non-use of contraceptives and pregnancy. The most frequent response given for becoming pregnant was, "It just happened." This finding is similar to Freeman's (1977) research on abortion. Women in this sample were faced with unwanted pregnancies because they had not seen themselves as instrumental in planning pregnancies. As Freeman describes it:

> Pregnancy happened to them. Their experiences had trained them to be receptive, to value themselves in terms of others responses more than through their own contribution. They had no history of feeling what they did made any difference, but their own actions and decisions had value to themselves and others. (p. 510)

Trieze (1975) also found that women are more likely to see what happens to them as independent of their own behavior and more often attribute their successes and failure to external and/or unstable factors.

The second most frequent response was, "I wanted to be pregnant." Kuzhetsova (1983) reports similar findings regarding the need to be pregnant among divorced women in the Soviet Union. She suggested that some women try to cope with their loneliness by having a child outside of marriage, or that older women have children outside of marriage because they cannot find a husband, and seek consolation and companionship in a child. The next most frequent response was, "I didn't think I could become pregnant." These findings are also similar to Luker's Decision-Making Model (1975).

A small percentage of the pregnant group also reported feeling lonely and looked for these needs to be met in a sexual relationship. Cognitive psychologists have recently found that the way in which choices are presented, or framed, determine to a large extent whether we will take a chance or play it safe. People will usually take bigger risks to avoid losses than to achieve gains (Kemps, 1985). A woman may frame this thought in her mind as she enters an unprotected sexual encounter, and in order to avoid the loss of a man, or a sexual encounter, she takes a risk. She does not look at it is a way to achieve a gain, but to avoid a loss of "love," with no thought to the long-term consequence.

Self-esteem and Self-acceptance. Self-esteem is an important component of one's identity. Divorce and formation of a new identity will likely have some degree of impact on the concept and, in particular, the sexual self-concept. For women there may be desperation incurred by feeling unloved. As discussed by Hetherington et al. (1979), feelings of lack of self-confidence in the divorced person stemmed from their concerns about sexuality, dating, and interpersonal relations. As divorced women begin to understand new data about their identity, their self-concept develops and learning becomes a part of their behavior. Receptivity to this new identity may enhance the self-concept. A positive self-esteem is repeatedly linked to contraceptive use. In contrast, a poor self-esteem may encourage some divorced women to act impulsively and seek sexual gratification to relieve feelings of rejection and loneliness.

It is my feeling that poor self-esteem drives some divorced women to seek sexual gratification in hopes of enhancing self-esteem. Data from the study and scores on the Rosenberg Self-Acceptance Scale ($z = 2.87$, $p < .004$) do suggest that contraceptive users feel more positive toward themselves. Seventy percent of the pregnant group and 90% of the not pregnant group also reported that they liked themselves.

Relationship to Adolescent Contraceptive Behavior. An important deduction in this study is the similarity of the findings with previous research done on adolescent sexual and contraceptive behaviors. Those who have experienced a pregnancy after divorce, began sex at an earlier age, married at a younger age and stayed married less time. During this time, they also began to have children. While no exact data was collected in this study as to exactly at what age they began to have children, this was discussed in the interview. It is my sense that they also had children at an early age and some were teenager mothers. Data does show they have had more pregnancies than the not pregnant group. Many of the former were poor contraceptors while married, and continued to be after divorce.

Implications for Clinical Practice. As the number of divorced women rises, it is important for the therapist to be cognizant of their needs and attempt to help the client achieve the skills necessary to live as a single person.

The following guidelines are recommended for counseling the divorced single woman.

1. Establish rapport.
2. Access lifestyle.

    a. Is she sexually involved? How often?
    b. Does she have a significant relationship?
    c. Does she have a reproductive life plan?
    d. Would she like more children?
    e. Assess how she is using denial. Bring her attention to the need for birth control. Does she believe she is infertile due to a risk which has not led to pregnancy?
    f. Assess values regarding sexuality. Determine if values are in conflict with her behavior.
    g. Assess client's perception of self; are her perceptions positive or negative?

3. Take a careful contraceptive history.

    a. Assess contraceptive behaviors in the past and present.
    b. Determine contraceptive methods she has used or is using at this time.
    c. Assess her likes or dislikes about the methods used.
    d. Assess circumstances that led her to discontinue or consider discontinuing the method.
    e. Determine to what extent she engages in sexual intercourse without using contraceptives.
    f. Assess knowledge and preconceived ideas related to contraceptive methods.
    g. Assess if knowledge related to ovulation is correct.

4. Implement comprehensive, careful counseling.

    a. Be quiet and listen – avoid the information giver, parent role.
    b. Utilize a positive approach, based on her goals. Teach her to set realistic goals.
    c. Do reality counseling. Point out inconsistencies and circumstances that led to non-use of contraceptives.
    d. Give her permission to have a sexual relationship.
    e. Teach her social skills: how to flirt, date, and make friends.
    f. Teach her the mechanics and importance of achieving a healthy self-esteem.

SUMMARY

According to previous research, early sex, marriage, and child-bearing perpetuates lower social class, less education, limited income, lack of goals, dependence, and divorce. Possibly once divorce happens, a crisis occurs of "Who am I?" The cycle begins again and a male relationship is sought to meet dependency and esteem needs. Again, old behavior patterns come into play and sexual involvement without contraceptives occurs. Only this time they are not adolescents, but women who have been married, have raised children, are chronologically older and supposedly more mature. It seems that the sexual and contraceptive behaviors that were started in adolescence (with the resultant social situation and personality characteristics) are being repeated in adulthood.

This finding has implications for health care professionals that are concerned with preventing teenage pregnancies. Young girls need to be taught the process of goal setting, the value of independence, assertion skills, clarification of sexual values, and decision-making skills at an early age, preferably beginning in elementary school.

The divorce process and its aftermath causes a loss and a change that may temporarily or permanently affect one's thought, feelings, and direction. Sexual decision-making and contraceptive use are important elements of this modification in thought processes. An important characteristic of sexual decision-making is knowledge of one's self; the aspect of self which is most important in self-esteem. Vital to the task of achieving an independent identity is a knowledge of one's own sexuality. Some divorced women may be experiencing an inadequate self-esteem, identity, and self-awareness. This may influence their choice in sexual decision-making. Contraceptive risk-taking may occur because of loss of one's identity, self-esteem, and self-awareness. Some intense, immediate experiences can serve temporarily to strengthen ones' identity and self-esteem. "Such activities frequently have a strong element of risk-taking that can function as a psycho-social defense mechanism and defend against feelings of identity uncertainty" (Logan, 1978, p. 505).

A woman may be less likely to make effective sexual decisions and take adequate contraceptive measures if she enters into an interpersonal relationship with extravagant hopes, lacks identity, has feelings of incompetence, has unstable feelings toward herself, needs to be dependent, is unable to monitor her own behavior, misperceives the messages of others, is not able to explore sensitive topics in depth, chooses avoidance or retreat from threatening confrontations, or lacks personal goals and aspirations.

Perhaps the inability to create or maintain satisfying relationships causes some divorced women to depend on coital activity as a compensatory strategy for maintaining closeness. Their deficiency in communication skills and ability to monitor behavior may make it impossible for them to discuss clearly and responsibly the issues of contraception necessary to avoid unplanned pregnancies. Unplanned pregnancy may be, to some extent, the outcome of their inability to deal on a logical level with normal human fears and insecurities, particularly in the area of one-to-one relationships. There may be ambivalent feelings about intercourse and conflicting demands for affection.

Historically, however, the capacity of a woman to conceive and bear children has also provided her with an identity, a network of social relationships, a meaning for her life, and the source of her self-esteem. To bear and rear children is primary for some and sometimes the only measure of worth. If that assumption is true, then it would seem logical that "unwanted pregnancies" may in fact be "wanted pregnancies."

REFERENCES

Beckham, E., & Adams, R. (1984). Coping behavior in depression: Report on a new scale. *Behavior Research Therapy, 22*, 71-75.

Cook, A. (1981). Better safe than sorry. *Nursing Mirror, 153,* 24-26.

Foriet, K.G., & Foriet, J.R. (1978). Correlates of contraceptive behavior among unmarried U.S. college students. *Studies in Family Planning, 19*, 169-174.

Freeman, E. (1977). Influence of personality attributes on abortion experiences. *American Journal of Orthopsychiatry, 47*, 503-513.

Gebhard, P.; Pomeroy, W.; Martin, C.; & Christenson, C. (1958). *Pregnancy birth and abortion*. New York: Harper Brothers.

Glick, P. (1984). American household structure in transition. *Family Planning Perspectives, 16*, 205-210.

Hetherington, E.M.; Cox, M.; & Cox, R. (1979). *The aftermath of divorce* in

J.W. Stevens and M. Matthews (eds) *Mother-child, father-child relation*. National Association for Education Young.

Kuzhetsova, I. Quoted in Moskoff, M. (May, 1983). Divorce in the U.S.S.R. *Journal of Marriage and the Family*, 419-425.

Logan, R. (1979). Identity diffusion and psycho-social defense mechanism. *Adolescence, 13*, 504-507.

Luker, K. (1975). *Taking chances. Abortion and the decision not to contracept*. Berkeley: University of California Press.

Maxwell, J.; Sack, A.; Frary, R.; & Keller, J. (1977). Factors influencing contraceptive behaviors of single college students. *Journal of Sex and Marital Therapy, 13*, 160-164.

Pohlman, C.W. (1969). *The psychology of birth planning*. Cambridge, Mass.: Schenkman.

Rosenberg, M. (1965). *Society and the adolescent self-image*. Princeton: Princeton University Press.

Scanzoni, J. (1975). *Sex roles, lifestyles, and childbearing*. New York: Free Press.

Snyder, M. (1974). The self-monitoring of expressive behavior. *Journal of Personality and Social Psychology, 30*, 526-537.

U.S. Bureau of the Census (1983). *Statistical abstract of the United States*. Washington, D.C.: U.S. Government Printing Office.

Walshok, M. (1972). *Unconventional role commitments and sexual permissiveness in women studies*. Unpublished manuscript. Bloomington, Ind.: Institute for Sex Research, Indiana University.

Weiss, R. (1975). *Marital separation*. New York: Basic Books.

Zelni, M., & Kantner, J.F. (1977). Sexual and contraceptive experience of young unmarried women in the United States, 1976, 1971. *Family Planning Perspectives, 9*, 55-71.

Women, Sexuality, and Disabilities

Sandra S. Cole

Society is still struggling with the negative concept that disabled people are asexual and could not possibly have concerns or problems regarding sexuality in the same way as able-bodied people. It seems difficult for society to perceive sexuality in any other context than among "pretty people": the domain of the healthy and beautiful. In a recent article in the *Village Voice* I read:

> The general public does not think of handicapped people as sexual beings because handicapped people seem to be so radically different from them that it is very difficult to realize that they have feelings just like their own. When they meet handicapped people they are so busy worrying about whether they can communicate with them, how intelligent they are, and how much help they want or resent, and perhaps even being repulsed by drooling, an external urine bag, or lack of eye contact, that the last thing which occurs to them is whether they would like to go to bed . . . Handicapped people are forbidden and sex is forbidden so it's no wonder that the sexuality of handicapped people is doubly forbidden. (*Village Voice*, 1987)

This mythology undermines the basic understanding of sexuality which has been defined as "the integration of physical, emotional,

---

Sandra S. Cole is Professor of Physical Medicine and Rehabilitation at the University of Michigan Medical School. She is certified as a Sex Counselor and Educator by the American Association of Sex Educators, Counselors, and Therapists. She has specialized in the sexual concerns of persons with physical disabilities for eighteen years, with a special focus on sexual exploitation of disabled persons.

intellectual and social aspects of an individual's personality which expresses maleness or femaleness'' (Bogle, 1980).

During the last eighteen years, literature has been developed on the topic of sexual concerns of persons with physical disabilities. Audio-visual materials, training and educational programs, services, and self-help information have been carefully created to provide a basis of understanding of sexuality and disability, a subject which for many carries a double taboo. However, in the author's recent review of the literature, it was found that there is still significantly less information available (in all forms of media) which addresses the unique sexual concerns of women with disabilities than there is for disabled men or able-bodied women; and specific information for this group remains very inadequate. One particular example is the lack of material for parents of disabled girls which could guide and assist them in the subtle role of parenting around issues of sexuality, femaleness, and disability.

Women with disabilities may have special concerns regarding sexuality, sex functioning and sexual health—partly because there may be physical differences between them and able-bodied women and partly because there may be circumstances which have prevented or precluded them from acquiring basic sex education or information about sexuality along the way as they were developing into adult women. They may have questions or concerns about their role in society, their role as a woman, femininity, self-image, family, sexual function specific to their disabilities and, perhaps, questions concerning fertility and pregnancy.

This article reflects general, broad stroke images of some of the real issues about sexuality and disabled women and is written for therapists who might work with them.

It is important for the therapist to have a basic understanding of disability and its impact. The following indicators can assist in organizing one's perception and knowledge about disabilities, the vast differences among disabilities and the ways in which they influence an individual's life. If a disability is *congenital* (such as cerebral palsy or spina bifida), then the child from birth or early childhood will integrate this disability into all aspects of sexual development. Sexual maturation inevitably will occur within the context of the disability. In many situations, chronological age of the child will not be consistent with the maturational or emotional age. Many factors can influence this delay—such as mobility limitations which require a great deal of physical assistance in all or many activities, lack of privacy including the area of personal hygiene, and other daily living experiences which can interfere with spontaneous learning about sexuality. We recognize that much acquisition of sexual knowledge and experience is gained privately, quietly, secretly, or spontaneously.

A congenitally disabled child can experience a great lack of privacy due to extensive personal care needs and perhaps unrealistic assistance or protection from the family who wishes to protect the child from emotional injury by an insensitive society. The child may experience isolation from peers because interaction takes organization, planning, effort, and assistance. Mobility limitations and lack of privacy are significant factors in altering or limiting natural sexual development, education, and values.

If a disability is *acquired* and gender role and sexual development of the individual is interrupted, additional implications are to be noted. Expectations and descriptions of masculinity and femininity are already in place as an able-bodied person, and personal goals are being pursued toward acquiring the societal traits expected in order to fulfill the role of being a "real" man or woman. When these hopes, dreams, and plans are interrupted by the onset of an acquired disability, a convolution is experienced in the family and within the individual, and massive life changes will be experienced. Intimate experience, information, and education about sexuality may be affected and limited by a disability. It is helpful to identify at what stage in life the disability occurs. It is easier to understand what might be happening to the individual as the result of a disability given information regarding the stage of psychosexual development in which the injury occurred, and therefore what losses to sexual identity she may be experiencing.

An adult woman who has experienced a physical disability after achieving womanhood will be more likely to recognize and define specifically the losses she faces in her own female role and self-esteem. This is very important information to factor into her currently stated problem. These types of disability might include cancer, heart condition, amputation, spinal cord injury, and other kinds of traumatic injuries. Adult onset of diseases can affect her self-concept as a woman and may cause great and real concern regarding fertility and pregnancy. In addition, some of these disabilities may be life threatening.

There are also important differences between a disability which is *stable* and one which is *progressive*. A stable disability can be understood, management techniques can be learned, and a lifestyle can be pursued with realistic goals and reliable expectations. A progressive disability can be experienced as slow or quick progression, or as a state of exacerbation, and remission episodes and can produce additional concern because of feelings of lack of control over one's life. Spontaneity, the ability to plan ahead and fulfill dreams and goals may be severely compromised and replaced with anxiety, fear, and lowered self-esteem.

Being aware of these different classifications of disabilities will assist the therapist in understanding the impact of the disability on sexual development and sexual function and can greatly facilitate discussing these issues.

It is advised that the therapist seek local medical practitioners as consultants for descriptions and definitions of the specific disability so that medical implications can be more easily understood. Questions need to be asked regarding how the disability will affect mobility, fertility, sensation (including the ability to experience genital sensation), and any other limitations unique to that particular disability which may be relevant to understanding this person's sexual concerns. In addition, it may be helpful for the therapist to have a resource text available on medical aspects of sexual health (e.g., Kaplan, 1974; Kolodny, 1979). If the therapist is equipped with knowledge about disabilities and their differences, he or she will be in a position to provide tremendous assistance to the disabled person who seeks counsel. It is generally recognized that what is commonly needed by the client with a disability is accurate and substantial sex education, information, and basic counseling. For the most part, women with disabilities have had no interaction with medical professionals who understand the subtleties involving sexuality and disability. If a dialogue among disabled women and professionals in sexual and mental health can be created, then many women would experience advocacy, assistance, and sex education for the first time.

Psychological support, accurate information, and validation contribute to one's sense of health and well-being. An unsupportive environment can lead to a decrease in self-esteem, difficulty in relationships, activities, and work. There are many myths about people with disabilities, particularly women, and it is understandable that sometimes disabled people begin to believe and buy into these myths themselves, especially if there is no one to assist them with optional thinking.

As a young girl is growing up, she is shaping her femininity and her definition of her own sexuality. Some sexual development experiences are inevitable and, as the Sarrels (1979) point out, how a child experiences the impact of first time events such as menstruation, development of axillary hair, and genital changes must be assessed in the context of his or her family culture and values. (Having a disabled child also has a significant impact on the family values, and this impact will be felt by the child.) Many factors work together in the imprinting of sexual values being acquired by this young person such as role models, spontaneous experiences, family roles and rules, violation of family roles and rules, basic sex education and information, ability to maintain and have relationships, and the child's own experiences in her daily living environment. When a disability is also a factor, it is suggested that situational changes in natural sexual development will occur. For example, it is common for families, in an effort to protect the disabled child, to withhold information about sexuality altogether. The parents may not understand the critical importance of information itself and, with good intentions, may overprotect the child from information and experiences or both. Isolation can be the result and it then becomes more difficult for the child to interact with peers, particularly around sexual issues. If the child has not even acquired the "language of sex" in order to dialogue, flirt, tell stories or "brag," then she may experience further isolation from peers.

A disabled young person often experiences excessive touching because of necessary health care tasks by family members, personal care attendants, and health workers. Situations commonly arise wherein the child is handled so frequently that he or she may not even acknowledge or be aware of the separateness and ownership of his or her own body. Often medical professionals or other caretakers do not stop to identify and negotiate necessary touching of a disabled person, sometimes resulting in further loss of autonomy.

Disabled children may spend many hours alone in front of TV because it is physically difficult or impossible to get around and be with friends. Many times disabled children, isolated from peers and uniformed about sex, are left to learn about sex and sexuality through a one-dimensional format such as television. Unrealistic experiences are observed in sexual acting out, sexual innuendos and sexual dialogue, frequently with an absence of specific or accurate information regarding birth control, pregnancy, risks, morals, or values. In these situations, children may not understand the subtleties and unrealities and may come away with misplaced and inaccurate understanding of images about women, sex roles, and behavior as portrayed on TV. In a culture where sexuality in general is often described through humor, double messages, and in sexist and exploitive ways (particularly by the media), it is difficult for any family to adequately prepare children, particularly females, with a realistic perspective about sexual health and values.

Beginning at puberty, some disabled girls may need assistance in menstrual hygiene care, thus adding conspicuousness and a loss of privacy to this sensitive, personal event. In addition, a disabled child may have trouble distinguishing appropriate touch from inappropriate touch and will be predictably a strong candidate for sexual exploitation (Cole, 1987).

Adolescent disabled girls have the same ideas, hopes, and dreams about sexuality as able-bodied girls. They will have learned the gender role expectations set for them by the media and others and may experience difficulty if they lack more substantive educational information about sexuality and sex function. In addition, their expectations may come in conflict with the family which may have consistently protected or overindulged the child and not permitted her to "grow up." This can be identified in situations such as insisting the disabled "girl" dress in youthful clothes and stay "girlish" even though she may be seventeen. In many cases the families are intensely concerned about the sexual and emotional vulnerability of the daughter and hope that "nothing bad" will happen to her. They may, therefore, encourage her to wear youthful clothing and to stay a safe little girl. The families can mistakenly assume there may be no sexual life ahead of her and protect her from this perceived bitter reality with youthful clothing and little-girlish ways. The result can be, of course, that the young emerging woman may become societally handicapped in learning how to conduct herself as a sexual woman. She will be infantilized.

It is commonly recognized that, because of mobility limitations and other family perceptions about disability, disabled girls and young women are frequently not given much opportunity to practice and understand their emerging sexuality in ways which able-bodied girls do, even though we recognize that the more opportunity one has to explore and understand one's own sexuality, the more responsible one can be for the results.

During dating and courtship years, opportunities for establishing relationships may be additionally influenced by a lack of ability to acquire transportation to participate in classroom or group experiences where other young people might be available. The continued lack of privacy for adolescents and young adults will certainly restrict risk-taking behavior and delay opportunities to gain a realistic understanding of their sexual selves.

All of these factors are helpful in understanding and working with an adult disabled woman. It is more difficult to talk about current sexual issues and problems without an understanding of the backdrop from which this disabled woman emerges. She may need basic sex education and information first.

In addition, the disabled woman herself may anticipate that the able bodied professional, particularly in sexual health, will *not* have a very good understanding of what it is like to have a disability and may be hesitant to trust. Therefore, a thoughtful therapist will take the time to learn about disability and to ask sensitive questions which will identify the real issues.

Experiences of infantilization, being treated as a "pretty" or "poor little girl," and perceiving diminished gender role expectations of herself from society will contribute to poor body image and self-concept. As previously mentioned, these women may have been overprotected by their families or may have lacked spontaneity in learning the secret sexual messages commonly learned during the childhood and development of able-bodied women. To some degree, the personal cost of omission of accurate information is far greater than the cost of being rejected. Families, which include extended "family" such as caretakers, teachers, healthcare providers, and clergy, play a major part in influencing and facilitating the development of the sexual profile of the disabled woman.

Women with disabilities may be keenly aware of deficits in their lives but may also be unable to change the situation in a way which would provide them with opportunities to reach out, make desired adjustments, and be assertive about themselves. It is important for therapists to understand some of these special issues in working as problem solvers and therapists of women with disabilities.

Although disabled women are generally able to fill the traditional role of marriage and motherhood, and in most cases fertility is not affected, it is a myth that there are no limitations or problems for a disabled woman in her traditional wife and mother role. Society may regard her as "fortunate" to have done so much, and she may not have any permission or opportunity to discuss her normal frustrations or problems. Conversely, many congenitally disabled women say that they were programmed to become super career women because their parents never perceived them as eligible for the traditional "female role." In addition, society values physical appearance in women more than in men, thereby adding an extra disadvantage. It is not surprising to learn that the statistics for divorce among disabled women are higher than for disabled men. The ingredients for such a dilemma are set long before the woman enters into marriage (Shaul, 1979).

All women experience discrimination in the workplace, including self-limiting attitudes learned through gender role socialization, and in the lack of control, information and options concerning reproduction. For disabled women, the restrictions are greater, and it is interesting to note that for many the larger issue of oppression may not be sexism but discrimination from the able-bodied society (Deegan, 1985). The insensitivity of the able-bodied society may render a disabled woman feeling as if she may not even be "in the race."

She may never have had the experience of flirting, being courted, exploring, being harassed, or objectified. Most able-bodied women experience problems in being treated as a *sexual object* whereas many disabled women experience being treated as an *asexual object*. The experience of the able-bodied woman can be devastating in feelings or social status, but being treated as asexual can be even more so. For example, the disabled woman may never have an opportunity to make a choice about a partner or marriage or to be perceived as having lost anything, including this choice, since she is viewed as asexual.

Some disabled women find themselves in sexual victim situations which they may accept or may not even recognize as exploitive because they have been and may always be victims of societal neglect and abuse. Kohlberg (1966) points out that children learn "I am a girl" and then adopt role attributes. Disabled women, however, learn "I am disabled" first and may secondarily learn to understand femininity. The scene is set for this woman in our society when a predominant characteristic or a label is "disabled" and not "woman." A sense of rolelessness or the absence of sanctioned role characteristics for disabled women can result in feelings of anonymity and isolation or, as has been described, "A psychological sense of invisibility" (O'Toole & Weeks, 1978). She may feel completely sexually alienated through her experiences.

The result of the situation of being viewed as outside or ineligible for sexual competition can be painful, demeaning, and humiliating. It can also result in an inability to access sexual information which would enable disabled women to be more sexually independent. Many women remain strongly connected to their families or have intense close friendships with family members in part because of perceptions of a hostile outside environment.

Disabled men and women are encouraged to be helpless, non-assertive, non-sexual, passive, dependent, grateful, and apologetic for a less than perfect body in a society where physical appearance is often the measure of "value" (Dailey, 1979). Physically disabled women probably have more in common with basic issues of discrimination than they do with sexuality issues with able-bodied women. Women with disabilities express a common mistrust of perceptions of able-bodied women and feminists (Kent, 1977).

Additional limitations may be experienced when disabled women are not viewed as feminine. They may need custom made clothing for non-traditional body shapes and may not be able to wear "fashionable" clothing or shoes. In our culture sex role cueing places a large value on clothing and fashion. Disabled women may have a very limited income with which to make non-essential purchases, such as high fashion clothing, entertainment, gifts, or travel. It is understandable that through these limitations and frustrations, women can develop self-defense mechanisms which are sometimes viewed as "unbecoming" or "pushy." In general, women are viewed as more circumspect in their communication patterns; and, for a variety of reasons including speech limitations, disabled women may be viewed negatively as "too direct," "too loud," "calling too much attention to themselves" or "inappropriate" and may be subject to increased rejection (more so than disabled men). Further, because of the sexual cues around body language, women who are unable to sit in "ladylike" positions will also inevitably experience disapproval.

On the other hand, there are some interesting and positive consequences as a result of these disenfranchising situations for many disabled women. A woman who is able to see the narrow and restrictive path of able-bodiedness may actually feel freed up from the sexual competition and standards of beauty. Many report that they *are* able to focus on their career, choose styles and clothing which work for them regardless of "fashion," and be more uniquely themselves. Becker writes, "We are first and foremost sensitive human beings with a terrific sense of accomplishment after all of the horrible, but challenging, experiences we have been through" (1977). These pluses of experience, strength, understanding, self-fortitude, and, often, compassion, are frequently not really recognized or understood by the able-bodied society, but may be the cornerstone of societal survival for disabled women.

Some negative experiences which may be the result of society's perception of disability and women may include increased domestic violence, giving up of reproductive freedom because of medical pressure not to bear children and an inaccurate perception that disabled women would be unfit as mothers or even sexual partners (Fine, 1985). However, because the economic situation is often grim for disabled women (i.e., inability to find employment or employment at lower status and paying positions), many seek marriage as an economic necessity (Perlman & Arneson, 1982). Such situations can be particularly difficult for these women if they are ill-equipped to enter into a marriage relationship because of lack of knowledge or socialization.

It is ironic that many disabled men who succeed in society and who have partners give great credit to their partners for helping them along the way toward their success but that disabled women are less likely to have partners and may be less able to feel successful in filling the "women's role" (Fine, 1985). Sometimes success is undermined and discredited, and a successful professional or independent lifestyle is viewed as the *only* choice the disabled woman had because she was not *able* to get a partner. It is easy to see how society goes around and around with these myths and expectations. Nevertheless, we all must be cautioned about our own views of disabled women. It would be easy to be sympathetic, to pity, or to simply shrug and feel helpless ourselves. However, disabled women are neither helpless or hopeless, nor are they necessarily fragile, bogged down, and trapped in their situations. They do, however, often lack the informational tools and experiences more readily available to able-bodied women in their developing years.

Sometimes participating in sexual and intimate activities can be anxiety producing for disabled women.

> Yet an even more basic problem, for me at least, is my mistrust of my own body. Intellectually I know that sexually I can perform . . . yet at what may be called a sub-intellectual level, I doubt my body's ability to give another pleasure. Rarely does my body give *me* pleasure. When I tell it to do something as often as not it does exactly the opposite, or else it flares out in wild tantrum-like motions. How could my body possibly conform to the wishes of an expectant, excited lover? This is the question I still ask myself. (Sutherland, 1987)

Some limitations in sexual function for disabled women have to do with physical limitations of hands and mobility. For instance, if a woman has limited hand function, inserting a diaphragm can be difficult, if not impossible. It would therefore require her to communicate with a partner and gain assistance from the partner or to make another choice for birth control. The most important skill in all of this is the ability to communicate honestly and directly with the partner, informing and instructing where necessary, which may be a problem in itself for the disabled woman. Many women wear catheters for the collection of urine. Catheters require regular maintenance, and the procedure must be done carefully and consistently. They can be viewed as inconvenient, particularly at times of sexual intimacy since we are told that sex is a natural function and sexual expression "should" be spontaneous. This can lead to feelings of embarrassment, conspicuousness, and vulnerability.

The presence of pain can have a distinct limitation on a woman's ability to participate in intimate sexual expression, including intercourse. Since it is a "hidden" aspect of disability, it may not be observable to a partner, and it is not uncommon for the partner to view reluctance in sexual activity as withholding, rejection, or lack of desire. Many times these perceptions are unspoken and the partner takes this perceived rejection personally, creating a dilemma for the couple. It would be helpful for the therapist or counselor to make practical suggestion for convenience in positioning and to enter into active discussion with the woman regarding creative options which will lead to greater opportunities for enjoyment of sexual activity (Becker, 1978; Hossler & Cole, 1983; Shaul & Bogel, 1978).

Kolodny (1972) documented unusual information in a study of long-term affects of diabetes on women's sexuality. He discovered through interview that "44 of 125 diabetic women (35.2%) reported complete absence of orgasmic response during the year preceding inquiry, whereas only 6 out of 100 non-diabetic women (6.0%) reported non-orgasmic function during the same period." Not only is this information medically important to link diabetes and female orgasmic dysfunction, but also to reveal that anorgasmic women with diabetes may have previously been diagnosed with "lack of sexual desire," "personality dysfunction," or "poor technique." It is understandable that this added stigma can have devastating effects on these women. An important recommendation to therapists is to avoid leaping to the assumption that the woman's attitude or lack of information is exclusively responsible for the sexual dysfunction.

Similarly, one must be equally cautious not to label the dysfunction the direct result of the disability. A thorough and careful examination, both medical and psychological, should assist the professional in making a realistic diagnosis. Again, therapists are encouraged to seek medical consultation with rehabilitation specialists in the area of the disability. Coupled with their own unique knowledge of sexual function and sexual health, realistic problem identification and goal setting can occur.

Further physical limitations can be experienced in sexual activity due to the presence of braces, crutches, and other assistive devices and apparatus. A woman may state that she feels more vulnerable or "less sexy" in braces, splints, or a wheelchair. Similarly, some disabilities, i.e., spinal cord injuries, can result in a decrease or cessation of lubrication, thus making coitus painful and difficult and creating situations which can tear or damage the labial skin. Since a woman with a spinal cord injury has no feeling of vaginal sensation, she should be encouraged to use additional lubrication (saliva, Lubrin, water soluble jelly).

A woman without sensation in the genital area might be encouraged to participate in sexual intimacy with the lights on as an option so that she will be able to receive the visual feedback of pleasure and intimacy and will be able to enjoy her partner's responses as well. For many individuals, being able to have visual feedback increases their own sexual responsivity.

Therapists will be alerted to the fact that disabled people have had to deal forthrightly and objectively with their bodies—more so than able-bodied people. Their bodies have been handled and touched by medical professionals over extended periods of time—perhaps years. The therapist or counselor, therefore, may be able to speak more candidly and directly about private and sexual matters with a disabled client during counseling and education than with an able-bodied client. Although education may start at a more basic level than other able-bodied clients, the ability to be open and informative will be facilitated by the fact that a person with a disability has a long experience dealing directly with information regarding his or her body. It is, however, ironic that disabled people have experienced explicit handling of their bodies for medical reasons but, at the same time, have often experienced a total void in sexual expression or experience and perhaps have never spoken or been spoken to directly about sexuality.

It is appropriate here to again alert the therapist to the very large possibility that the disabled woman may have experienced exploitation, molestation, or rape at some point in her life and that she may not realize that she has been exploited. Questioning in this area should proceed in direct relationship to her sexual knowledge. Society may perceive a disabled woman as vulnerable. As a result, she may have been sexually exploited–whether or not she was aware of the fact that it was exploitation (Cole, 1987).

One study, conducted in Seattle, Washington among developmentally disabled persons, indicates that the percentage of sexually abused victims among disabled people was higher than in the able-bodied population and that the percentage of disabled victims who recognize their perpetrator was 99%, compared to 80-85% of the able-bodied victims (Ryerson, 1984). This clearly implicates the "extended family" of a disabled person who may need an attendant, family members, and other persons directly involved in assistance with mobility and personal care. These "incestual" intrusions in some cases may have been the only form of affection experienced by the disabled woman and, therefore, she may have remained silent in order to maintain her place in the family, her friendship, or to avoid losing the person on whom she is dependent for services rendered. She may also be unaware that the affective gestures are inappropriate.

Many women who have experienced such exploitive situations do not realize it for many, many years or are not willing to tell (Cole, 1986). Once the story is told for the first time, the natural grieving process beings; and, as is true for many able-bodied women, it does not seem to matter that there may have been a lapse of several years between the incident and the telling. The unconscious fully remembers the experience, and the anxiety, rage, and feelings of helplessness appear as post-traumatic stress. In such situations it will have been compounded by time, and the stigma and other limitations of having a disability. Affirmation, validation, and sex *education* in a supportive environment are essential ingredients in these counseling circumstances.

The basic message for therapists working with disabled women on issues of fertility and dysfunction is to consult with a health professional who has knowledge or expertise about the specific disability. Although these individuals may not be specialists in gynecology or obstetrics, they will know the implications of disability in terms of sensation, mobility, and function. This information, coupled with the patient's personal history and emotions, will identify some of the target areas for counseling. In addition, it might be helpful to further consult with an obstetric/gynecologic specialist for future recommendations. Keep in mind, however, that these specialists may not be familiar with the disability issues.

Be alerted to the fact that disabled women will often report that they have been advised not to produce children because of inappropriate assumptions by medical professionals that they will be unable to be successful in child rearing. Some may have experienced unwanted and unnecessary tubal ligations or hysterectomies for pregnancy prevention.

There are a limited number of articles available on pregnancy and child-rearing for disabled women. Only a few offer solid advice and a good basic philosophy for working with the client (Asrael, 1986; Verduyn, 1986).

Professional education is needed to help able-bodied therapists learn about disability. We should continue to recommend that this type of training be included in all counselor/therapist education. Basically, disabled people need education and counseling to fill in some of the missing pieces they may not have had available to them during their sexuality development. Disabled people are creative and adaptive; and the facilitative, respectful role of a therapist is expeditious.

Being familiar with the language of disability is an advantage for all counselors in any situation. Opinions vary both personally and geographically as to appropriate usage – whether the words be "differently abled," "dis-abled," "handicapped," "physically challenged," "handicapper," or "physically disabled." It is generally regarded as being in unfortunate poor taste to use the word "disabled" as a noun. The more acceptable phrasing is a "disabled woman," a "disabled person" or an "individual with a disability."

A strong recommendation to therapists would be to conduct a thorough assessment of the true and underlying issues which women with disabilities may have before launching into a therapeutic pattern which is already familiar to the therapist. It is my experience, and that of my colleagues, that women with disabilities in particular lack information, education, and simply an opportunity to discuss and understand the basic issues and tenets of our society in the role of being a sexual woman.

Parents should be encouraged to learn and teach their disabled children about sexuality at an early age in order to provide them with information, decision-making and risk-taking skills which will enable them to more fully experience natural sexual development in an insensitive society. Parents of adult disabled persons need to view their children as sexual individuals. This perception will validate the sexuality of the disabled family member and may be one step to removing a barrier or social restriction.

Local advocacy groups, such as Centers for Independent Living, can be of great assistance to therapists working with disabled persons. They are knowledgeable, creative, and pro-active in advocating for disabled persons. They usually have a great deal of information available for educating the community and are also able to participate in in-service training, conversations, and even consultations as peer advocates where appropriate.

Some helpful suggestions for interacting with women with disabilities are:

1. When in doubt: ASK.
2. Do not be parental or overattentive (disabled people are not fragile).
3. React without pity (pity reinforces the idea that a person with a disability is inferior to the able-bodied person).
4. If you wish to know about the limitation: ASK (select an appropriate time).
5. Do not worry about slips of the tongue (such as "Do you *see* what I mean?" when speaking with a blind person. Natural dialogue communicates a form of acceptance).
6. Simulate a handicap for a few hours, including public contact.
7. Recognize that persons with physical limitations are people, and be yourself (Topp, 1985).

Our worst ugliness was our blindness to our own beauty.
And our fear, more than death, was rejection from each other.

Pintauro

REFERENCES

Asrael, W. (1986). Today's challenge: Childbirth education for women who are physically disabled. *NAACOG Update Series*, New Jersey, Continuing Professional Education Center, Inc.

Asrael, W. (July-August, 1982). An approach to motherhood for disabled women. *Rehabilitation Literature, 43* (7-8), 214-218.

Becker, E.F. (1978). *Female sexuality*. Illinois: Accent Publications, Cheever Publishing, Inc.

Bogle, J.; Hudgins, G.; Peters, L.; Shaul, S.; & Wysocki, J. (1980). *A manual for service providers*. Washington: Ebon Research Systems. (DHEW – Region X, Family Planning, 1321 Second Avenue, M-S 833, Seattle, Washington 98101).

Campling, J. (Ed.) (1981). *Images of ourselves: Women with disabilities talking*. London: Routledge and Kegan Paul.

Cole, S.S. (1986). Facing the challenges of sexual abuse in persons with disabilities. *Sexuality and Disability, 7* (3/4), 71-88.

Dailey, A. (1979). Physically handicapped women. *Counseling Psychologist, 8*, 41-42.

Deegan, M.J. & Brooks, N.A. (Eds.) (1985). *Women and disability: The double handicap*. New Brunswick: Transaction Books.

Duffy, Y. (1981). *. . . all things are possible*. Michigan: A.J. Garvin and Associates.

Fine, M. & Asch, A. (1985). Disabled women: Sexism without the pedestal. In *Women and disability: The double handicap*. New Brunswick: Transaction Books.

Hale, J.; Norman, A.D.; Bogle, J.; & Shaul, S. (1977). *Within reach: Providing family planning services to physically disabled women*. Washington: Planned Parenthood of Snohomish County, Inc.

Hossler, C.J. & Cole, S.S. (1983). *Intimacy and chronic lung disease*. Michigan: The University of Michigan.

Kaplan, H.S. (1974). *The new sex therapy: Active treatment of sexual dysfunctions*. New York: Brunner/Mazel Publications.

Kent, D. (1977). In search of liberation. *Disabled USA, 3*, 18-19.

Kohlberg, L. (1966). A cognitive developmental analysis of children's sex role concepts and attitudes. In E. Maccoby, ed. *The development of sex differences*. Stanford, CA: Stanford University Press, 82-173.

Kolodny, R.C. (1972). Sexual dysfunction in diabetic females. *Medical Aspects of Human Sexuality, 6*, 98-106.

Kolodny, R.C.; Masters, W.H.; & Johnson, V.E. (1979). *Textbook of sexual medicine*. Boston: Little, Brown and Company.

Neistadt, M.E. & Freda, M. (1987). *Choices: A guide to sex counseling with physically disabled adults*. Florida: Robert E. Krieger Publishing Company.

O'Toole, J. & Weeks, C. (1978). *What happens after school? A study of disabled women and education*. San Francisco: Women's Educational Equity Communications Network.

Perlman, L.G. & Arneson, K.C. (1982). *Women and rehabilitation of disabled persons*. Virginia: National Rehabilitation Association.

Ryerson, E. (September, 1984). Sexual abuse and self-protection education for developmentally disabled youth: A priority need. *SIECUS Report*, Vol. XIII, 1, New York.

Sarrel, L. & Sarrel, P. (1979). *Sexual unfolding: Sexual development and sex therapies in late adolescence*. Boston: Little, Brown and Company.

Shaul, S.; Bogle, J.; Hale-Harbaugh, J.; & Norman, A.D. (1978). *Toward intimacy: Family planning and sexuality concerns of physically disabled women*. New York: Human Sciences Press.

Sutherland, P. (April 7, 1987). I want sex—just like you. New York: *Voice*.

Topp, D.M. (November, 1985). *Women with disabilities: Surviving stairs and stares*, paper presented GLCA Women's Studies Conference.

Verduyn, W.H. (1986). Spinal cord injured women, pregnancy and delivery. *Paraplegia, 24*, 231-240.

EPILOGUE

Tensions, Dilemmas and Possibilities for Understanding Women's Sexuality

Denise Webster

The following observations and questions reflect my need for discussion with others who are trying to understand women's experiences around a variety of developmental and situational events which are often conceptualized as "sexuality issues." As a nurse, I have been involved with what may seem to be some of the more concrete aspects of "sexuality," such as contraception, infertility, mastectomy, rape, and hysterectomy, as well as with presumably more abstract sexuality concerns including sexual identity/orientation/preference and a variety of problems associated with changes in body image.

Increasingly, I find myself asking, What is sexuality? The research and clinical literature range from the general (everything that you are, and everything that happens to you) to the extremely spe-

Denise Webster is a feminist nurse psychotherapist who recently moved to Colorado to direct the graduate program in psychiatric nursing. Her life-long inability to maintain a consistent perspective on anything has forced her to become a reluctant scholar and has driven her friends and family to the brink on many occasions.

Paper presented at the annual meeting of the Advanced Feminist Therapy Institute, May 16, 1987, Chicago, IL.

cific (how many orgasms you have had in the past week). Intermediate definitions tend to be operationalized into sexual identity, body image, satisfaction in socially-defined "sex roles," sex-role stereotyping, knowledge of physiological sexual response patterns, and "satisfaction" reported by a sexual partner. Biological, psychological, social, cultural, spiritual, and interpersonal levels of experience are seldom acknowledged as being interrelated in complex and relatively unstable, therefore unpredictable, ways. All contribute to a woman's unique sense of herself "as a woman."

I'm not sure if I used to know what "sexuality" meant and forgot, or whether the meanings of the word have become so varied that nobody knows what anyone is talking about. Or have the norms which informed the meanings been so radically shaken that new meanings must be identified and put into language that reflect new realities? Maybe we never really knew what it meant, and some of us just pretended that we did.

I know that other women are also confused. When Alice Dan and I did a small survey about sexuality with a group of industrial nurses who were often consulted about such issues, we found a pattern of responses which may be typical. Asked to define sexuality, the open-ended responses included "differences between males and females," "stimulation to orgasm," "cultural norms," "self-awareness," "the relationship between men and women," and "instinctive responses to another—especially eye contact." When asked what kinds of problems they were consulted about, most were concerned with reproductive problems, sexually transmitted diseases, or "sexual dysfunction," but also included concerns about job discrimination and balancing home and work responsibilities without help. The issues which they found most difficult to deal with included homosexuality, infidelity, battered women, abortion, rape, and "lack of satisfaction in the act itself."

In a group study of "self-care responses to threats to sexuality," we asked women about the experiences of natural menopause, premenstrual syndrome, and mastectomy. Among other research aims, we wanted to know how women themselves defined their sexuality. We had to abandon that attempt when endless confusion about the complexity of the data threatened to scuttle the entire project. We found, for example, on a question asking for a description of a "sexually attractive woman" that we often got multiple and highly contradictory responses from individual women. Often they said they couldn't answer, since they never thought about women "that way." Or they would tell us what they thought "society" presented as attractive, "what men saw as attractive," as well as what their significant other felt was attractive, usually in terms which described a woman's physical appearance. Pressed to come up with their own definitions, they might respond in physical terms, but also in terms of "being interesting," "showing concern for other people," "being intelligent," and "radiating a healthy vitality." Asked, then, if she considered herself to be sexually attractive, the responses often reflected entirely different criteria than any of the preceding lists!

The political and personal tensions generated by the attempt to analyze these data brought into sharp focus the volatility of the topic. Despite the atmosphere among the researchers of mutual respect and a history of successful work on many other projects, it seemed we were left with "agreeing to disagree" about how we could accurately and honestly communicate what women were telling us. We were struck with the tendency of the women to "define themselves in relation to others' views and to harbor polyvalent(?) (certainly more than just ambivalent) images in relation to their experiences and feelings "as women." Could it be that low reliability on scales which seek attitudes about women's sexuality is highly valid?

As a therapist, I find myself asking questions about the questions we ask. What is sexual "dysfunction"? Who decides? Based on what "norms"? When what is called "normal" sexual behavior/thoughts/feelings can be redefined at frequent intervals within one's lifespan, between generations, and within different cultures, how do we know if "we/they" are "normal"? Has confusion between the "sexual revolution" and the women's movement led women to confuse sexual conquest (their own and other's) with a promise of "freedom," which somehow still eludes us?

I had more questions than I thought I had the answers to. Why is it so important to label ourselves and others vis-à-vis sexuality? I find myself ruminating over Audre Lorde's caution that we cannot dismantle the master's house using the master's tools. Whose need is it to sexualize every object, activity, and emotion in the human repertoire? Labels based on sexuality seem like other labels to be yet another means of creating hierarchies and ways to discriminate.

And yet, what happens if we don't label? Labels are important ways of naming our realities, our truths, of legitimating our experiences. They help us to know who we are and where we fit—"with whom our lot is cast and from where we get our strength." I recall Adrienne Rich's observations that to deny, through silence or distortion, the personal and political fact that women love women, is to participate in perpetuating the invisibility of those who are not/cannot/will not be collaborators in the demand for "compulsory heterosexuality."

What if, with the best of intentions, we cannot label? What if none of the labels fit? What language do we use then and how do we communicate our experience? We know the woman who stays in the marriage "for the sake of the children," perhaps engaging in sexual activity with her husband at prescribed intervals, with little shared warmth or communication. If she feels most alive, most whole, over a cup of coffee with her dearest female friend—is she "straight"? If one is celibate, by choice or circumstances for a certain period of time, are one's sexual credentials revoked?

For many, the term "bisexual" doesn't fit, because it puts into the forefront only one part of a relationship which is distorted by such a label. In common usage, it implies "I am capable of enjoying sex with anyone," denying the other dimensions of relating that have little to do with sex. It puts in the background some of the issues around intimacy which women describe in studies being done at the Stone Center. To describe oneself as bisexual may in fact, as Woody Allen says, double your chances for a date on Saturday nights, but what does it do to someone to take on such a label if it doesn't fit? To sexualize what might really be a need for connectedness, a desire for mutuality and cooperation, rather than sexual sport or physical release? Other terms are no less confusing. It is quite possible to be "psychologically androgynous" and yet maintain an active homophobia. Somehow the term "pansexual" conjures images of activity with small animals and possibly one's personal computer.

My hardest questions come when I find the theories and the

words cannot help me in trying to work with women who are in pain.

> "I'm just afraid of dying. The loss of the breast isn't that important." Do I wonder if she's denying?
>
> "I used to think I was straight, and then I thought I was a lesbian, and now I don't know what I am." Do I help her pick a label? Do I find her a self-help group for "revolving closet door" syndrome?
>
> "When he used to want sex, he would signal by coughing when we got in bed." I laugh. She laughs.
>
> "My oldest brother started with me when I was five. Then my next brother and then the next. When my younger brother was ten I tried to seduce him." I cry. She cries.
>
> I worry later that my responses are "wrong." What would be "right"?

REFERENCES

Aletky, P. (1984). Research methodology in human sexuality issues: Problems and potential. In H.I. Lief & Z. Hock (Eds.). *International Research in Sexology*. New York: Praeger, 151-157.

Bernhard, L. & Dan, A. (1986). Redefining sexuality from women's own perspectives. In D. Webster & T. Hughes (Eds.). *Nursing Clinics of North America, 21*(1).

Caplan, P. (Ed.) (1987). *The cultural construction of sexuality*. New York: Tavistock Publications.

Dworkin, A. (1987). *Intercourse*. New York: The Free Press.

Jackson, M. (1984). Sex research and the construction of sexuality: A tool of male supremacy? *Women's Studies International Forum, 7*(1), 43-51.

Katchedourian, H. (1979). The terminology of sex and gender. In H.A. Katchadourian (Ed.). *Human sexuality* Berkeley, California: University of California Press, 8-34.

Lorde, A. (1984). *Sister outsider*. Trumansburg, New York: The Crossing Press.

Rich, A. (1979). *Lies, secrets and silence*. New York: Norton.

Rich, A. (1980). Compulsory heterosexuality and lesbian experience. *Signs: Journal of Women in Culture and Society, 5*(4), 631-660.

The Stone Center for Developmental Services and Studies at Wellesley College. *Work in Progress* papers and tapes. Wellesley, Massachusetts 02181.

Vance, C. (1985). Pleasure and danger: Toward a politics of sexuality. In C. Vance (Ed.). *Pleasure and danger*. Boston: Routledge & Kegan Paul, 1-27.
Webster, D.; Dan, A.; McElmurry, B.; Bernhard, L.; Lewis, L; & Huddleston, D. Unpublished study of Self-Care Responses to Threats to Women's Sexuality. Nursing Research Emphasis Grant, Doctoral Programs in Nursing, Division of Nursing #NU 0 1048 03.